ARCHETYPES OF THE FAMILY IN LITERATURE

ARCHETYPES
of the FAMILY
in LITERATURE

SVEN ARMENS

UNIVERSITY OF WASHINGTON PRESS
Seattle and London

Quotations from *The Complete Greek Tragedies,* edited by David
Grene and Richmond Lattimore, are reprinted by permission of The
University of Chicago Press: translations by Richmond Lattimore,
Oresteia (1953) and *The Trojan Women* (1958), © by The Uni-
versity of Chicago Press; by David Grene, *Oedipus the King* (1942),
© by The University of Chicago Press; by Elizabeth Wyckoff,
Antigone (1954), © by The University of Chicago Press; by Robert
Fitzgerald, *Oedipus at Colonus* (1941), © by Harcourt Brace & Co.;
by Rex Warner, *The Medea* (1944), © by John Lane, The Bodley
Head Limited, London, England. Quotations from *The Hero with a
Thousand Faces,* by Joseph Campbell (Bollingen Series XVII, Pantheon Books), and from *The Origins and History of Consciousness,*
by Erich Neumann, translated by R. F. C. Hull (Bollingen Series
XLII, Pantheon Books), both © by the Bollingen Foundation, are
reprinted by permission of the Bollingen Foundation.

*Dedicated to Kathleen, Karl, and Sharon
and the memory of my Mother and Father*

Preface

As a work of literary criticism, this study has a twofold intention: first, to examine certain literary depictions of the parent-child relationship; and second, to investigate how imagery grounded in this relationship is utilized in poetry and drama to provide a mode of communication beyond that of rationally formulated statement. As a contribution to literary criticism, I believe such a study offers both further substantiation of the aesthetic theory of archetypes (that is, that certain basic human situations and roles are constantly repeated and receive similar literary presentations from age to age), and a fresh approach to a topic hitherto investigated only in the novel.

My primary approach to family relationships is based on the principle that a child encounters two fundamental formative factors within his family circle—the patriarchal demands of the father and the nurturing care of the mother. One of the briefest summaries of this position is contained within a monograph by Erich Fromm, "The Oedipus Complex and the Oedipus Myth" (Anshen, *The Family*, p. 341):

> Matriarchal culture is characterized by the emphasis on ties of blood, ties to the soil and the passive acceptance of all natural phenomena. Patriarchal society in contrast is characterized by respect for man-made law, by the predominance of rational thought and by the effort to change natural phenomena by man. . . . In the matriarchal concept all men are equal since they are all the children of mothers and each one a child of Mother Earth. A mother loves her children all alike and without (limiting) conditions, since her love is based on the fact that they are all her children and not on any particular merit or achievement; the aim of life is the happiness of man and there is nothing more important or dignified than human existence and life. The patriarchal system, on the other hand, recognizes obedience to authority as its main virtue. The principle of equality is replaced by a hierarchical order in society and state, ruled by an authority just as the family is dominated by the father.

In applying these principles to certain purposively selected well-known literary texts, I have employed two chief symbols: the *Physical Hearth* or fireplace around which the primary family unit groups itself with bonds of mutual affection, and the *Sacred Fire*, the altar devoted in Greek and Roman times to the worship of a deified ancestor and his patriarchal demands. I have attempted to integrate certain anthropological and sociological concepts that bear upon the opposition of these forces wherever they seemed to illuminate the text. Obviously, my commentary is Jungian in orientation, thus the importance of the Bollingen Series (XX) of Jung's *Collected Works* and the reference to the studies of

Erich Neumann. I have also found such studies as Margaret Mead's *Male and Female* and the volume of essays compiled by Ruth Nanda Anshen, *The Family: Its Function and Destiny*, of invaluable assistance.

After a positing of the basic oppositions in an introductory chapter analyzing two poems of Tyrtaeus and G. M. Hopkins, I proceed to a further elucidation of the principles of matriarchy and patriarchy, illustrating the concepts through exegeses of a few selected scenes from Greek tragedy (with stress upon the *Oresteia* of Aeschylus and the Oedipus plays of Sophocles). The following chapters demonstrate the exemplification of these concepts in two plays of Shakespeare: *Hamlet*, an obvious choice, useful in exploring the archetypal relationships of the father, mother, hero, and maiden; and *King Lear*, a tragedy which not only depicts a double violation of both hearth and sacred fire but also the reachievement of a family covenant in the reconciliation of Lear and Cordelia.

Although much of the preliminary work on this study was accomplished under the favorable circumstances afforded me by a grant of a research professorship by the Graduate College of the University of Iowa in 1957, my concluding chapter, as is much of the best of modern criticism, is indebted to the brilliant *Anatomy of Criticism* by Northrop Frye. I have sought to show here, as briefly as possible, how an understanding of the dominant conceptions above both informs and enhances full poetic communication. As a theoretical chapter of literary criticism, it is intended to clarify the combined methodologies of Frye, Cleanth Brooks, and Erich Auerbach in the preceding chapters.

Because of the somewhat controversial nature of this material, I should like to absolve the following of any responsibility for my conclusions even as I express my thanks once more for their most welcome assistance: Professors Rhodes

Dunlap, Ralph Freedman, and Clark Griffith of the English Department of the University of Iowa; Professor Roger Hornsby of the Classics Department; and the late Professor Manford Kuhn of the Department of Sociology and Anthropology. Elsewhere I should like to thank Professors George P. Elliott of Syracuse University and Professor Harry Levin of Harvard University for their efforts on my behalf.

Again, I would offer my gratitude to my colleague, Professor W. R. Irwin, whose guidance in the preparation of any manuscript is always invaluable. My appreciation also to Walter F. Loehwing, late dean of the Graduate College of the University of Iowa, the present dean, Duane C. Spriestersbach, and Professors Baldwin Maxwell and John C. Gerber of our English Department for their aid in obtaining subventions for the present project.

Publication of this work has been financed by a grant from the Learned Publications Fund of the University of Iowa, which is administered by Duane C. Spriestersbach, dean of the Graduate College.

I wish to thank the following for permission to quote from copyrighted material: Bollingen Foundation for *The Hero with a Thousand Faces,* by Joseph Campbell, and *The Origins of Consciousness,* by Erich Neumann, translated by R. F. C. Hull; Cambridge University Press for *Prolegomena to the Study of Greek Religion,* by Jane Harrison; Clarendon Press, Oxford, for *Oxford Book of Greek Verse in Translation,* edited by T. F. Higham and C. M. Bowra; Faber and Faber Ltd for *Collected Poems 1909–1962* and *Selected Essays,* by T. S. Eliot; Harcourt, Brace & World, Inc., for *Collected Poems 1909–1962* and *Selected Essays,* by T. S. Eliot; Harper & Row, Publishers, Incorporated, for *The Family: Its Function and Destiny,* edited by Ruth Nanda Anshen; Harvard University Press for *Early Greek Elegists,* by C. M. Bowra; Lawrence and Wishart Ltd for *Aeschylus and Athens,* by

George Thomson; Penguin Books Ltd for *The Odyssey*, translated by E. V. Rieu; Routledge & Kegan Paul Ltd for *Contributions to Analytical Psychology*, by C. G. Jung, and *The Origins and History of Consciousness*, by Erich Neumann; The University of Chicago Press for *The Complete Greek Tragedies*, edited by David Grene and Richmond Lattimore; Methuen & Co Ltd for *Greek Tragedy*, by H. D. F. Kitto.

SVEN ARMENS

University of Iowa
February, 1965

Contents

ARCHETYPES OF THE FAMILY IN LITERATURE

CHAPTER

I

Two Poems, Two Flames

To cast concept in the form of image dramatized would seem to be the major task of the poet. Explication of the achievement, however, often demands that the critic render once again a visualization of the particular action involved. In studying the two formative factors encountered by a child within the family circle, the authoritarian demands of the father and the nurturing care of the mother, one might oversimplify the issue by posing a small domestic scene wherein the father, threatened by some abrogation of rule, rebukes the child with a slap or harsh word, and the child, puzzled, hurt, and confused, runs to the mother for comfort. But in the infinite variety of literary depictions of the parent-child relationship, there would seem to be ramifications of response far beyond these simple gestures.

For example, we might, in seeking to discover those archetypal patterns which cut across mere cultural manifestation, turn, as much modern criticism inevitably does, to certain anthropological reference. In the now famous study of the primitive puberty rites of the Arunta (Baldwin Spencer and F. J. Gillen, *The Arunta*), we discover a typically significant instance of indoctrination. After instruction in the basic precepts of the tribe, the youth deemed eligible for entrance into the elite male group is compelled to submit to a rather terrifying ordeal. While "bull-roarers" prance about him on every side, representing the voice of the ceremonial demon, he is placed upon a shield by his uncles and subjected to a ritual circumcision. When the priests have accomplished their task, symbolically separating him from the world of childhood and the feminine, he is roused "in a more or less dazed condition . . . attended to, and congratulated by the men to whose estate he has just now arrived. 'You have done well,' they say; 'You did not cry out.' "[1]

As commonly interpreted, such ritual substitutes the male phallus for the female breast as the focal point of consciousness. A late circumcision of this sort, especially at puberty, constitutes an act of rebirth whereby the son is separated permanently from the mother and made fit for acceptance into the "men's house" of patriarchal society. The reason for such an ordeal, according to Erich Neumann, one of Jung's most perceptive disciples, involves a schooling of the will, a subjection of the ego to the fortifying elements of fear, hunger, and pain so as to inculcate within the *consciousness* of the male child the criterion of manliness.

The rites of puberty, like all initiations, "aim at producing something supra-personal, namely that part of the individual which is transpersonal and collective. . . . Hence the production of this part [represents] a second birth, a new generation through the masculine spirit, and is accompanied by the inculcation of secret doctrines, ancestral knowledge, and cosmic lore, in order to sever all ties with the purely familial existence of the immature."[2]

Given the prohibition of women to partake in, or even be present at, such ceremonies, it is obvious that all such rites of initiation seek to free the son from an image of himself as the helpless infant dependent upon the mother and to create for him a conscious image of the Hero. Such an image is undoubtedly very ancient, probably prehistoric, but, to substantiate, we may cite in further evidence one of its first literary manifestations in western culture, the seventh of the fragmentary elegiacs of Tyrtaeus, that rather mysterious figure whose martial poetry supposedly urged the Spartans on to victory in the second Messenian war:

> Noble is he who falls in front of battle
>   bravely fighting for his native land;
> and wretchedest the man who begs, a recreant,
>   citiless, from fertile acres fled.
> Dear mother, ageing father, little children
>   drift beside him, and his wedded wife;
> unwelcome he shall be, wherever turning,
>   press'd by want and hateful penury;
> He shames his folk and cheats his glorious manhood;
>   all disgrace attends him, all despite.
> Come then,—if beggars go unheard, uncared for,
>   spurn'd in life and in their children spurn'd—
> with courage let us battle for our country,
>   freely spending life to save our sons.
> Young men, stand firm and fight, stand one by other;
>   base retreat and rout let none begin.
> Be high of heart, be strong in pride of combat;
>   grapple, self-forgetting, man to man.
> Forbear to fly, deserting men grown older—
>   stiff about the knees, in honour old.

O foul reproach, when fallen with the foremost
 lies an elder, hindermost the young—
a man whose head is white, whose beard is hoary,
 breathing out his strong soul in the dust,
In nakedness his blood-wet members clutching—
 foul reproach, a sight no gods condone!
Naked he lies where youth were better lying—
 sweet-flow'rd youth, that nothing misbecomes.
Grown men regard the young, women desire them—
 fair in life, in noble death still fair.
Be steadfast then, be strong and firmly rooted
 grip the ground astride, press teeth to lip.[3]

As we know, under the Spartan system of military communism, all other attributions of nobility were regarded as trivial when compared with those demonstrated by the Warrior-Hero in his guardianship of the State. As a member of an exclusively military caste, the Spartan citizen was probably subject to the complete control of an authoritarian code from the moment of his birth, when it was decided whether he was worthy enough to live for the State, until the moment of his glorious death when he was allowed to die for it. His education consisted primarily of physical hardening and combat training; at the age of seven he was removed from his home to live in youth barracks; at the age of twenty he began adult participation in military affairs; and from thirty to sixty his prime purpose in life was full military service. His early rewards were social approval and an equal share in the spoils of conquest. When he attained the status of an Elder, his reward was active participation in the government.

Such an orientation may be considered somewhat unique even in the history of western culture, yet it manifests elements to be found in many later patriarchal societies. For the Tyrtaean hero, the State was his true home, and the possibility of dismissal from the common table of its strict regimen constituted his main source of anxiety. In this poem, then, it is the threat of exile, as pictured in the "wretched recreant" deprived of his share in the "fertile acres" of Messenia, which provides the hero his chief impetus for valor. Lack of wealth, in one sense, becomes symbolic of cowardice and nonacceptance. By extension, failure to conform to absolutist doctrine and human frailty in combat become the crimes which inhibit a man's fulfillment. Failing to grasp the ideals of his society, the inept one is dismissed in exile, "citiless," back to the dark earth which alone is willing to receive him.

As failure, he destroys not only himself but his family. He shames his father who had sought to give to the State a hero after his own image; he shames his mother who might have rejoiced at his death in battle, but who can only mourn at such defection; he shames his wife and children and bequeaths to his sons only the image of a weakling. Thus Tyrtaeus presents as a warning to the youth of his poem the picture of the exile, the citiless drifter, "unwelcome . . . wherever turning, / press'd by want and hateful penury," a shame and a disgrace to all. "Come then," he urges, if you would not be this scorned and penurious beggar, "battle for our country" and in the exercise of courage "freely spend [your] life to save our sons"; that is, die to perpetuate the patriarchal mode.

Although the Tyrtaean elegiac is primarily hortatory in intention, beneath this urging to martial endeavor one perceives in the poem a peculiarly "masculine" form of logic. The maintenance of order demands military exploit; successful military exploit demands unquestioning obedience to the authoritarian Word of Command; and this, in turn, necessitates the abrogation of individual thought. One is forced to conclude that the patriarchal mode of what might be termed "societal reasoning" demands the nonfunctioning of both individual and "humanistic reason" to preserve that which is assumed to be of self-evident value to all reasonable men.

Thus, though Tyrtaeus' invocations to "be strong in pride of combat," to be steadfast, and to forget oneself imply that military heroism really springs from the warrior's own free will and proud sense of aspiration, the threat implicit in his exhortation vaguely recalls Dr. Johnson's ironic definition that "patriotism is the last refuge of a scoundrel."

The contradiction inherent in such logic compels one to ask whether such "patriarchal altruism" can be rightly considered a valid expression of love? Most specialists in this area would agree that the finer forms of such an emotion involve a devotion to something external, an abandonment of all self-aggrandizement in order to achieve the betterment of the beloved object—the gift and whatever sacrifice is entailed in the giving are intended to ensure the realization of some potential latent within the recipient. But is this the end held out by the old schoolmaster, Tyrtaeus? Is the sacrifice demanded by Spartan authority in any way similar to that offered by Oedipus? Is the resultant boon in any way a means of guaranteeing any substantial growth or beneficence? Or does the plea reveal ultimately only the narrowly circumscribed interests inherent in all castes of authority?

The injunction to love, meant to be taken personally by each individual youth, is couched in the most *general* terms: "Young men, stand firm and fight." But once the exhortation is made, the poem's focus of interest shifts immediately to those whose preservation is of prime concern, the elders. The older warriors are not to be deserted in battle, and it is the possibility of their defeat which gives rise to the image of shame which youth must at all costs seek to prevent—"O foul reproach" when the honorable elder falls "with the foremost," clutching his shattered genitalia. Obviously, the shattering of the instruments of procreation suggests not only the loss of the male's capacity to bequeath organic life, but also, in this bloody image, the loss of a masculine spiritual capacity—

the elder "is . . . breathing out his strong soul in the dust." Such is "a sight no gods condone," a sight to stir the anger of all ancestral deities who find in this shameful neglect of age, authority, and honorable repute a crime against themselves and the whole hierarchical order which they have instigated and willed to the minds of their descendants. Religious sanction is invoked in substantiation of the propriety and necessity of military heroism.

The point at issue would seem to be whether the "love" expended on the preservation of the State can be deemed beneficent when it demands the sacrifice of individual life for the maintenance of hierarchical order and a particular, if not provincial, law and status quo. Tyrtaeus' poem affirms this "love" and urges youth to fall in the forefront of battle as evidence of an abnegation of the personal self in behalf of the more worthy elders. What we may term the Spartan inversion is summarized in the reproachful lines—"Naked [the elder] lies where youth were better lying— / sweet-flow'rd youth, that nothing misbecomes." All the promise of youthful potential, all the glory of youth's sensual response, all the often manifest beauty which makes youth so splendid that "nothing misbecomes it"—all this must be offered on the altar of Ares to preserve the ancient guardians of order. In this act of sacrifice, youth is promised a patriarchal "heaven on earth," the attainment of status, the splendor of an heroic repute which will deny the image of reality, his own dismemberment and death on that very battlefield.

TWO POEMS . . .

Far different from this exhortation to the fulfillment of self as Warrior-Hero is the devotional lyric of medieval Europe, limited, without doubt, by its specific religious orientation, yet capable also of revealing certain basic responses. As the

Tyrtaean fragments create symbolic images of the Archetypal Masculine as Hero and Father, so the following well-known poem depicts images of the Archetypal Feminine as Kore (Maiden) and Mother:

> I Syng of a myden Þat is makeles,
>   kyng of alle kynges   to here sone che ches.
>
> he cam also stylle   Þer his moder was
> as dew in aprylle,   Þat fallyt on Þe gras.
>
> he cam also stylle   to his moderes bowr
> as dew in aprille,   Þat fallyt on Þe flour.
>
> he cam also stylle   Þer his moder lay
> as dew in aprille,   Þat fallyt on Þe spray.
>
> moder & mayden was neuer non but che—
> wel may swych a lady   godes moder be.[4]

As in most lyrics of this sort, the Virgin Mary serves as the intercessory source of salvation; the emotional tone of the poem bespeaks a simple piety and an instinctual turning to the Good Mother of Christianity for protection. Mary is praised as the catalytic agent between God and man, between the spirit in the flesh and the flesh seeking to free the spirit; in her archetypal role of the Madonna she gives birth to the Bambino, the Son of Light, who is to save the world from worldliness. She is not only the vessel of birth but also the vessel of rebirth, the beauteous earth that receives the "heavenly" dew and effects a spiritual transformation. In giving birth to Jesus, Mary, traditionally, gives a new day, a new birth to humanity.

As the provider of both physical and spiritual life, Mary is depicted in these lyrics in a variety of relationships to Jesus: she is the pure maiden or Kore to whom the Annunciation is made; she is the nursing mother or Madonna; she is the grieving mother of the Crucifixion; and she is the joyous mother who has seen her Son fulfill His divine potentiality. Throughout, and most important, she is the revelatory instrument of an understanding based on faith. In Erich Neumann's terms, she is both the archetypal Good Mother of the secular vegetation mysteries, the actual fruitful source of organic being, and the archetypal Virgin of the spiritual inspiration mysteries who, through the transforming emotion of love, enables man (the son as Hero) to achieve transcendent being.[5]

This role of catalytic agent is explored and fully elaborated in the following poem of Gerard Manley Hopkins, both a priest and medieval scholar:

> Wild air, world-mothering air,
> Nestling me everywhere,
> That each eyelash or hair
> Girdles; goes home betwixt
> The fleeciest, frailest-flixed
> Snowflake; that's fairly mixed
> With, riddles, and is rife
> In every least thing's life;
> This needful, never spent,
> And nursing element; 10
> My more than meat and drink,
> My meal at every wink;
> This air, which, by life's law,
> My lung must draw and draw
> Now but to breathe its praise,
> Minds me in many ways
> Of her who not only
> Gave God's infinity
> Dwindled to infancy
> Welcome in womb and breast 20
> Birth, milk, and all the rest

But mothers each new grace
That does now reach our race—
Mary Immaculate,
Merely a woman, yet
Whose presence, power is
Great as no goddess's
Was deemèd, dreamèd; who
This one work has to do—
Let all God's glory through,   30
God's glory which would go
Through her and from her flow
Off, and no way but so.

   I say that we are wound
With mercy round and round
As if with air: the same
Is Mary, more by name.
She, wild web, wondrous robe,
Mantles the guilty globe,
Since God has let dispense   40
Her prayers his providence:
Nay, more than almoner,
The sweet alms' self is her
And men are meant to share
Her life as life does air.
   If I have understood,
She holds high motherhood
Towards all our ghostly good
And plays in grace her part
About man's beating heart.   50
Laying, like air's fine flood,
The deathdance in his blood;
Yet no part but what will
Be Christ our Saviour still.
Of her flesh he took flesh:
He does take fresh and fresh,
Though much the mystery how,

Not flesh but spirit now
and makes, O marvellous!
New Nazareths in us,   60
Where she shall yet conceive
Him, morning, noon, and eve;
New Bethlems, and he born
There evening, noon, and morn—
Bethlem or Nazareth,
Men here may draw like breath
More Christ and baffle death;
Who, born so, comes to be
New self and nobler me
In each one and each one   70
More makes, when all is done,
Both God's and Mary's Son.
    Again, look overhead
How air is azurèd;
O how! nay do but stand
Where you can lift your hand
Skywards: rich, rich it laps
Round the four fingergaps.
Yet such a sapphire-shot,
Charged, steepèd sky will not   80
Stain light. Yea, mark you this:
It does no prejudice.
The glass-blue days are those
When every colour glows,
Each shape and shadow shows.
Blue be it: this blue heaven
The seven or seven times seven
Hued sunbeam will transmit
Perfect, not alter it.
Or if there does some soft,   90
On things aloof, aloft,
Bloom breathe, that one breath more
Earth is the fairer for.
Whereas did air not make

This bath of blue and slake
His fire, the sun would shake,
A blear and blinding ball
With blackness bound, and all
The thick stars round him roll
Flashing like flecks of coal,   100
Quartz-fret, or sparks of salt,
In grimy vasty vault.
  So God was god of old:
A mother came to mould
Those limbs like ours which are
What must make our daystar
Much dearer to mankind;
Whose glory bare would blind
Or less would win man's mind.
Through her we may see him   110
Made sweeter, not made dim,
And her hand leaves his light
Sifted to suit our sight.
  Be thou then, O thou dear
Mother, my atmosphere;
My happier world, wherein
To wend and meet no sin;
Above me, round me lie
Fronting my forward eye
With sweet and scarless sky,   120
Stir in my ears, speak there
Of God's love, O live air,
Of patience, penance, prayer:
World-mothering air, air wild,
Wound with thee, in thee isled,
Fold home, fast fold thy child.[6]

The devotion of the medieval saint, who suffered in his prayers and laments the very agony of Christ himself, is also characteristic of Hopkins. In his so-called "terrible sonnets," he experiences a personal crucifixion in terms of a spiritual dryness, a sense of being overburdened by his priestly task, and a threatened divorce from the sustaining nourishment of his God. But the opposite state of achieved communion, of the *"dulcedo Dei"* of delight in the sweetness of the proffered love of Christ, is, as in these medieval lyrics, just as strong an element in Hopkins' total perspective. In both emotional states the soul's need for intimacy with Christ tends to be pictured in terms of physical images, images of hunger and thirst, images even of a grotesque spiritual drunkenness or heartburn, images which, in their echoing of medieval poetry,[7] voice the necessary grounding of the infinite in the finite.

When we turn to the imagery of "The Blessed Virgin Compared to the Air We Breathe," we see that the comparison of Mary, the sufferer of childbed pain, to the physical air which sustains each living human organism is but a valid extension of this medieval poetic mode. In seeking to convey man's tenuous knowledge of Mary's symbolic role, Hopkins is employing devices similar to those of the poets who sought to convey the irrational, but heartfelt, significance of what seemed at the time to be the most crucial of all relationships. In using functional images expressing the full scope of this emotional intimacy, Hopkins, too, seeks to mirror that unconscious faith which demands visible fulfillment, but which can be conveyed to finite apprehension only through imbuing the figures and actions of religious love with the vestments of daily reality. As Hopkins reflects attitudes wholly characteristic of European medievalism, he also manifests the archetypal Artist-Hero's desire to probe the mysteries of universal experience. Perhaps this is why his poetry, though it is interwoven with Roman Catholic dogma, seldom seems dogmatic. The personal figures of a personal religion are transmuted into transpersonal images as common to the species as the air we breathe.

Seeking a force analogous to the spiritual force of the Blessed Virgin, Hopkins employs this very image of the air, the physical gases which embrace the earth and sustain its organic life. The poem begins by immediately designating these gases as the "world-mothering air." The air which surrounds every least part of the human body nestles the poet like the arms of the nursing mother, the arms of love which offer the child complete protection, recalling for him the warmth and nourishment of his intra-uterine existence. Its necessity is similar to that of the encompassing womb or the fruitful breast. As "this needful, never spent, and nursing element," it feeds the body with a sustenance of even more importance than one's daily meals. "Life's law" demands its constant presence, thus, as analogous image, it speaks of a mode of physical satisfaction beyond that represented by the hunger pole of satisfied sensual appetite (ll. 1–12). Similarly, the physical body of the mother sustains the embryo and infant, but her presence, like that of the inevitable air, implies more than temporary satisfaction; it is the continuing fount of love, and therefore, of life. It cannot be confined to a ritual performed but three times a day. Thus Mary, like the air, becomes more than a source of nourishment; she becomes the very source of existence.[8]

As Hopkins equates these two and contemplates their mysterious powers, he recognizes that the semantic use of the term, *anima*, to designate both air and soul, breath and spirit, serves also to depict the double role of Mary herself who is not only the all-accepting Good Mother providing for Christ an earthly home within her womb, but also, through her mercy, the intercessory agent of God's spiritual grace. Subtly, though with infinite clarity, the poem proceeds to reveal Mary's double nature, first, through this analogy with the air, and then, through a further analogy with God Himself. As God incarnate in the flesh of Jesus is both the embodiment of infinity and the archetypal human child, so Mary is both a fertility goddess of physical nature and the means of humanity's achieving spiritual life: she "mothers each new grace / That now does reach our race." Through her sympathetic action of welcoming God in His fleshly role, she gains the capacity to communicate with Him on a spiritual basis and to transmit the prayers of her fellow fleshly beings. Through this welcoming of Christ, and through her organic nourishment of the Bambino or Holy Child, she displays a form of human maternal love which is so great as to entitle her thenceforth to be the agent of God's own greater offering of grace. Regardless of any doctrinal designation of Mary of Nazareth as the recipient of the Annunciation, her expression of human mother love manifests a mode of selfless giving (*agape* or *caritas*) sufficiently splendid to earn divine approval (ll. 13–33).

The image of the air is then amplified so that it becomes the all-encompassing mercy of God which is epitomized in the figure of Mary herself. The gift of mercy, like the gift of air, is God-created and evidence of His grace. It is made comprehensible to man in the figure of Mary, who, in reflecting associations with the personal mother, evokes a further vision of divinity in its absolute perfection. This vision, in so far as it may be comprehended, is not based on any rational conviction but on an unconscious extension of man's earliest emotions. He feels this mercy as subtly as he feels the air around him. Its attributes—giving, forgiving, and compassion—thus constitute a "wondrous robe" which "mantles the guilty globe" in the warmth of total acceptance. Justice is abnegated by a so-called "higher" code; punishment as the instrument of legality has no place in Mary's all-embracing benevolence:

Ave Maria, gratia plena, Dominus tecum, benedicta tu in mulieribus et benedictus fructus ventris tui, Jesus.

Thus Mary becomes, as God's agent, more than the conveyer of His mercy, she becomes "Mercy" herself, the means whereby the efficacy of God is made available to man. As the biological mother is the source of the organism's physical life, and as all men share equally in the sustenance of the air, so in their spiritual communion with Mary, all men share equally in an all-enveloping mercy (ll. 34–45).

"If I have understood," says Hopkins, appealing to that form of higher wisdom which transcends rational conviction, Mary is the mother of "all our ghostly good" or spiritual welfare; she is the manifestation of God's willingness to give of Himself. Through His grace, she gives birth to that possibility of Redemption which allays and countermands for mankind the doom of original sin ("the deathdance in his blood"). In the image of the medieval *Totentanz*, Hopkins seeks to depict the force of death against which the maternal principle of life must struggle. Here, the figure of Mary offers not only continuing life, an opportunity to realize human potentialities, but also an escape from mutability through the partaking of Jesus' redeeming sacrifice. Through her, man is bequeathed his emotional capacity to respond to that love which is supposedly the spirit of Christ within him. His "soul," a term used here by Hopkins to suggest an agency capable of both divine "feeling" and reason, through such union, is continually reclothed in the spiritual "flesh" of mercy just as the spirit of Christ was clothed in the bodily flesh of Mary ("though much the mystery how").

As all Christian imagery insists, this possibility of redemption is not to be considered a static pool, but an eternally flowing river of grace as blood or milk, always "fresh," immutably dynamic, and ever present to those who would come to refresh and nourish themselves. It is not, however, in any sense a Heraclitean river of flux,[9] but, as the poem would have it, a stream of immortal life giving birth to "new Nazareths in us," cities of individual rebirth where, in Thomas à Kempis' terms, we may constantly grow into Christ's likeness. Here, the immutability of Christ's grace and the possibility of our own rebirth in an *Imitatio Christi* is conveyed in a wonderfully apt metaphor: Nazareth, the city of Jesus' conception and thus of our own potential rebirth, is equated with the womb of Mary where a continual process of growth takes place, where the nourishing lifeblood of mercy is always available through the umbilical cord of prayer. The living air drawn into the mother's lungs is, in a sense, breathed by the child in the womb, and in the Nazareth of Mary's womb, "man . . . may draw like breath" to that drawn by Christ himself and thereby share in a similar atmosphere of love. In doing so, "men . . . baffle death," the suffocation which occurs when the heart is deprived of air, blood, and life-giving divine grace. "Who, born so, comes to be / New self and nobler me . . ."—the merciful womb of Mary, rather than the men's house of patriarchal society, is to be the true city of rebirth. Nazareth is Bethlehem for those who will share the brotherhood of Christ. Through participation in such action, Hopkins is assured that we may escape worldly motivation to become, like Jesus and Mary, blossoming trees of *caritas* giving the shade and refreshment of love to all who would seek it (ll. 46–72).

Similarly, the natural beauty of the air serves, like such trees, to transmit and transform light. The essence of air is its transparency, which functions analogically here as a mode of revelation. Looking upward, we see through Hopkins' delighted eyes "a sapphire-shot, / Charged, steepèd sky," as much an image of man's aspiration as is the sun which illumines it. Yet, both sky and sun come to man *through* the air, the agency which transmits this ineffable glory in all its varied colors with "each shape and shadow" perfect. It does not "stain light"; it does not distort our perception of the beauty blooming there; but "with its one breath more, / Earth is the fairer for" its mitigating influence. And yet, air is not ornamentation but necessity, it is the intermediary force of cooling intercession between the pure glory of the fiery sun and man who needs the warmth of sunlight for his very life. The living organism cannot endure the intense purity of such heat; man needs the intervening ministration of the merciful air to temper the solar gift or else "the sun would shake" the earth to ashes.

In his definitive study of Hopkins, W. H. Gardner interprets this solar threat of destruction thus:

> Such "bare glory" was the wrath, vengeance and destruction attributed to "god of old." It was the advent of Christ and the Holy Family that made meekness and love the prime aspirations of the religious in the Western world. Hopkins took the realistic view that man's apprehension of God is mainly emotional; hence man, a mere child in relation to such mysteries, must attain to the Infinite Father through the tender spiritual motherhood of Mary.[10]

From this perspective, the Old Testament Jehovah, in His more extreme manifestations as the guardian of the Old Law, and the proponent of strict obedience to authority, is equated with the intense purity of the unsheathed sun, a force of all-consuming power. Images of destruction, especially those of fire, are now commonly accepted as symptomatic of a patriarchal solar orientation of the psyche. The "blear and blinding ball" of the poem becomes equated with that untempered justice and vengeful punishment characteristic of all cultures seeking the birth and maintenance of order. In contrast to the anthropomorphism which naturally reflects a projection of this effort, Hopkins, in his attempt to explicate the essence of the New Testament Gospels, equates solar light with Christ's compassion, thus emphasizing God's beneficent forgiveness as the primary manifestation of divinity. In like fashion, the ethereal Mary, as the quasi-human Good Mother, serves to transmit this merciful light of love in terms comprehensible to the human heart which has experienced such love in earthly infancy and childhood. Through the re-evocation of such previous associations, man can understand the import of divine tenderness, not with the limited and distorting perspective of the finite intellect, but with the emotional perception of his "heart" whose responses lead him to communion with Mary, his fleshly *and* his spiritual mother. Through her, Christ's love comes to him with no diminution of its splendor or its efficacy, but with the additional "one breath more" of human tactile intimacy which earthly love "is the fairer for" (ll. 73–102).

Climactically, the dichotomy between maternal tenderness and patriarchal authority is elaborated as evidence of differing modes of emotional and intellectual apprehension. As the air further glorifies the sun and heaven through disseminating the varied colors of the spectrum, so Mary, in providing the physical means whereby divine love can express itself in a sacrifice comprehensible to the human understanding, transforms the sunlight of God into the mild grace of Jesus. Thus divine love becomes "much dearer to mankind" in its tempered effluences than it might be when experienced in its intensity. We note a most significant qualification in the following lines (108–09)—"Whose glory bare would blind / Or less would win man's mind." Pure sunlight is equated with the goal of complete knowledge attained through perfect reason.

But Hopkins rejects any such prideful aspiration that God can be known through the efforts of patriarchal "witt." Any epistemology which seeks to approach God through positing the validity of logical assumptions is deemed, by Hopkins, inadequate—in winning man's mind it would becloud his perception. However, through Mary, "we may see him / Made sweeter, not made dim, / And her hand leaves his light / Sifted to suit our sight." Softened by the maternal mode of tenderness which supplants Old Testament subjection to authority (*"le roi le veut"*), God's essence becomes satisfactorily available to our weakened spiritual insight. In this surpassingly lovely image, the kindly hand of the interceding and consoling mother sifts the bright glare of pure divinity through the leaves of her human compassion so that it will "suit our sight," fall quietly upon our eyes (ll. 103–13).

The poem concludes with Hopkins' direct address to Mary praying that she be "my atmosphere; / My happier world, wherein / To wend and meet no sin." Establishing the vivid personal communion which he feels for this "dear Mother," Hopkins pleads that she envelop him completely like the air with the "sweet and scarless sky" of her merciful innocence. In coming alive through the breath of her perception, he prays that he, like Jesus, may become truly her son, and that in being continually aware of the spiritual aspects of living, he may achieve his identity as a servant of God. He prays that he may hear always her gentle voice speak in his ears "of God's love, . . . of patience, penance, [and] prayer," the maternal attributes available to man in his quest for an *Imitatio Christi*.

Hopkins in his affirmation, much like Yeats in his dubiety, seems to suggest that this communication of spiritual values is possible only on the basis of participation in a prior physical union. The gentle touch of the air and the subtly sifted warmth of the sunlight elicit responses from the human psyche which are primarily sensual in origin, although they may be transformed into emotions which themselves are capable of eliciting revelations. As in T. S. Eliot's *Ash Wednesday* (Part II), where the mystical Lady of Intercession feeds "to satiety / on [the sinner's] legs . . . heart . . . [and] liver" so that his dead bones may "shine with [the] brightness" of God's acceptance, so here Hopkins propounds his meaning through sensory images: the tactile envelopment of the air which sounds in his ears and stimulates purity of vision is prayed for as the source of ultimate understanding.

But the final analogy of the poem is even more daring: the achievement of this "happier world" is designated as a re-achievement, with added understanding, of uterine serenity. The word "atmosphere" connotes not only the all-enveloping air but also the all-enveloping gentle waters of the womb; the air is again "the world-mothering air" which will enable the transfigured poet to be reborn within the womb of Mary ("Wound with thee, in thee isled"). Her all-encompassing mercy is but a spiritual manifestation of the warmth of the uterus, and as Jesus found a means to human life there, so, Hopkins suggests, man may find in Mary a means to a higher life. As he prays Mary to "fold home, fast fold thy child," the poet evokes, through these images of nurturing, certain unconscious associations which provide means for him to express his belief that we are all the children of Mary's love in the reachieved serenity of an acceptance by God (ll. 114–26).

. . . TWO FLAMES

Those acquainted with the analytical psychology of the late Dr. Jung will recognize that the responses discussed above reflect, if only in a somewhat peripheral fashion, his conception of the archetype. To summarize briefly: Jung posits a human mind which acts as a repository of certain transpersonal images common to the species. Grounded in the evolutionary processes of mankind, these images are actually "thought feelings," universal components so deeply rooted in the psyche that they are bound to manifest themselves in all human action. The poet, as seer, is an organism so refined that he is capable of perceiving them and expressing them for us.

In his *Origins and History of Consciousness*, Erich Neumann shows how these archetypes may be fragmented, separated from a larger, undifferentiated mass. This produces not only a variety of individualized manifestations but also evidence of coherent archetypal groups and symbol canons which may be ordered through analysis into categories. Assuming, then, the archetype's possession of an "eternal presence" as well as a "symbolic polyvalence" (that is, a multitude of variable expressions), one can perceive the possibility of such categorization in the manner in which they divide themselves into polarities according to a principle of opposites: birth and death, youth and age, toil and rest.[11]

In examining the poems of Tyrtaeus and Hopkins, the polarity, mother and father, is immediately recognizable. We would associate with its expression two archetypes which we may term the *Physical Hearth* and the *Sacred Fire*, each possessing a variety of symbolic expressions grounded in our shared psychical experience. As is commonly accepted, it is from the psyche that we derive all "images," images which convey not only the likeness of some originally perceived object, but also the result of its exposure to our reaction to it. These images are bound to be highly personal, without doubt, yet, because of the basic similarity of much human experience, they may also be considered as manifesting a transpersonal quality, mirroring man's continuing conflict with unavoidable external forces: "Man that is born of a woman is of few days, and full of trouble."

It is obvious that the family must serve as the agency of much of this archetypal imagery. As the fount of most early experience, we encounter there love and, occasionally, hate, acceptance and rejection. Within this context, we find the varying promise of the book of Genesis, generation, mutability, and dissolution; and, pending unfortunate neuroses or psychoses, joy, grief, and aspiration. The archetypes which reflect these responses are, of course, not primarily "ideas," but, more like the figures of myth and dream, instinctual apprehensions bodying forth our perceptions of certain vital relationships, contacts which, though not fully understood, speak in emotional overtones to us of mother, father, maiden, child, and, perhaps, mysterious shape of terror.[12] Sociologists look to the family as the basic social unit; psychologists find in family relationships the origin of those unconscious powers whose expressions, repressions, and sublimated tendencies shape man's personal destiny; even theologian and philosopher find in the family environment the source of many cherished moral conceptions.

Thus the poet (dramatist or novelist), attempting to re-create life, seeking verbal equivalents for such subtle response, is often compelled to rely heavily upon those basic experiences encountered when we were first drawn out of our infantile egoism and presented with other identities, with an environment much colder than the womb, with new situations, tension, and conflict. The child cannot control the situation, force acceptance, demand tenderness, or refuse authority; but as a result of these initial recognitions, even this imagined figure can respond or retreat. Whether, symbolically speaking, he basks in the warmth of a caress or perhaps, in aggressive retaliation, rises in anger to bite the hand that somewhat indifferently feeds him, makes a large difference. The extensions expressed by one "choice" or the other seemingly underlie the entire future evolution of the personality. Psychological exploration has made it quite clear that man cannot spring into life with any expectation of being welcomed by a loving family group. Instead, he encounters formative influences, a feminine presence, a masculine presence, and a group situation. The interaction of these forces, the differing images they provide for emulation, the tensions of conflict and cooperation, this, as we know it, is family life, for the poet, a major source of symbol, theme, and significant content, the matrix of the emotions suggested by our introductory poems.[13]

The Images of the Physical Hearth. If, for purposes of discussion, then, we may assume a complex of family symbols, certainly the dominant symbol of such a canon would be that of the *hearth*, whether it be the crude mass of burning sticks around which a primitive family grouped itself to share its particular crises or some more modern equivalent. Obviously, all such symbolic hearths must have their genesis in this ancient group huddled about the ashes of a prehistoric *place of fire* in an attempt to protect themselves from a hostile sphere of cold and mystery. Here, within the family circle, the basic experiences of an almost bestial existence take place —copulation, birth, nursing, the family meal, sleep, and death. It is an environment whose symbolic extensions are difficult to delimit. We can imagine it being a world of male hunters and female guardians of the camp, or, in an even earlier stage, a world of single hunters and single hearths, but, whatever it might have been, the simple contrast reflected suggests two differing roles played by man and woman, even two differing attitudes toward the goals (or "heavens") of human aspiration.[14]

In exploring these complex interrelationships, both Erich Neumann and Erich Fromm acknowledge, in addition to the work of Freud and Jung, the prior investigation of an early nineteenth-century cultural anthropologist, J. J. Bachofen, who, in his now somewhat discounted *Das Mutterrecht* and other studies, sought to distinguish between matriarchal and patriarchal cultures. Neumann and Fromm insist that, despite certain limitations, such as an overemphasis on the actual existence of matriarchal cultures, many of Bachofen's theories, though of doubtful sociological accuracy, still possess validity as insights later substantiated by various depth psychologies.[15]

Ignoring, then, the sociological structure of Bachofen's work, one may still posit the existence of a possible matriarchal stage of human development in which the archetype of the Great Mother was dominant. As in the "Asian orientation" characteristic of the Creto-Mycenaean aspects of Greek myth and legendary history, this goddess seems to have functioned not only as the representative of the fertility processes of Nature but also as representative of an equally mysterious agency of fate. She stood, symbolically at least, for certain aspects of the mythical "Great Dragon of Mystery," unknown forces whose shadowed emanations remain as challenge to man's rational capacity.[16] Evidence abounds of many strangenesses, fecundating animal goddesses and totems, generative figures of earth and ocean whose powers only later became the property of patriarchal gods. In Egypt, tree goddesses give birth to the sun; in Greece, transfigured woman weaves and spins each individual destiny. Everywhere one finds a host of female deities functioning as creatures of instinct, mirroring man's physical alliance with nature.

These transformations of the Archetypal Feminine seem to indicate, as opposed to a later world of patriarchy characterized as "solar," "conscious," and "rational," the existence of a mythical primordial matriarchate which may be designated as "lunar," "unconscious," and predominantly nutritional, concerned, as is the infantile stage of man, with hunger and its satisfaction through food.[17] It is a world based on the undeniable priority of the mother as a physical source. "Man that is born of woman" comes from the womb as the result of a mysterious natural phenomenon; *he* is the passing sower of seed in the ever-present soil; *he* may be blown away by the wind, but *she* will remain forever to welcome new passersby.

According to analytical psychology, the root of such a

conception lies in the psychobiological effects of such feminine blood mysteries as menstruation and pregnancy which
led the primitive to conceive of the mother as "the sheltering
structure" within which *all* the mysteries of life take place,
"preservation, formation, nourishment, and transformation."[18] In this symbolic vessel character, woman functions
primarily as the Good Mother who transforms her blood to
milk, sustaining man as his protective container and cup of
life. Compelled by biological necessity, if not by her very
nature, to first fulfill the role of the nurturing parent, she
takes on herself those associations allied with care and tenderness. In addition, given the mandatory division of labor entailed by a primitive environment, she comes to embrace the
roles of food gatherer and sustainer of the camp. In all of
these, she performs as nurse, feeder of the fire, feeder of the
child; for the uterine warmth of her body, she substitutes the
physical warmth of the hearth.[19]

This is relatively clear; one need say little more about the
image of the Good Mother other than that embodied in the
commentary on Hopkins' poem. However, in terms of a
larger masculine experience of the feminine, it would be
imprecise to limit the interpretation of matriarchy to this one
figure. In another study, *The Great Mother*, Neumann makes
much of the splitting of this basic archetype into the two
opposing images of the Good and Terrible Mothers. Family
associations with a personal mother, or her surrogate, have led
most men to some conception of the former, a fertility goddess still, but one who gives birth to tenderness as well as life.
By contrast, other feminine associations, or a personal failure
in the mother-child relationship, have led some to images of
woman as the Archetypal Temptress or Terrible Mother,
figures comprehensible to the mind in the images of the
succuba, the deceiver, the denier of love, all of those forces,
which, through containment or neglect, place obstacles in the

path of the hero-son seeking his independence or the fulfillment of his quest.[20]

For the Hero, however, conscious choice is not made easily.
The evil aspects of the Archetypal Feminine do not always
display themselves in patently repellent shapes. For example,
early in Book I of Spenser's *The Faerie Queene* (cantos ii–v),
the Red Cross Knight encounters the figure of Duessa, the
feigned virgin, who, in her maidenly innocence seems the
very prototype of the Kore, yet, as the deceitful creation of
the wicked Archimago, she is, in reality, not the promise of
harvest but an agent of physical and spiritual sterility. Spenser
presents her in such a way that we must ask whether the
emotion known as love may not be actually a disguise for lust,
a cloak to hide the truth of an inexorable process leading only
to some form of death, or worse, to the deformity of the
growing personality. The portrayal thus forces upon us the
realization that the Kore may become the Archetypal Temptress who promises, with teasing allurements and duplicity, an
intoxicant vitality and ecstasy, but who, when possessed,
unveiled, reveals only that moral ugliness which leads man to
madness and impotence. What the hero yearns for as his
victory turns out to be the "sinfull house of Pride." Through
mistaking Duessa (falsehood) for Una (truth), the Red Cross
Knight is rendered a child in the world of morality.

To fall under the lure of Lilith, to hear the Siren song, to
approach the couch of Circe without divine aid, to yield to
the serpent stare and tongue of Eve, all these lead to the
fixation of the hero in the woods of digression, his arms weak,
his mind in a stupor, his quest forgotten, his purpose lost. The
delusions of intimate communion hover before him as light,
but such light is the *ignis fatuus* which leads him into exile and
deprivation. He awakens, if at all, not in Book II's "Bowre of
Blisse" but in Orgoglio's dungeon.[21]

Thus, Spenser insists that to obtain valid communication

with woman, and through her, communion with deity, the hero must disavow the "masque of Cupid" which represents a debasement of love; the Red Cross Knight must seek, instead, the "house of Holinesse" where he can be taught "repentance, and / the way to heavenly blesse" (I.x).

How is this to be accomplished? After the Archetypal Temptress, Duessa, has been stripped of her false beauty (I.viii), Una, like Mary, an intercessor in behalf of Truth, resolves to bring the weakened knight to a certain ancient manor which can only be regarded as an elaborate allegorical version of the Physical Hearth. Here, the Youthful Hero meets first the figures of *Fidelia* and *Speranza*, virgins, portrayed in the image of the Kore, who provide for him the inspiration for his quest, who incite him with visions of God's grace, justice, and offering of free will, who comfort him with the possibilities of God's aid as he undergoes his purgatorial discipline. But it is their sister, *Charissa*, portrayed as the Good Mother, who is eventually chosen to instruct him "in every good behest, / Of love, and righteousnesse, and well to donne. . . ."

> She was a woman in her freshest age,
>   Of wondrous beauty, and of bountie rare,
>   With goodly grace and comely personage,
>   That was on earth not easie to compare;
>   Full of great loue, but *Cupids* wanton snare
>   As hell she hated, chast in worke and will;
>   Her necke and breasts were euer open bare,
>   That ay thereof her babes might sucke their fill;
> The rest was all in yellow robes arrayed still.
>
> A multitude of babes about her hong,
>   Playing their sports, that joyd her to behold,
>   Whom still she fed, whiles they were weake and young,
>   But thrust them forth still, as they wexed old:

And on her head she wore a tyre of gold,
Adornd with gemmes and owches wondrous faire,
Whose passing price vneath was to be told;
And by her side there sate a gentle paire
Of turtle doues, she sitting in an yuorie chaire.

[I.x, 30–31]

As Demeter planted the effigy of the corn god, who, through his ritual death, would guarantee harvest, so *Charissa*, the exemplar of married love, plants in the hero's mind "the ready path to heaven," the means and mystic way of accomplishing his hero-task of slaying Satan, the Dragon of Evil. Calling up as his guide the "auncient matrone, *Mercie*," *Charissa* sends him to her "holy Hospitall" where he encounters the seven Bead-men who teach him the matriarchal virtues of feeding the hungry, clothing the naked, comforting the sick and oppressed, praying for the dead, and caring for their widows and orphans (xxxvi–xliii). Once indoctrinated in these Christlike tasks, the Red Cross Knight is conducted to the hermit, *Contemplation*, where he learns *intellectually* of the meaning "of God and goodnesse." "His mind . . . full of spirituall repast," he is conducted to the visionary hill of revelation where he views the New Jerusalem of God's ". . . chosen people purg'd from sinfull guilt, / With pretious bloud, which cruelly was spilt / On cursed tree, of that unspotted lam, / That for the sinnes of all the world was kilt" (lvii). Thus, through *Charissa*, the youthful Hero learns his lesson, the full import of his road of trials and its spiritual culmination: only in an *Imitatio Christi* can he become the Savior-Hero, St. George.

Although there are patriarchal overtones in Spenser's allegory, the basic role of the Good Mother is fully elucidated: she is to guide the growth of the hero until a transformation mystery occurs. Through her capacity for bearing and releasing life, she is to teach him the meaning of *caritas*. This capacity becomes, in a later stage of development, the capacity to inspire, and so the Child, or Bambino, as in Hopkins' poem, will obtain the means of accomplishing his quest. Mere physical strength, and the ability to grow and function well, become, under her aegis, moral strength and the ability to perceive spiritually. Thus the Good Mother obtains her archetypal existence not only as a source of tangible protection but also as the means of man's achieving further recognition of the *anima* and a knowledge of compassion, "the matriarchal wisdom of the soul."[22]

Out of the sensual world of birth and nursing, she brings to the world, and to the individual, symbolic sacrifices of blood and milk which are to lead the untutored to the sublime visions of benevolent purpose. Transforming physical into spiritual reality, she gives always with tenderness, with no thought of retraction, the male child as Hero, the pursuer of light, the female child as Kore, the new fount of permanence.

The Images of the Sacred Fire. Manifestly, the idea of progress leads away from such a primitive orientation. Even at its best, demonstrating such close, but restricted, ties, the environment of the Physical Hearth cannot provide a large enough area of endeavor for human effort. Man must leave the warm hearth to probe the "Swamp of Mystery" beyond the firelight.

Thus, if we continue to explore these wells of early experience, we must confront next the hypothetical entrance of a huge, perhaps blood-stained, figure who intrudes upon the hearth to startle the infant and child. It is the image of the Father as Hunter, or Warrior, returning to assert his status, to demand certain prescribed modes of action. If, by any chance, there is a conflict over his right to impose his will upon the family, he must certainly triumph, for he provides the more desirable "animal" food, the winter's staple; he builds and fashions the more complex tools; he provides communication with the external world. He is the one who knows "reality," the best hunting grounds, the best place to pitch camp, the most effective way of keeping off marauders. Above all, he represents that one invaluable contact with other males who together recognize the inevitability of communal grouping as the best means of attaining security. Thus he gains his right to impose authority.

This will is to be expressed *within* the family by the establishment of a hierarchy and graduated spheres of duty and privilege, *outside* the family by demanding that his own family group observe those customs which enhance, glorify, and solidify patriarchal dominance. Even before these vague dictates are formulated into elaborate religio-magical, societal, and political structures, the primitive Father satisfies for his family group the need of a strong figure who can guarantee the hearth some form of safety from external threat. In both primitive and heroic age depictions of the male, one discovers a fierceness of facial expression, wildly staring eyes, obtruding veins, a mouth easily imagined fanged as that of the ravenous beast. It is a picture of the utmost power, a picture of obsession and purpose; it represents the fury of the raging river, the ominous brow of the thundercloud:

> And what shoulder, & what art,
> Could twist the sinews of thy heart?
> And when thy heart began to beat,
> What dread hand? & what dread feet?
>
> What the hammer? what the chain?
> In what furnace was thy brain?
> What the anvil? what dread grasp
> Dare its deadly terrors clasp? . . .

Tyger! Tyger! burning bright
In the forests of the night,
What immortal hand or eye,
Dare frame thy fearful symmetry?

To Blake, the fury of the tiger's natural force was as apt to
be found in man as were the evidences of divinity. Confronted with this overwhelming strength in the figure of the
father, the face of the child turns pale with fear and he
cowers from the threatening storm, the raised hand. However, when this force becomes his mentor at the pubertal
period of initiation, he experiences a new possibility. Suddenly, he is aware that he too can possess this power, he too
can be as the river and the thunderbolt. The revelation of the
strength latent within him, as it is demonstrated in the
grown father, makes him seek guidance for his aspiration.
Such guidance is not to be found in the matriarchal environs
of the Physical Hearth, but is readily available if he will but
heed his father's cry from the doorway of the Sacred Fire. It
is a call to knowledge and power but it is also a call to pain.
Through the circumcision of primitive ritual, or some other
test, the male child is allowed to prove himself worthy of
acceptance into the patriarchal womb of the men's house
where indoctrination into secretly formulated codifications
will serve as new nourishment. Once reborn, he can attain
further skill and further acceptance through the skillful use of
weapons designed for the continuing defense of the patriarchal group. Through these means, his dreams of dominance
and power can be realized.

Theoretically, the archetypal Father figures of masculine
dominance manifest their control in two ways: through denying the expected paternal strength and assistance, and through
the assumption of the "right" to punish. Thus it is by taking
the great step from a world of almost total acceptance to a
world embodying demands and the possibility of rejection

and punishment that we are led from the primordial Physical Hearth to the ancient Greek and Roman altars with their dominant symbol of the Sacred Fire. At this now sanctified stone, formulated worship in terms of hymns, prayers, and libations to the entombed fathers of the Ancestral House attest to a patriarchal usurpation of the harmonious mutual acceptances of the matriarchal world. The growth of a conscious awareness of the ego and its environment leads man from an almost bestial state of existence to a human condition wherein precisely ascertained relationships and rules of order become the primary concerns. Oversimplified, the power of the Sacred Fire inheres in its capacity to deny, to say *no*.[23]

At first, then, it might seem that any literary analysis concerned with the family would deal with the relatively easy problem of whether the hearth has been preserved or violated. But when one recognizes, despite a multiplicity of cultural variance, the essentially differing basic roles of the mother and the father, it becomes apparent that we are actually concerned with two hearths, and that the preservation of the one may very likely involve the violation of the other. The Sacred Fire may evolve out of certain attitudes displayed by the Hunter at a primitive stage of development, but these attitudes cannot become fully crystallized into a code until a much more advanced state of civilization has been attained. The Hunter's demand for authority can only be transformed into an enduring force with man's later capacity to order social behavior. However, before this can be accomplished, the male must usurp the prerogatives gained by matriarchy through its power of giving physical birth, an act which makes all of his own accomplishments minimal, relegating him to a subordinate role within the environs of the Physical Hearth. This usurpation involves two processes: a derogation of the value of the matriarchal role and its customs, and a glorification of the patriarchal mode. In exalting patriarchy, the dominant Elders of the group seek, first of all, to solidify their customs by imbuing them with supposedly unbreakable religious, social, and political sanctions. These sanctions are themselves patriarchal creations, and thus the mode becomes self-justifying, self-glorifying, and self-perpetuating. The usurpation process then continues as an unabated and archetypal action just as long as these sanctions of the patriarchal consciousness succeed in subduing the unconscious, instinctual expressions of the matriarchate.

Without doubt, the Hearth and the Sacred Fire have much in common: both serve the pragmatic purpose of cooking the family meal; both serve as a gathering place for family contact. The Physical Hearth, however, since it is equated with the Good Mother's instinctual tenderness, serves as a more or less *natural* source of warmth, nourishment, and communion. The role of human fatherhood, on the other hand, is a *learned* role, and by extension the Sacred Fire, also, is the product of trial and error, of an authoritative formulation designed to create and perpetuate an Ancestral House. Margaret Mead bases such action on a desire for "ancestral expectancy," a desire to establish a way of life based on a specific cultural heritage. Within this formulated family of well-born ones, the chosen members, having assumed for themselves certain aristocratic prerogatives, come to feel obligated to a code or set of rules to which the natural family of the Physical Hearth is not subject.[24]

In his study, *The Ancient City*, Fustel de Coulanges traces one such development of a code from its beginnings in the early family to its eventual culmination in the "religious and civil institutions" of classical Greece and Rome. It is a story of the Father and Elder as patriarchal authorities.

We know that primitive man had some conception of an existence after death, and that, among the early Greeks, the spirits of the dead preferred to remain near home. There is something rather pathetic about this desire to care for the dead, to pour libations and place a pittance of food upon the grave in an attempt to restore the completeness of the family circle, to give warmth again to the poor dead creature and assure him that his place by the fireside has been kept for him, that he is still loved and welcomed. It is this feeling of piety toward parents and home that leads initially to the growth of ancestor worship, the deification of a deceased Elder whose soul lived on in its underground tomb waiting the daily appeasement of its hunger and thirst.

But almost immediately the element of fear seems to have been introduced, a fear that the tutelary deity of the household, when not reassured of continued family respect, might turn into a malevolent spirit. If the living patriarch as priest neglected the proper burial ceremonies or failed to offer the funeral repast, then the distressed and rejected spirit would gain his revenge on the family by becoming a shade, visiting all sorts of disasters on the house that scorned him. The son who neglected these ceremonies was actually committing a form of parricide, and, worst of all, could be considered guilty of depriving the living family of the wisdom, consolation, and general beneficence of its household god.[25]

Of all the mandatory rules of conduct in this worship, the most important seems to have been the establishment of a Sacred Fire, an altar on which "there had always to be a small quantity of ashes and a few lighted coals." This fire was never allowed to go out because its extinction indicated the extinction of the body of the ancestral god who animated it.[26] The fire was always to remain pure; one did not burn trash in it, nor commit a crime in its presence; even the natural union of the sexes, so much a part of the love and warmth associated with the Physical Hearth, was forbidden in its vicinity. In its purity the Sacred Fire served as a protective power and a source of morality; it enjoined "purity of heart, temperance, and wisdom," all the "higher," or solar, attributes of patri-archy. Yet, in its demand for obedience and the authoritarian imposition of order, it also threatened punishment and death to those who sought self-fulfillment in any but the accepted mode, thus providing a justification for all future patriarchal defense of the status quo.

The religion of the Sacred Fire, then, was definitively exclusive, offered only to the obedient, to blood relations, participated in only by the nearest relatives, jealously guarded from outside intrusion. In contrast to the reverence for and acceptance of all life characteristic of the Physical Hearth, the religion of the Sacred Fire involved a pattern of rejection, not only of alien neighbors, but also, to a lesser degree, of the lower members of the family hierarchy. It tended to become a patrimony, a heritage of rites, obligations, and privileges be-queathed by the father to the eldest son, often leaving even mother, daughter, and younger son to share in it only as submissive adjuncts.[27]

Such a patrimony led quickly to the development of the Ancestral House which came to represent the aristocratic bond maintained by the male members of a family and the spirits of their revered ancestors who inhabited not only the family tomb but the altar stone of the Sacred Fire as well. Eventually, expansion of this religiously dominated family organization led to the formation of further patriarchal con-federations, the clan, phratry, tribe, and ancient city. Social order became the final solar goal of the Sacred Fire as it sought its perfection.[28] Denying the environment of the Physical Hearth as incapable of discrimination, the Elders formulated precise rules of acceptance to avoid the continued formlessness of nomadism. When admission to an exclusive society could only be gained through presentation by one's father at an initiation ceremony, then authority could prevail, the inept could be rejected, and the sacrificial meal shared only by the worthy who would continue the approved pursuits of the particular patriarchal idealism involved.

To comprehend the Tyrtaean mode, then, and the absolutism of Spartan authority, one must realize that the founding of a city-state was a sacred act, the choice of site, a decision of the gods, and the result, a fatherland with a Sacred Fire of its own. The right worshipful Elder as priest and father figure, whether he was king, prytane, or archon, maintained this fire, conducted the sacrificial rites, and presided at religious festivals in hopes of preserving the welfare of the State, his fellow Elders, and their worthy descendants. Thus it was that the "wise old man's" knowledge of liturgical directions, his religious authority, led to his becoming codifier of the group law; as mediator between man and his god, he became, by extension, magistrate, judge, and military chief. Since he was so favored by the gods, and his legislative regulations with regard to marriage, divorce, and property rights were considered to be divinely inspired, his word was law, its validity as a sacred injunction was not to be questioned.[29] Unfortunately, as De Coulanges indicates, the letter of the law became everything—"The value of the law [was] not in the moral principle that it contains, but in the words that make up the formula."[30] And so even Socrates can ask of Crito, "Are you so wise as to have forgotten that compared with your mother and father and all the rest of your ancestors your country is something far more precious, more venerable, more sacred, and held in greater honour both among gods and among all reasonable men?" If one disagrees and "cannot persuade [the State] in accordance with universal justice," then, as Socrates asserts, one must obey the dictates of its military and its courts of law.

Yet, such obedience has its own rewards. In his excellent discussion of the Tyrtaean fragments, C. M. Bowra seeks to explicate "two closely related conceptions, the ἀνὴρ ἀγαθός

or good man and his ἀρετή or excellence."³¹ In these poems,
the good man achieves his goodness, or nobility, through
"fall[ing] in front of battle." In so doing, he manifests his
essential excellence, that capacity for devotion which makes
him a proper *man* or hero:

> No man proves that he is good in war,
> Unless he bravely face the bloody carnage,
>   Standing by the foe to strike him down.
> This is man's excellence and finest guerdon,
>   Fairest glory for the young to win.
> A good for all the city, all the people,
>   When a man stands up in battle's front
> And flinches not, nor thinks of base withdrawal,
>   But sets heart and spirit to endure,
> And with his words makes brave the man beside him:
>   So the good man is revealed in war.
>
> For him young men and old make lamentation,
>   All the city weeps with sad regret;
> Well known to men his grave is, and his children,
>   Children's children and those after them.
> His good name dies not nor his noble glory:
>   Under earth he liveth evermore.³²

In addition, then, to the hope of actual material spoil and
sensual indulgence, obedience offers (as in fragment #7) the
approval of the Elders and the admiration of women; but
more, it provides a standard of behavior: the good man is the
good soldier and citizen. As Bowra puts it, "Tyrtaeus' soldier
fights not for himself but for his city; he fights not alone but
in regiments; his honor comes not [primarily] from an anon-
ymous posterity but from his countrymen. He is a citizen
before he is a hero, and he only becomes a hero by being a
good citizen."³³ The heroic world of individual combat in
which the warrior-hero met his challenger to prove their

comparative strengths and skills yields to a world in which the obedient salute to the Word of Command is the prime gesture of the hero. Man's aspiration for immortality was to be satisfied through the remembrance of his feats in battle, his capacity to conquer that universal fear of death which inhibits the Warrior-Hero's prowess. Those who survive in security will bequeath him new life and resurrection as the incarnate figure of heroic memory.

Thus, according to such patriarchal conceptions, it was to the binding religious and civil authority of the Sacred Fire that a man owed his primary allegiance. If he lost this through failure to conform, he was, as we have noted, threatened with a wretched exile, to be unwelcome and disgraced "wherever turning." Such banishment, of course, involved not only the loss of his honor, his family, and his goods, but worst of all, his gods—exiled from the locale of his Sacred Fire and his city worship, he lost the protecting, guiding power of patriarchal providence.

In a larger context, the exclusiveness of the Sacred Fire led inevitably to antagonism between the religious groups of any two cities. Possessing different founding fathers, often enemies of one another, how could they unite in a common form of worship? The communion of the Physical Hearth yields, then, to a further isolation of warring factions, each obsessed by a desire to maintain in total purity its own particular code. Yet, this compulsion for autonomy, this insistence on the sovereignty of each State, resulted also, within one's own city, in the suppression of individual liberty. Supported by religious sanction, the formulations of political authority became an inhibiting force far greater than any the mother might impose on the developing psyche. The maintenance of the status quo demanded full obedience and the subjection of any conflicting natural sentiments: children belong more to the

State than to their parents; a man's private life is not really his own.

Thus, initiation into a selective "men's house" would seem, eventually, to result in an adoption of the individual by the paternity of the State, functioning as a sort of superego shaping social and moral beliefs in the mind of the citizen. And thus the State risks becoming the source of certain destructive images, of models which encourage aggression, tyranny, or a submissive apathy in the form of an unthinking conformity. These, plus a whole host of personality-inhibiting guilts and anxieties, warp the personality of the citizen just as the family father might warp the personality of the child. In such primarily patriarchal documents as Plato's *Republic*, not to mention the Tyrtaean fragments, the citizen-child is deprived of natural affection because it is considered a contaminating and weakening force. Adherence to "reason" as a complete guide to moral action is deemed sufficient for all societal purposes. The solar ideal of wisdom is meant to blend with the phallic ideal of courage to create that *arete* which is the goal of the ideal city-state.

But children *as children*, as the objects of parental love, are missing from this picture. In the background of this theoretical ideal there seem to be the echoes of Bacon's partial censure of those who have given "hostages to fortune," and the disgust evoked by the urinating Yahoo infants of Swift's *Gulliver's Travels*. To use, but not to care for the child, suggests one of the chief causes of that later subtle frustration felt by patriarchy as its quests, even when successful, prove, emotionally, not wholly satisfying. For the patriarchal realm would seem to be, basically, a childless realm, and its births seem, somehow, always inadequate, lacking in organic vitality. What cannot be tangibly produced (and fondled) cannot be loved. Deprived of the actual birth experience, the masculine psyche is, supposedly, unable to accept fully the image of the child which, symbolically, reminds it of its limitations. Thus it turns to other births, the rituals and laws of the Sacred Fire, hoping to find in these versions of itself the immortality denied the secondary role of the sower of seed. The life which the male cannot produce from his inept body must be found in the formulating mind. To render this life significant in terms of religions, philosophies, and laws, man must *use* those whom he controls to create his churches, his books, and his courts. In such patriarchal roles, he must, in Fielding's phrase, "employ hands" to attain his objectives. And in choosing and rejecting, discriminating instead of accepting, he finds anew the taint of that mutability which destroys his births.

The new Youthful Hero, who is to become the later Elder, appears on the scene to choose and reject in his own terms, and the earlier birth becomes a moment's empty triumph to be followed again by frustration:

> I met a traveller from an antique land
> Who said: Two vast and trunkless legs of stone
> Stand in the desert. Near them, on the sand,
> Half sunk, a shattered visage lies, whose frown,
> And wrinkled lip, and sneer of cold command,
> Tell that its sculptor well those passions read
> Which yet survive, stamped on these lifeless things,
> The hand that mocked them and the heart that fed;
> And on the pedestal these words appear:
> "My name is Ozymandias, king of kings:
> Look on my works, ye Mighty, and despair!"
> Nothing beside remains. Round the decay
> Of that colossal wreck, boundless and bare
> The lone and level sands stretch far away.
>   [Shelley, "Ozymandias"]

The Family Covenant: Looking back on the sources of such imagery, it is evident that the initial realizing of the Physical

Hearth involves a basic dichotomy in the pursuit of the Kore. On the one hand, we have a realistic thrashing in the brush; on the other, an inner quest for loveliness, the capturing of symbolic Spring. Both are aspects of what is commonly termed "love," the former reflecting the exercise of masculine strength, the latter, an effort on the part of the mutable male to ally himself with eternal matter. The symbolic rape leads, without doubt, only to social chaos, the destruction of the weak and innocent; but the latter motivation, with its implications of a more permanent union, suggests the possibility of some enduring fount of tenderness, a gift transmitted by human male and female to their helpless offspring.

The embodying of such an emotional bond, even for the primitive, implies some notion of the family, evocative of a covenant meant to ensure the stability and preservation of this initial communion. In this covenant, the value of the Feminine may be renewed. Repeating an archetypal pattern, the male rejects the masturbation of his egoistic pursuits to turn, as in his youth, back to the joy of his first possession of the Kore, finding again in his rediscovery of love, the extended meanings of fertility, the reality of a life external to himself (and more enduring). As the primitive found latent in the Kore the image of the Good Mother, provider of life, nurse, guardian of his fire, gatherer of his plants and fruits, contact with Demeter, the elementary goddess of the earth, so, in a compatible relationship with a woman, man becomes aware of his *anima*, the personality beyond himself who, in complementing his powers, will assist him as the "helpmeet" in all his crucial experience. An idealized image, undoubtedly, but, as part of an informing archetype, an image of permanence, or constancy, to which he may turn for strength when, and if, his chosen journey becomes too arduous. In terms of Spenserian allegory, she is the Faerie Queene herself, Una, Britomart, and the hope of marital love held out by the poet as one of the ultimates of the Hero's quest.[34]

To summarize, despite a variety of modifications, one perceives in this dynamic orientation a clear pattern of influence: birth from the mother, initiation by the father, conflict between the two forces, and a choice of one of two possible resolutions, a dominant identification with one of the primary images, or the achievement of harmony through synthesis. Emotion insists on expression, authority insists on an intellectual justification of its actions, both components are inevitable, and often, irreconcilable. Thus birth and initiation, respectively, as the exemplars of biological inevitability and cultural patterning, may be regarded as the key crises of any person's experience. Birth into life and birth into society, selfless giving and the imposition of duties—these are the primary forces encountered within the family. The *instinct to cherish*, represented by maternal tenderness responding sympathetically to the chaotic pains and joys to which man is subject, is always in conflict with a *will to regulate*, represented by paternal authority seeking the general welfare of a larger group. The mother, as the exemplar of the former, may give life spontaneously and prolifically, but, according to patriarchy, she cannot, as the symbol of the unconscious, control it—" 'tis an unweeded garden / That grows to seed, things rank and gross in nature / Possess it merely."

The matriarchal mode, then, is to be equated with the passions, with blind, undifferentiating impulse. To the patriarchal consciousness, those who love often seem incapable of discrimination; they love irrationally, often with little regard for the larger communal issues. Matriarchy will love that which may destroy itself and society with it; the Kore and Mother may love so strongly, so blindly, that they will smother rather than encourage growth—departing from their own societies, they may even come to love aliens. Because love cannot control itself, it is thought that feminine impulse must be curbed by the reins of a controlling intellect lest it weaken the very foundations of social order. For it is obvious to reason that men are *not* equal in their actions beyond the Physical Hearth; some must be guided by authority lest they destroy rather than build. Progress, even justice, demands an order transcending any individual's desire to love, forgive, or reaccept. Upon this basis, patriarchal intellect insists that the welfare of the communal group (or State) necessitates the greatest of all sacrifices, the subordination of the family and its rights.

More basic questions, of course, occur: how is it that a simple biological impulse can be transformed into such a profound emotional bond between the partners involved and the children resulting from such union? By what means do these orientations affect the growing individual within the family? Has he been so malformed by an overidentification with one parent or the other that he perpetuates the antagonisms of these forces, or has he experienced the possibility of harmony in such a way that a productive union of tenderness and authority will inform his own later actions?

It appears to be the emotional structure of the family which provides the initial "set" for all future development.[35] Acceptance or rejection are the primary determining experiences; participation or exile are the chief results. For example, one may analyze the usages to which the family fire is devoted at mealtime. If the values of the Physical Hearth predominate, the sharing of meals becomes more than mere ritual; it becomes a re-embodiment of the original nursing process which leads to tender warmth, satisfaction, and a sense of communion for the entire group just as participation in Mary's mercy constituted the living air of life for Hopkins. On the other hand, should the values of the Sacred Fire predominate, custom and sacramental obedience to Tyrtaean authority rule, and the possibility of exile from the kitchen table becomes both a threat and a source of anxiety. If one does not "behave," one must leave; both father and the gods will be displeased. From this latter source arises the sense of isolation and helplessness felt by the archetypal exile, whether he be Job, the infant undergoing his birth trauma, the child dismissed from the table, the young initiate, or the disobedient member cast out from his clan. Authority justifies the imposition of law to prohibit disordering impulse; patriarchal severity punishes the well-meaning "historical" Saul while matriarchal forgiveness in the person of Jesus reaccepts the penitent sinner.

For literary purposes, two dominant dramatic patterns may be seen as constantly recurring: the actions of a character may be interpreted as suggesting the formation of an emotional covenant, a bond of tenderness to nourish the flickering blaze of the Physical Hearth; or they may suggest separatism and the formation of aggressions which blow like cold winds from the external patriarchal world to threaten the extinction of this warming flame. The consciously executed authority of the Sacred Fire produces conflict, it assigns duties, it poses quests, it insists on obedience even to the extent of Shakespeare's Henry IV demanding of Hal, "be like me," but it seldom evokes a reciprocal covenant between willing participants. Complete communication asks for more, demanding emotional commitment, intense identification, and a sharing of experience which transcends even the coincidental bond of blood.

Thus, the distinctive morality of the Family Covenant is meant to encourage a mode of action beyond precise and legal justice. In the morality of acceptance, the positive roles of the Archetypal Masculine and Feminine are meant to reflect one another: as Cordelia forgives Lear so must he forgive her; as

Mary gives birth to Christ so He gives birth to her capacity for mercy. Such benevolism ranges all the way from the commonest earthly *caritas* to the most exalted spiritual beneficence:

> . . . what man is there of you, whom if his son ask bread, will he give him a stone? Or if he ask a fish, will he give him a serpent? If ye then, being evil, know how to give good gifts unto your children, how much more shall your Father which is in heaven give good things to them that ask him? Therefore all things whatsoever ye would that men should do to you, do ye even so to them. . . .

From this perspective, all communication based on particularized custom becomes actually a narrowing of man's full scope of communion. The Sacred Fire rejects, the Physical Hearth embraces—and this becomes symbolically true also of their spiritual extensions. The images of the Sacred Fire involve pain and deprivation; those of the Physical Hearth are to be associated with maternal love, a love given not only to the worthy but to the exile. The Gospel teachings of Jesus are for "the poor and . . . broken-hearted."

It is in this sense that the ambiguous figure of Jesus becomes a part of the symbol canon of matriarchy, functioning as a force of "eternal life" and spiritual growth. The biological organism is consumed in the fire of experience, but its burning may give a beautiful flame, a flame to be nourished through love so that it burns well, gives good warmth and good light. The Sacred Fire, despite its capacity to found religions and civilizations, would seem to be, all too often, composed of the slow coals of a stubborn idea which smolders obstinately, giving little light and less warmth. As the symbol of the Ancestral House rather than the functional flame of the Physical Hearth, it may replace the spontaneous with the plotted, the instinctual with the formalized, the sacrificial acts of benevolism with the graspings of self-aggrandizement.

Re-examining the fragments of Tyrtaeus in this light, one perceives the irony implicit in a patriarchal insistence on obedience to authority as the chief virtue (ἀρετή) of the good man. In begetting the desired social image, the Spartan youth is urged to show his respect for the Fathers of his society by sacrificing himself in their behalf. Obeisance to hierarchical order demands that he be the ritual victim. The reproachful image of the fallen Elder, the ancient warrior, clutching "his blood-wet members" represents a shameful reversal of order, a distortion of the rite of circumcision whereby it is the blood of the child that should properly be shed in evidence of his worthiness to be a candidate for the men's house of his group. To revisit this pain upon the already proven Hero is an act of shame not to be borne by patriarchal discipline. Such affronting of authority would undermine all status, all law, and all "justice."

By contrast, the Madonna-Bambino relationship, exemplified in Hopkins' poem, demonstrates an image which contradicts completely the sacrifice of youth in war. The yielding of youth to the arms of death constitutes an act of harshness directly opposed to the tenderness of the Blessed Virgin who holds in her arms the gift of life. In contrast to her reverence for human existence, the patriarchal mode of Tyrtaeus subjects the child, the exultant creature who plays in the sunlight and romps in the wind, to the demands of the State, which has other uses for him. No longer can he shout in his sensual response, "I am therefore I am"; his recognition of self and identity must now be couched in the Cartesian *"cogito, ergo sum."* Only consciousness of his function can give him existence and reality. When the Word of Command is hurled from the doorway by the Father's intervening superego, he must abandon those elements to which he responds so naturally to come home, do his chores, learn his books, become a man, a soldier, a contributing member of society, and, eventually, an Elder himself poised in the doorway to repeat the patriarchal cry.[36]

Yet, behind all such solar episodes of ascent, in the primordial recesses of man's intuition, there remains the sense of a world in which, "Human life is determined to a far higher degree by the unconscious than by consciousness . . . directed more by archetypal images than by concepts, by instincts than by the voluntary decisions of the ego."[37] It is the world of the Physical Hearth which precedes the Sacred Fire, a world where the maturation of the Kore into Demeter creates the archetypal portrait of the Madonna and Child. Through these images, the Hero supposedly learns that which provides humanity spiritual nourishment, strength, and insight. As Hopkins' poem puts it, through "Mary Immaculate, / Merely a woman," man may glimpse the wondrous powers of love, their capacity to accomplish the seemingly miraculous (cf. ll. 13–33). Here, where such miracles occur, this portrait of intimacy offers a conception of total communion, the possibility that a giving of the self to pain may create tenderness. From this arises the corollary image of the Family Covenant, the magic circle within which Hero and Kore, each as fully productive personalities, transcend all physical ties to transmit themselves as images of masculine and feminine maturity to their children.

Thus, whether it be the recurrent "Swamp of Mystery," the area of ignorance beyond his wisdom, or "the winter of his discontent," which dismays him, man may turn, in fantasy, at least, back to this source of knowledge to escape the impositions of that tyrannical logic which sends men out to slaughter. Abjuring the fallacious Word of Command, he may find in the matriarchal mode of feeling an epistemology which, though it cannot effectively deny pain or joy, will satisfy him as a living organism.

In this light, we may ask of our cited poems is the Bambino merely mass, unformed matter to be shaped only on the lathe of externally imposed patriarchal demands? Can there be a reconciliation in unity of the contradictions presented to the child by the archetypal Masculine and Feminine in their roles of father and mother? When a family groups itself about the hearth-fire, or the kitchen table, does a transformation mystery take place yielding, in the intercourse of its participants, evidence of "soul," the possibility of a spiritual covenant? In the Tyrtaean fragment, there is a secular injunction, "Young men . . . be high of heart, be strong in pride of combat"; in the Hopkins poem, a prayer, "Stir in my ears, speak there / of God's love. . . ."

CHAPTER

II

Inceptions in Greek Tragedy I: Oresteia

BECAUSE of its close associations with myth as well as ancient religion, Greek tragedy has served as a fertile source of archetypes. Yet, though the protagonists of these plays share with us a common human plight, they can hardly be likened to people whom we know. As noted, they are rather representative of certain symbolic equations: the Father is the State, the Mother is the Family, the Child, all youthful humankind thrown into the arena of conflicting experience. As Aeschylus, Sophocles, and Euripides depict the struggle of man to ascertain the roots of moral order, vast emotional forces come into contention with the evolving rationality of the age, manifestations of a primordial unconscious arise to cloud the solar light of consciousness.

With regard to the masculine dominance of Greek society,

Bowra comments, "It has its noble and impressive side, but it also means that in the Greeks we miss the gentleness and tenderness which often soften the asperities of masculine life when women share the activities of men and bring their own point of view to them."[1] The Greek family, then, is to be conceived of in terms of the Sacred Fire rather than the Physical Hearth, and, although family loyalty plays a large part in an individual's moral choices, still the emphasis is primarily on blood ties and kinship customs rather than on natural affection.

Such an orientation naturally assumes the existence of a strong man, the hero, eponymous or not, who unites disparate elements under his banner, whether it be to trap the wild beast, protect the incipient community, or systematize ritual worship. Thus, despite the confusion of myth, legend, and history which restricts our knowledge of these early periods, one fact seems clear from the Homeric epics, that the various Greek city-states were originally limited patriarchal monarchies. Usually, the king, who served as commander-in-chief, court of final appeal, and high priest, claimed direct ancestry from the god and founding father of his particular State, thus lending religious sanction to his acts and decrees. Seeking the counsel of his fellow nobles and the tribal elders who compose his retinue, he exercised irrefutable privilege through making crucial political decisions. The bulk of the communal wealth was his; its protection depended upon his repute as warrior-hero in single combat and his ability to incite his followers to aid him in its protection. His authority became the very source of the preservation of the State, and since he was supposedly in contact with divinity, his version of the then uncodified law, which we would regard as mere custom, became *the law*, to all intents and purposes.

However, with the codification of law, the dispersal of wealth, and the development of more complex administrative organization, the authority of the city-state supplanted that of the epic hero. This change is especially noteworthy in the tone of the Tyrtaean fragments where injunctions of allegiance to the State replace praise of individual heroism. Sparta represents an extreme case, but Athens also demonstrates the patriarchal mode of allegiance—with one important difference embodied in her rejection of the chivalric horse of Poseidon for the olive tree of her patron goddess, Athene. Throughout all of her political and social changes from aristocracy to tyranny to democracy, Athens stressed the cardinal virtues of prudence and temperance as well as fortitude; from the incipient codifications of Solon to Plato's *Republic* we have manifested here a patriarchal concern with the ordering of society in an image of justice best suited to guarantee the maximum communal welfare.

Such a concern mirrors, as does the law of the Old Testament, the possibilities of beauty inherent in the solar aspirations of the Archetypal Masculine. That patriarchy has misused its authority, that it has relied on mere strength to enforce its statutes when threatened by equally valid or invalid authorities, that it has consciously distorted law for its own preservation, dims, but in no way obliterates, the light for which it strives. The failure of light in the sociopolitical realm is but a further example of archetypal patriarchal frustration. All utopias are seemingly the products of Artist-Heroes, all actual states, primarily the products of Warrior-Heroes. In a sense, the former is always the result of the latter because these often intellectually formulated (though visionary) utopias spring from a dissatisfaction with the way actual States have turned out. The hope of order corrupted, in dismay, the Artist-Hero visualizes a new sphere of perfection, an art work embodying an imaginary rational ideal.

But such visionary schematizations, though based on the finest philosophizing, seem also to reflect the orientation of the Physical Hearth, for the basic motivation would seem to involve more than a mere desire for order, positing in addition, a yearning for a state (in both senses) of serenity. Thus patriarchy confronts an ultimate dilemma: to achieve the social state analogous to the individual state of intrauterine serenity, it must usurp all manifestations of the matriarchal culture to which it owes, perhaps, its own existence.[2]

AGAMEMNON: THE PHALLIC HERO

In distinguishing the types of motivation, effort, and achievement originating at the Sacred Fire, analytical psychology describes two basic heroes, the phallic hero who devotes his quest to sensual satisfactions and material rewards, and the solar hero who finds fulfillment only in a less egoistic, more spiritual giving of himself to self-transcending endeavor. The study of each demands some examination of their relationship with woman.

Throughout the *Odyssey*, Penelope is presented as ultimately unequal to the task of maintaining the Sacred Fire unblemished. Only the return of Odysseus can restore and purify the Ancestral House. But the *Odyssey* not only presents us with a patriarchal version of the Good Mother as inadequate, confined to her loom, a parcel of property to be despoiled by suitors and disregarded by a maturing warrior-son, it also introduces us to various images of the Terrible Mother in the roles of temptress, witch, and monster (the Sirens, Calypso, Circe, and Scylla). The contrasting images, and an implied patriarchal debasement of woman, receive specific demonstration in Hades (Book XI) when Agamemnon, confronting Odysseus, reviles Clytemnestra as his accursed wife, the treacherous harlot who would not even draw his eyelids down in death:

And so I say that for brutality and infamy there is no one to
equal a woman who can contemplate such deeds. Who else
could conceive so hideous a crime as her deliberate butchery
of her husband and her lord? Indeed, I had looked forward
to a rare welcome from my children and my servants when I
reached my home. But now, in the depth of her villainy, she
has branded not herself alone but the whole of her sex and
every honest woman for all time to come.

[ll. 426–34]

Odysseus sympathizes,

Alas! . . . All-seeing Zeus has indeed proved himself a relent-
less foe to the House of Atreus, and from the beginning he has
worked his will through women's crooked ways. It was for
Helen's sake that so many of us met our deaths, and it was
Clytaemnestra who hatched the plot against her absent lord.

[ll. 436–39]

In response, Agamemnon draws a final moral:

Let this be a lesson to you also. . . . Never be too gentle even
with your wife, nor show her all that is in your mind. Reveal
a little of your counsel to her, but keep the rest of it to yourself.
Not that *your* wife, Odysseus, will ever murder you. Icarius'
daughter is far too sound in heart and brain for that. . . .

[ll. 441–46]³

Throughout the patriarchal literature of ancient Greece,
the wise and obedient Penelope is opposed to the evil wife and
mother, Clytemnestra. But what are the usual terms of de-
marcation? Penelope is wise because she is submissive and
tends the loom beside the Sacred Fire; she is ever faithful to
her lord, Odysseus, ensnared though he may be on paradisal
isles with Calypso and Circe. Her acceptance hints at one of
the earliest sources of the "double standard." Clytemnestra,
on the other hand, is rendered monstrous not only because she
slays the Warrior-Hero, Agamemnon, the lord and priest of

the Ancestral House, but also because she is strong and capable, as depicted in the *Agamemnon* (ll. 10–11), almost masculine in her prowess.

Searching an explanation for such characterizations, we must admit that the clouds which, in early Greece, hide the usurpation of an older matriarchy by a denying, conquering patriarchy are almost impenetrable, and the interpretation of matter such as the matriarchally oriented Cretan ritual, a mystery in all senses. Yet, the perpetuation of the worship of the figures of Demeter and Kore, even in the complexities of the Eleusinian mysteries, signifies a continuing concern with the powers of matriarchy: of what use is any speculation upon form, material, or essence unless there be human life in the first place? Plato may dismiss the "poets" in an attempt to purge the State of the irrational, but, in so doing, he tends also to dismiss the Family Covenant, to substitute for the beauty of tactile intimacy, the beauty of abstract form.

This opposition between the rational and irrational is, of course, one of the major problems explored by the tragic dramatists, who often use the varying images and symbols of the family to create scenes of conflict which blend reverence for the inestimable capacities of the human organism with an attempt to gain, through the intellect, some understanding of their function. Turning to Aeschylus, "heir of an aristocratic tradition going back to the tribal society of primitive Attica,"[4] we may inquire whether he adheres fully to the patriarchal conventions of the Homeric epic?

According to George Thomson's study (*Aeschylus and Athens*) of the evolution of the Greek State from tribal groups, in the *Oresteia* primitive myth, legend, and ritual have been so enriched in significance that "the vicissitudes of the House of Atreus appear in retrospect as the battle-ground of human progress."[5] In this ancient trilogy of violations against the family and the State, of opposition between the Physical

Hearth and the Sacred Fire, the archetypal family is subjected to most violent distortions. In a grotesque nightmare, the father allows the uplifted knife to slash his little daughter, the mother creeps up on the father with the all-enmeshing net of doom, the son prepares to cut his mother's throat—it is a scene of horror worthy of the most surrealistic painting of a black and gory Id. And yet, at the conclusion of *The Eumenides* we have one of the most exalted presentations of the formulation of justice and moral order ever to receive literary demonstration.

How are we to reconcile these seemingly unalterable oppositions? Perhaps, only through a recognition of the power of poetic drama as an aesthetic catalyst. It is quite apparent that much of the emotional vitality of Greek tragedy derives from its preoccupations with the infinitely subtle relationships of parent and child, with the perpetuation or disruption of a Family Covenant; and yet, at the same time, such drama offers complete evidence of an intellectual concern for moral order, an order linked almost inevitably with the preservation of society. No matter what catastrophes the myriad defeating circumstances of experience may visit upon those doomed to be the executors of this preservation, the welfare of the communal group must transcend that of the individual.

In studying how these two dominant concerns reflect the tension between matriarchal feeling and patriarchal codification, and how the ramifications of this tension intrude upon spheres of activity far beyond the peripheries of the family circle, one would note that there has been a good deal of speculation, supported by some archaeological evidence, that the pre-Hellenic religious cults of Minoan Crete and Mycenae worshiped as their principal deities female goddesses whose attributes were later assimilated and transformed within the figures of the patriarchal Olympian goddesses, Hera, Athena, and Artemis.[6] These early indigenous goddesses seem to possess many of the characteristics of both the Good and Terrible Mothers; they were fertility symbols, domestic and agricultural deities, nourishing and protecting Earth-mothers of the primitive Physical Hearth—but they were also snake-goddesses of the tomb, deities of stultification and death. Their usurpation by the gods of the predominantly patri-archal cults of the invading Achaean cultures seems to have resulted in a general debasing of the status of woman, actually representative of a social and political conquest; the Homeric poems are thought to "represent . . . the tradition of a Northern conquering race, organized on a patriarchal monog-amous system vehemently distinct from the matrilinear cus-toms of the Aegean or Hittite races, with their polygamy and polyandry, their agricultural rites, their sex-emblems and fer-tility goddesses."[7]

Thus, for the Northern invaders to achieve supremacy, it was necessary that the older customs be denigrated; by sym-bolic extension, for man to escape his slave-role as procreative servant, it was necessary that he invent new doctrines, codes which exalted masculine rights and the deeds of Warrior-Heroes. The laws of these aristocratic chieftains are evolved to strengthen their position politically as well as psychologi-cally, and with the growth of the Sacred Fire and the An-cestral House, the older religions are contemptuously treated as the superstitions of a native peasantry. Thus, Hera, often considered to be an indigenous mother-goddess, is subordi-nated, if not ridiculed, by the immigrant father-god, Zeus; Penelope, the mother of the Physical Hearth for which Odys-seus yearns, is constantly portrayed as the usurped and com-placent female who cannot cope with the demands of the external world after her lord has departed.

Superior strength is but one explanation of usurpation, but the literature of ancient Greece abounds with further ex-amples of a denial of feminine worth. Characterized by an attempt to avert evil, early Greek myth, under patriarchal dominance, tended more and more to depict this evil in the form and actions of woman. Pandora, an early version of the sacred Kore, became, under patriarchy, the irresponsible female who loosed all hardships upon mankind. The demonology surrounding the worship of chthonic gods was employed by patriarchy to substantiate their own views; they pictured many evil sprites in female form: Harpies (winged female demons who snatched objects off to destruction), Gorgons (female monsters who slew men with a glance), and an infinite variety of sprites representing old age and death. But these are not all. There are the Sirens, embodiments of the Archetypal Temptress in birdlike shape whose fatal songs and beauty would lure men away from home to die; there are the Sphinxes, part human, part lioness, whose prophetic powers are used only to ask unanswerable riddles with the resultant visitation of plagues on patriarchal societies. There are above all the Erinyes, the angry Furies, the souls of the unavenged dead, whose double form of woman and hell-hound demonstrates the horror felt by the Greeks at any offense done to ancestral ghosts. And there are Helen, Clytemnestra, and Medea.[8]

If at Mycenae, where it is said that the figure of Agamemnon came to be worshipped (even as a form of Zeus), Clytemnestra represented the vestigial powers of an earlier Minoan goddess, then the necessity of her usurpation and debasement becomes obvious. It is an action as necessary for social order as the condemnation of the matriarchal Ashtoreth by the invading, patriarchally oriented Israelites. Still one must ask whether the Clytemnestra of Aeschylus' *Oresteia* is the same monster as that depicted in Homer's *Odyssey*, or is there partial evidence suggesting that she may be also the outraged mother of the Physical Hearth, justified in her instinctual reactions by the unwarranted deeds and egoism of the Warrior-Hero, Agamemnon?

According to Fromm, Bachofen regards this trilogy as "a

symbolic representation of a last fight between the maternal goddesses and the victorious paternal gods":

> Clytemnestra had killed her husband, Agamemnon, in order not to give up her lover, Aegisthus. Orestes, her son by Agamemnon, avenges his father's death by killing his mother and her lover. The Erinyes, representatives of the old mother-goddesses and the matriarchal principle, persecute Orestes and demand his punishment, while Apollo and Athene (the latter not born from woman but sprung from the head of Zeus), the representatives of the new patriarchal religion, are on Orestes' side. The argument is centered around the principles of patriarchal and matriarchal religion, respectively. For the matriarchal world there is only one sacred tie, that of mother and child, and consequently matricide is the ultimate and unforgivable crime. From the patriarchal point of view, the son's love and respect for the father is his paramount duty and therefore patricide is the paramount crime. Clytemnestra's killing of her husband, from the patriarchal standpoint a major crime because of the supreme position of the husband, is considered differently from the matriarchal standpoint, since "she was not related by blood to the man whom she killed." The murder of a husband does not concern the Erinyes, since to them only ties of blood and the sanctity of the mother count. To the Olympian gods, on the other hand, the murder of the mother is no crime if it is carried out as revenge for the father's death. In Aeschylus' *Oresteia*, Orestes is acquitted, but this victory of the patriarchal principle is somewhat mitigated by a compromise with the defeated goddesses. They agree to accept the new order and to be satisfied with a minor role as protectors of the earth and as goddesses of agricultural fertility.[9]

Examining the text, we see that from Agamemnon's death Clytemnestra derives a sort of ecstasy which reflects the naturalness of a purely emotional response—". . . and as he died he spattered me with the dark red / and violent driven rain of bitter savored blood / To make me glad, as gardens

stand among the showers / of God in glory at the birthtime
of the buds" (ll. 1389–92). Further, in self-defense, she ad-
dresses the Chorus of Argive Elders, pointing out their double
standard of judgment:

> Now it is I you doom to be cast out from my city
> with men's hate heaped and curses roaring in my ears.
> Yet look upon this dead man; you would not cross him
>   once
> when with no thought more than as if a beast had died,
> when his ranged pastures swarmed with the deep fleece of
>   flocks,
> he slaughtered like a victim his own child, my pain
> grown into love, to charm away the winds of Thrace.
> Were you not bound to hunt him then clear of this soil
> for the guilt stained upon him? Yet you hear what I
> have done, and lo, you are a stern judge.
>   [ll. 1412–21][10]

The patriarchal doom of exile threatens Clytemnestra, but
she is moved only to self-defense, for, to her, the murder of
Agamemnon is an act of righteousness similar to Antigone's
burial of Polyneices, a means of purifying the Physical
Hearth. Although the mode of her propitiation imitates that
of the Sacred Fire, the imagery employed in this speech recalls
the fertility rituals of the earlier matriarchal cults and their
agricultural milieu: the driven rain of Agamemnon's blood
revives the fertile fields of Clytemnestra's maternal emotions;
she has been cleansed by this sacrifice, and her capacity to
love again blooms like a garden "at the birthtime of buds."
Later, she pleads with Aegisthus and the Chorus for peace:

> No, my dearest, dearest of all men, we have done enough.
>   No more
> violence. Here is a monstrous harvest and a bitter reaping
>   time.

> There is pain enough already. Let us not be bloody
> now. . . .
> Thus a woman speaks among you. Shall men deign to
> understand?
>
> [ll. 1654–61]

Thus, it is only to the patriarchally oriented Argive Elders, who refuse to understand, and to the mad Cassandra that Clytemnestra need be completely "accursed bitch, . . . viper double-fanged, [and] Scylla witch." We note that, in retelling the tale of the House of Atreus (ll. 1214–41), Cassandra seems hardly aware that in her vision of the spectral children of Thyestes holding out their entrails, she is summoning to view the basic sin of this Ancestral House, the primal violation of a Physical Hearth duplicated in the slaying of Iphigenia. Atreus and Agamemnon are guilty of kinship murder, a violation, according to Professor Thomson,[11] of the blood line traced through female descent, but even more, they are guilty of an abrogation of their roles as fathers. Deprived of the object of her maternal love, Clytemnestra must act for the Erinyes of the dead Iphigenia in this first play of the trilogy just as her Erinyes function in the last play to pursue Orestes. By his choice, Agamemnon has prevented the transmission of tenderness from mother to child; by upholding authority, advancing the State, and insuring his own repute, he has interfered with the flowering of life, he has destroyed the Kore, the future Mother, Demeter.

What of Agamemnon's motivation? He is tortured by the demand that he stain his hands with maiden blood, the blood of his own house, yet he must ask himself, "How shall I fail my ships / and lose my faith of battle?" (ll. 211–13). As leader of the Achaean forces, he can give but one answer. Calchas must be obeyed, Artemis propitiated, so that the gods of the Sacred Fire of Atreus will not be distressed. But there is more to the problem than this. As King and Elder, Agamemnon is also responsible for the preservation of the State and its honor, defiled by the theft of Helen, threatened perhaps by the latent economic power of the cities of Asia Minor. As Statesman-Hero and Warrior-Hero, he has an authority to uphold, and a reputation to be preserved and enhanced. Unfortunately, in terms of Bacon's familiar essay, "Of Marriage and Single Life," he has given to fortune those hostages which "are impediments to great enterprise," so he is confronted with the archetypal conflict between Family and State. To achieve a resolution, Agamemnon reverts to single life, subordinating "the discipline of humanity" which he has learned at the Physical Hearth to the firmness demanded by lower patriarchy. Conscious rationalization supports his choice: the tearful Iphigenia is rejected in behalf of social exigency; the child of his "kind festive table" is sacrificed for the greater birth, the State; he and his troops will set sail for Ilium to destroy the alien hearth of Hector, Andromache, and Astyanax. Material concerns, political obedience, conquest, and the maintenance of law are exalted in this refusal of Agamemnon to yield to his emotions and preserve his child.

Seeking an explanation for Agamemnon's choice, we may recall the ordeal of the Arunta ritual which suggested certain archetypal masculine roles to be made available to the embryonic personality of the initiate. For Agamemnon, the father (and later, for Orestes, the son), the "life-experience" of all males represents, in essence, a form of the familiar "night-sea journey" of the mythic hero in both its "higher and lower" manifestations, a journey which inevitably involves pain and choice, a separation from the tender warmth and complete acceptance of the Physical Hearth and a continuing struggle to exist in an external world of conflict. Agamemnon, like all males, has two primary weapons with which to fulfill his goals, the strength of the Hunter, and the formulating capacity of the Elder, the priest of the Sacred Fire. In the Tyrtaean poems, or the world of the *Iliad*, the latter might suffice; we know that the warrior is not to shirk combat, that Hector must tear himself from the arms of Andromache to meet the challenge of Achilles. There can be no safety, no particularized law, order, and security without the subjection of the desires of other males; the Sacred Fire cannot be lit nor the Ancestral House established until the Warrior-Hero has made sure that they will not be extinguished or destroyed by a flood of competing, avenging blood. Astyanax must be thrown from the Trojan walls lest he grow up to avenge Hector; Telemachus can only be initiated into the world of men through his participation in the ritual of bloodshed; Penelope, patriarchal wife, mother, and property, can only be rewon through slaughter. And Hecuba must weep.

Analytical psychology finds the essential character of the Archetypal Masculine to be best represented by the attribute of *change* as manifested in both the higher and lower modes of patriarchy. Both are concerned with quest; the distinction lies in the differing means employed to attain the desired goal. In any specific case such as Agamemnon's, individual heroic action is to be evaluated in terms of motivation, whether the impulse to act springs from a desire to gratify the personal ego (ego-narcissism) or to bring the boons of perception and salvation to a waiting dependency (ego-benevolism). The infantilism of the former leads, supposedly, to acts of self-aggrandizement, to the appeasement of the ego's voracious appetite to think well of itself in terms of the approbation it gains from others; the comparative maturity of the latter leads to acts of charity, performed whether external approbation, or blame, be forthcoming or not.[12]

Agamemnon, in many ways, would seem to fulfill the image of the ego-narcissist posited above, the hero of lower patriarchy who seeks wealth, status, and control over others to compensate for subtly felt guilts or personal inadequacies.

Paradoxically, however, his efforts, as suggested earlier, seem to deny the masculine attribute of change, because, as inflexible Elder, he can only find stability in the maintenance of a *status quo* which guarantees him his authority and freedom from anxiety. His only peace lies in a continuing gratification of self, and thus he is compelled to deny such as Iphigenia the opportunity of fulfilling their individual potentialities. It is in this negative character of patriarchy that we find the most obvious demonstration of an archetypal problem: the psychical need for *change* in masculinity cannot be denied; yet, inevitably, patriarchal endeavor seems bound to the quest for stability. What can possibly result from such ambivalence but the frustration voiced in Shelley's "Ozymandias"?

As ego-narcissist and phallic hero, Agamemnon does not hesitate long; the confusion bred by such ambivalence must not be allowed to result in public accusations of ineptitude. Thus, he resolves his problem in line with Calchas' injunction to appease Artemis: obeying the dictates of the Sacred Fire, he will uphold the honor of these allied city-states; he will remain General of the Armies at all cost.

Such a decision, naturally, leads us to question his love of, and concern for, his family. Perhaps this conflict between lower patriarchal pursuits and the goals of the Physical Hearth may be clarified by an interpolation, by comparing Agamemnon and Clytemnestra with the chief protagonists of Euripides' ambiguously conceived *Medea*.

The "heroine" of this tragedy, who, as Terrible Mother, slays her children in vengeance, most certainly illustrates barbarian impulsiveness and irrationality, yet, like Clytemnestra, she also voices the worth of the Physical Hearth, suggesting, by implication, that the proper choice of a marital partner (cf. ll. 640–41) might conceivably contribute serenity and communion to human existence even in a world of suffering. To her, the sustaining of the Family Covenant is all important, even on the verge of her exile and infanticide:

What was the purpose, children, for which I reared you?
For all my travail and wearing myself away?
They were sterile, those pains I had in the bearing of you.
Oh surely once the hopes in you I had, poor me,
Were high ones: you would look after me in old age,
And when I died would deck me well with your own hands;
A thing which all would have done. Oh but now it is gone,
That lovely thought.

[ll. 1029–36][13]

However, since, in an egoism quite similar to that of Aga-memnon's, Jason has rejected her and their home with clever protestations that his sons deserve a "better chance in life," Medea can but confront the unhappy lot of woman:

. . . My friends, I only want to die.
It was everything to me to think well of one man,
And he, my own husband, has turned out wholly vile.
Of all things which are living and can form a judgment
We women are the most unfortunate creatures.
Firstly, with an excess of wealth it is required
For us to buy a husband and take for our bodies
A master; for not to take one is even worse.
And now the question is serious whether we take
A good or bad one; for there is no easy escape
For a woman, nor can she say no to her marriage.
She arrives among new modes of behavior and manners,
And needs prophetic power, unless she has learned at home,
How best to manage him who shares the bed with her,
And if we work out all this well and carefully,
And the husband lives with us and lightly bears his yoke,
Then life is enviable. If not, I'd rather die.
A man, when he's tired of the company in his home,
Goes out of the house and puts an end to his boredom
And turns to a friend or companion of his own age.
But we are forced to keep our eyes on one alone.

What they say of us is that we have a peaceful time
Living at home, while they do the fighting in war.
How wrong they are! I would very much rather stand
Three times in the front of battle than bear one child.

[ll. 226–51]

In this presentation of opposing roles, the voice of usurped matriarchy speaks aloud: the bringing of life, though it involves pain, though it is minimized by comparison, is of infinitely more value than Tyrtaean martial endeavor. To Medea, exile from a Greek patrimony is hardly important; questions of property rights, female subordination, and patriarchal law pale into insignificance when compared to the exile of family members from one another. To Medea, it is the death of love which constitutes the death of life. In his violation of the Physical Hearth, the ambitious Jason has destroyed not only the Family Covenant but whatever function and worth his wife might possess as an individual.

When Medea is deprived of her right to love, her emotions lose direction and begin to function chaotically; she can no longer think, she can but act. Without discipline, direction, and purpose, with all that is meaningful to her violated and destroyed, she can only yield to the anarchy of hatred, only function as a force of death herself. In the horrible scene of Glauce's and Creon's deaths (ll. 1136–1230), we have, in the clinging robe and fiery crown, the very symbols of misdirected emotion, anticipating her imminent murder of her children.

Yet, this cited speech would seem to query also whether these monstrous acts are to be regarded as any the more evil than the slaughter urged by Tyrtaeus? Rejection of life is the crime in both situations—only, in this domestic war, the ultimate culpability is harder to determine. Jason obviously does not care much for women: he wishes children could be born from another source; he accuses women of irrationality, inconstancy, and limited perspective; even Glauce, like Medea earlier, is but his means to an end. Like the Tyrtaean Elder, he is concerned only with the fulfillment of his worldly quest; he adheres to the principle that to be a Greek, to share in the ritual and law of the Sacred Fire is the only solid benefit (ll. 535–45), and that the sons he would steal from Medea deserve the chance to be raised in a *Greek* Ancestral House. Thus, in his attempt to establish for himself a greater Sacred Fire through alliance with Glauce and Creon, he comes to epitomize the very image of the egoistic patriarchal usurper. Euripides compels us to ask whether such effort is actually in accord with universal morality or only with the precepts of patriarchal custom.

Turning back to the *Oresteia,* we find Orestes, in *The Libation-Bearers,* confronted with similar transgressions by the masculine and feminine forces of his environment. Agamemnon, like Jason, has violated the Physical Hearth by sacrificing Iphigenia; Clytemnestra, like Medea, has violated the Sacred Fire by repaying him in kind. To whom does the chorus refer when it states ambiguously, "For God from mortals asks a stern / Price for the stain of kindred blood / In like disaster falling on their homes" (*Medea,* ll. 1268–70)?

Orestes immediately adopts the attitudes of the Sacred Fire. He will see Clytemnestra in no image other than that of Medea, the Terrible Mother and sorceress who kisses the dear hands of her young (ll. 1070–75) just as she is about to plunge a knife into their unwitting hearts. To him, she is the monster Greek patriarchy dreaded as the epitome of impassioned vengeance. Thus oriented, how could he possibly understand the complexities of her inner conflict? How could he, in his close identification with his father, see that Agamemnon, in yielding up love for status, must share in the image of such as Jason? For, after all, it is Agamemnon, the

Elder, who must answer the mourning of Hecuba for Astyanax in Euripides' *The Trojan Women:*

> O darling child, how wretched was this death. You might
> have fallen fighting for your city, grown to man's
> age, and married, and with the king's power like a god's,
> and died happy, if there is any happiness here.
> But no. You grew to where you could see and learn, my
>   child,
> yet your mind was not old enough to win advantage
> of fortune. How wickedly, poor boy, your fathers' walls,
> Apollo's handiwork, have crushed your pitiful head
> tended and trimmed to ringlets by your mother's hand,
> and the face she kissed once, where the brightness now is
>   blood.
> O little hands, sweet likenesses of Hector's once,
> now you lie broken at the wrists before my feet;
> and mouth beloved whose words were once so confident,
> you are dead; and all was false, when you would lean across
> my bed, and say: "Mother, when you die I will cut
> my long hair in your memory, and at your grave
> bring companies of boys my age, to sing farewell."
> It did not happen; now I, a homeless, childless, old
> woman must bury your poor corpse, which is so young.
> Alas for all the tendernesses, my nursing care,
> and all your slumbers gone. What shall the poet say,
> what words will he inscribe upon your monument?
> Here lies a little child the Argives killed, because
> they were afraid of him. That? The epitaph of Greek
>   shame.
> You will not win your father's heritage, except
> for this, which is your coffin now. . . .
>   [ll. 1167–93][14]

In terms of this passage, the orientation of the Physical Hearth suggests a concern with peace even amid chaos, but that of the Sacred Fire, despite all rational protestation, suggests no more than a triumphal procession paved with skulls (if not necessarily real skulls, at least the symbolic skulls of other crushed and defeated egos). Aristophanes' comic opposition of matriarchal peace and patriarchal war in the *Lysistrata* loses much of its humor when we realize that it more accurately reflects the problem which has caused the death of Astyanax. Hapless is the death of the innocent child thrown from the walls to appease the fears of the Greeks seeking future self-preservation. The tiny hands which offered love to an old woman are limp and lifeless; they will never hold a spear to threaten the Sacred Fire of the enemy. The State has been preserved at the price of a tremendous violation of the Family, and what can the old grandmother say? Bury the child as custom wills—but remember the burial rites of the Sacred Fire constitute only an empty gesture (ll. 1240–50). The child we loved at the Physical Hearth is dead and can no longer be warmed by such obsequies. And so with Agamemnon and Jason.

Like Hecuba, Clytemnestra rejects the values of a code which demands the abrogation of the Family Covenant. With the sacrifice of Iphigenia and the preference of State over Family, Agamemnon has ceased to be her husband. Like Jason, he has become for her an image of evil, the ambitious man whose lust for power leads to *hybris*. Instead of the conquering Warrior-Hero, she sees him as the Hunter stained with the blood guilt of Aulis and Troy, a blind man who brings home his concubine to flaunt his authority, a weak man who cannot resist the temptation to be as the gods. This is the man the Youthful Hero, Orestes, is called upon to avenge; and, thus, like Hamlet, he must make a moral choice. Bound by a primitive *lex talionis*, whether it be an older law or but a patriarchal adaptation, Orestes is committed to taking "an eye for an eye" so that the spirit of such a father will be pacified.

But this reciprocal blood lust is hardly to be associated with the Family Covenant; the Agamemnon mourned by Orestes and Electra is not the loving Father of a Physical Hearth. In greeting her brother as the "treasured darling of my father's house, / hope of the seed of our salvation" (ll. 235–36), Electra makes it clear that she is seeking a revival of their Sacred Fire, and that her brother is to her a father-surrogate, and perhaps a means of revenge against Clytemnestra, the mother-rival of her continuing subjection:

> . . . To call you father is constraint of fact, and
> all the love I could have borne my mother turns your
> way, while she is loathed as she deserves; my love
> for a pitilessly slaughtered sister turns to you.
> And now you were my steadfast brother after all. You
> alone bring me honor; but let Force, and Right, and
> Zeus almighty, third with them, be on your side.
> [ll. 239–45]

Orestes, in return, prays for both of them to the patriarchal Zeus as "orphaned children of [an] eagle-father" needing the god's assistance to recover their Ancestral House. He reminds Zeus that

> . . . We both
> are driven from the house that should be ours. If you
> destroy these fledgelings of a father who gave you
> sacrifice and high honor, from what hand like his
> shall you be given the sacred feast which is your right?
> [ll. 254–57]

The intimate association of religion, society, and State as patriarchal institutions is clearly elaborated, and Agamemnon, as in the *Odyssey*, is mourned as the Warrior-Hero treacherously slain at home, deprived of his chance for an honorable death on the field of battle. There is little indication of the mourning for a truly beloved father as in *Hamlet* ("A' was a man, take him for all in all, / I shall not look upon his like again"). There is every sign that Orestes, in addition to feeling the necessity of avenging this blasphemy, feels much more strongly than Hamlet that he has been deprived of the rightful lordship of his Ancestral House (ll. 479–80). Wounded pride, lost honor, and outrage accompany him as he faces Clytemnestra. But he is not only the agent of patriarchal justice, he is also the deprived and rejected child. Who can feel for a father he has rarely seen or a mother who prefers her paramour to her child? Orestes, the patriarchal son, is, seemingly, a man without knowledge of love.

The extent of Clytemnestra's rejection of Orestes is illuminated by the dream that she gave birth to and nourished a snake, the symbol here of the usurping son. Her guilt is obvious in the interchange between the Chorus and Orestes:

Chorus
    She laid it swathed for sleep as if it were a child.
Orestes
    A little monster. Did it want some kind of food?
Chorus
    She herself, in the dream, gave it her breast to suck.
Orestes
    How was her nipple not torn by such a beastly thing?
Chorus
    It was. The creature drew in blood along with the milk.
Orestes
    No void dream this. It is the vision of a man.
Chorus
    She woke screaming out of her sleep, shaky with fear,
as torches kindled all about the house, out of
the blind dark that had been on them, to comfort the queen.
So now she sends these mourning offerings to be poured
and hopes they are medicinal for her disease.

Orestes
   But I pray to the earth and to my father's grave
that this dream is for me and that I will succeed.
See, I divine it, and it coheres all in one piece.
If this snake came out of the same place whence I came,
if she wrapped it in robes, as she wrapped me, and if
its jaws gaped wide around the breast that suckled me,
and if it stained the intimate milk with an outburst
of blood, so that for fright and pain she cried aloud,
it follows then, that as she nursed this hideous thing
of prophecy, she must be cruelly murdered. I
turn snake to kill her. This is what the dream portends.
                                        [ll. 529–50]

Orestes' interpretation points out for us that Clytemnestra's crime is twofold, a murder of her husband *and* a banishment of her son to exile. Like Jocasta, violating her own Physical Hearth at the behest of Laius, she became culpable as an "absent mother"—when Orestes needed her, she was not to be found. This dream scene is replete with birth and nursing imagery, but the images are not to be associated with warmth, tenderness, and acceptance, but with the coldness of the snake and the tomb, the horror of bursting blood. The exiled Orestes returns to relight the sacred coals, but he is also motivated by a desire to reject in turn the negligent mother who refused to care for him and his sister. The extent of his hatred seems in direct proportion to his yearning for recommunion and that first intimacy which was later denied him. Thus, his deed of violence repeats the rejection of matriarchy embodied in a patriarchal initiation ritual; as the young Warrior-Hero, seeking in himself the image of his father, Orestes commits a great act of denial so that he may escape the defilement of his natural birth and attain rebirth as a fully masculine creation. The newborn son must be the upholder of the code of Zeus, the avenger of the House of Atreus and the dishonored Achaean forces, besmirched in their leader's death. What greater trial can he undergo as Hero than to slay his mother?

After the Chorus has cited a series of legends concerning the evil done by "female force [and] desperate love . . . [to] mortal men" (ll. 594–651), Orestes, justified by patriarchal authority in his curbing of the chaos which results from the free exercise of matriarchal impulse, proceeds to kill Aegisthus and his mother. He cuts the umbilical cord with finality, acting in strict self-control, refusing to weaken at Clytemnestra's attempted resurrection of the Madonna-Bambino relationship. This scene of pleading is worth the quoting since it introduces anew the plea for peace heard at the end of the *Agamemnon*. Hovering in the background of this interchange is Clytemnestra's hope for a renewal of tenderness, and her mistaken claim that now her justice (*dike*) has been accomplished, all may still be well:

Clytaemnestra
> Hold, my son. Oh take pity, child, before this breast
> where many a time, a drowsing baby, you would feed
> and with soft gums sucked in the milk that made you
>   strong.

Orestes
> What shall I do, Pylades? Be shamed to kill my mother?

Pylades
> What then becomes thereafter of the oracles
> declared by Loxias at Pytho? What of sworn oaths?
> Count all men hateful to you rather than the gods.

Orestes
> I judge that you win. Your advice is good.
>   [*To Clytaemnestra*]
>   Come here.
> My purpose is to kill you over his body.
> You thought him bigger than my father while he lived.

Die then and sleep beside him, since he is the man
you love, and he you should have loved got only your hate.
Clytaemnestra
I raised you when you were little. May I grow old with
you?
Orestes
You killed my father. Would you make your home with
me?
Clytaemnestra
Destiny had some part in that, my child.
Orestes
Why then
destiny has so wrought that this shall be your death.
Clytaemnestra
A mother has her curse, child. Are you not afraid?
Orestes
No. You bore me and threw me away, to a hard life.
Clytaemnestra
I sent you to a friend's house. This was no throwing away.
Orestes
I was born of a free father. You sold me.
Clytaemnestra
So? Where then is the price that I received for you?
Orestes
I could say. It would be indecent to tell you.
Clytaemnestra
Or if you do, tell also your father's vanities.
Orestes
Blame him not. He suffered while you were sitting here at
home.

[ll. 896–919]

The basic issues of the matriarchal-patriarchal opposition are
well demonstrated in this crisis: Clytemnestra speaks in terms
of the imagery of the symbolic Physical Hearth—"when you
were little . . . May I grow old with you . . . a friend's
house . . . It hurts women"; but Orestes, adamant in his

patriarchal purpose, can only reply in the terms of the Sacred
Fire—"You killed my father . . . You bore me and threw
me away to a hard life . . . You sold me . . . He suffered
[in war] . . . the man's hard work supports the women
who sit at home." The failure of their communication leads to
no renewal of intimacy, and Orestes attains his rebirth
through executing the word of Loxias, the seer, who declares
that this deed of matricide in defense of the Sacred Fire is just
and capable of being done with impunity.

Yet, before the third play even begins, the Erinyes enter in
harsh disagreement. They are female hell-hounds, voicing the
abrogation of a family bond; they are the symbols of Orestes'
repressed guilt. Coming in search of renewed vengeance, or
the only justice that instinct knows, they

> . . . stand for the tribal order of society, in which kinship,
> traced through the mother, had been a closer bond than mar-
> riage and the murder of a kinsman had been punished instan-
> taneously and absolutely by the outlawry of the murderer. . . .
> Apollo, on the other hand, whom the Athenians worshipped
> as "paternal" [patroios], proclaims the sanctity of marriage and
> the precedence of the male. And the issue turns on the fate of
> Orestes. The dilemma in which he has been placed reflects the
> struggle of divided loyalties characteristic of the period in
> which descent was being shifted for the sake of the accompany-
> ing succession and inheritance from the mother's to the
> father's side, and his acquittal will mark the inauguration of
> the new order which is to culminate in democracy.[15]

Thomson further suggests that, in *The Eumenides*, the debate
between the Erinyes and Apollo reflects a conflict arising
from the supplanting of an older conception of communal
possession of property by a new idea of private ownership.
During the posited period of an early matriarchate, the exile
guilty of kinship murder was automatically deprived of all

such communal privileges by his clan or tribe, but, with the formulation of patriarchal law, a higher authority took it upon itself to punish crime (and assign property). Thus such issues became matters of larger public concern just as the right to designate male heirs became the exclusive right of the father.

Under this new dispensation, the impulsive vengeances of the Erinyes seemed grossly irrational and chaotically impulsive; they had to be pictured as "black and utterly repulsive" (ll. 52–53). Apollo speaks of their origin in the "evil darkness of the Pit below Earth" (ll. 70–72), and their stated purpose in the play is but to satisfy "the deadly anger of the mother-snake," Clytemnestra (l. 127). Symbolizing a perversion of emotional energy from love to hatred, from goals directed toward maintaining life to goals bent on its destruction, the Erinyes, in their turn, accuse the younger patriarchal god, Apollo, of favoritism in allowing Orestes to escape to Athens. Howling for a bloody justice, they make him responsible for the violation of tribal custom.

Apollo's defense is illuminating:

> You have made into a thing of no account, no place,
> the sworn faith of Zeus and of Hera, lady
> of consummations, and Cypris by such argument
> is thrown away, outlawed, and yet the sweetest things
> in man's life come from her, for married love between
> man and woman is bigger than oaths, guarded by right
> of nature. If when such kill each other you relent
> so as not to take vengeance nor eye them in wrath,
> then I deny your manhunt of Orestes goes
> with right. I see that one cause moves you to strong
>   rage
> but on the other clearly you are unmoved to act.
> Pallas divine shall review the pleadings of this case.
>   [ll. 213–24]

Again, we may question whether this rationalization is but another instance of the Sacred Fire's adaptation of matriarchal principle for its own purposes. In asserting that "married love is bigger than oaths," Apollo may be implying the very opposite, thus seeking to justify the civil code of marriage, which, under the Sacred Fire, regards the wife as property. In order to minimize the blood relationship of mother and son, Apollo cleverly defends "sworn faith" as the basis of the Family Covenant, disregarding the actual emotional relationship involved in favor of a contractual obligation. The Erinyes are accused of seeking blind vengeance rather than the maintenance of the family bond (their later insight into the possible justness of this accusation prepares the way for their becoming Eumenides); yet, simultaneously, the laudation of "married love" by Apollo seems but a disguise for the maintenance of patriarchal authority. Legally speaking, he feels it more justifiable for Agamemnon to slay Iphigenia of kindred blood than for Clytemnestra to slay her wedded husband; thus, the issue: whether a wife dare exercise individuality and threaten established law, or whether she must remain entirely submissive no matter how outraged?

The resolution provided by Aeschylus in *The Eumenides* would seem to demonstrate his preoccupation with both the necessity of legally constituted authority and the informing tenderness of a maternal perspective. The text offers clear evidence of a patriarchal fear of the emotions based on two tenets: matriarchal custom limits the masculine ego; and matriarchal impulse inhibits intellectual clarity. Thus, as tribal law recedes into the unconsciousness and codified law gains conscious ascendancy, one perceives, at the Sacred Fire, a strange sense of dread felt at any overt manifestation of these early responses. Male society reacts strongly against any primitive "mysteries" which it cannot control.[16] The rejection of the Erinyes as matriarchal symbols is part of the Greek process of creating through rational law a realm of certitude.

One cannot deny that the reconciliation of these warring forces before the temple of Athene is weighted in favor of patriarchy; neither Apollo nor the patron goddess can be termed impartial. Apollo speaks in behalf of patriarchal privilege:

> The mother is no parent of that which is called
> Her child, but only nurse of the new-planted seed
> that grows. The parent is he who mounts. A stranger she
> preserves a stranger's seed, if no god interfere.
> I will show you proof of what I have explained. There can
> be a father without any mother. There she stands,
> the living witness, daughter of Olympian Zeus,
> she who was never fostered in the dark of the womb.
> yet such a child as no goddess could bring to birth.
>
> [ll. 658–66]

And in making her final decision, Athene asserts:

> It is my task to render final judgment here.
> This is a ballot for Orestes I shall cast.
> There is no mother anywhere who gave me birth,
> and, but for marriage, I am always for the male
> with all my heart, and strongly on my father's side.
> So, in a case where the wife has killed her husband, lord
> of the house, her death shall not mean most to me. And if
> the other votes are even, then Orestes wins.
> You of the jurymen who have this duty assigned,
> shake out the ballots from the vessels, with all speed.
>
> [ll. 734–43]

Facing such a dominant orientation, the Erinyes can hardly triumph; tribal custom must be subordinated to "the reorganization of the law of homicide effected under the rule of the aristocracy."[17]

Athene's deciding vote acquits Orestes and restores the

Ancestral House to its rightful owner, but of more importance, of course, is her legendary institution of the Court of the Areopagus with its guarantee of trial by a jury of fellow citizens.[18] This ancient Athenian institution embodies for Aeschylus all of those attributes of reason, moderation, and fair persuasion (ll. 971–75) which the Athenians found in their patron goddess. The solar idealisms embodied in her symbol, honor in war, creativity in peace, clarity of intellect at all times, are to be considered gifts of inestimable worth. The substitution of an ordered law, based on moral justice and administered by an impartial court, for the chaos of "diverse and incompatible" sanction comes to light as the finest of all patriarchal births.

Yet Thomson emphasizes that Athene, in endorsing Apollo's point of view on paternity, is but "laying down the cardinal principle of the Attic law of inheritance," a principle which completely denies all property rights to women.[19] The necessary submission of women for the development of private property represents, then, the triumph of patriarchal authority, and Aeschylus' resolution serves to enhance the male prerogatives of the Sacred Fire and the dominance of the State over the Family. It confirms an archetypal patriarchal pattern whereby the Hunter, Agamemnon, turned Elder, devises a ritual to enforce a code of conduct upon the youthful initiate, Orestes. Bound by a prescribed image of the Hero, the "night-sea journey" of the young man can only result in further confirmation of accepted law with all its variable elements. Thus Orestes, like the youth of the Tyrtaean fragments, may be considered a victim of his father's hybris, his desire for status and that honor to be derived from the slaying of such as Priam and Astyanax. Actually, Orestes is denied the right of *change* or choice—he loses his individuality to become but an extension of his dead father's ego, joint-murderer, perhaps, of his sister, Iphigenia.

What, then, of the problem of the unavenged matricide, the violation of the Physical Hearth? Does Aeschylus, preoccupied as he is with religious morality, ignore this issue? We may recall the choral invocation to Zeus early in the *Agamemnon*, a prayer to the patriarchal god "who guided men to think, / who has laid it down that wisdom / comes alone through suffering" (ll. 174–78). Here (ll. 160–83), implied again, is that archetypal frustration deriving from the ultimately inadequate processes of the intellect; the more extended the analysis, the greater the recognition that all may be vanity, and that, in Sophocles' terms, no man may be called happy until he has crossed the final threshold free from pain. To admit this, and yet to pretend that Orestes' acquittal constitutes the culmination of the *Oresteia*, would be to attribute to Aeschylus a mere blatant defense of patriarchy.

Such is not the case. Despite the monstrous forms with which they were invested by a patriarchal tradition, Aeschylus seems to recognize in the Erinyes a rightful association with the Physical Hearth. Although he uses them, at first, to represent an inversion of value, to depict through this imaged horror what happens when familial tenderness is abrogated by the exercise of civil authority, he reinverts their role at the end of the trilogy to depict a rechanneling of psychic energy from hate to love, paralleling, of course, Clytemnestra's earlier translation of love to hatred. As with Sophocles and Euripides, mystical transformation is resorted to in an effort to suggest the spiritual factors in human existence which, in the worship of Dionysos and Orpheus,[20] persisted simultaneously in Greece with an attempted clarification of the intellect.

In terms of the basic symbolism of this study, the transformation of the Erinyes (Furies) into Eumenides (Gracious Ones) under the aegis of Athens represents the correction of a distorted perspective, actually, the reachievement of a unity such as one might find in a Family Covenant. In similar fashion, authority and justice are tempered by tenderness and mercy; universal moral order adopts the matriarchal principle that wisdom must partake of love. The acceptance of the Eumenides at the hearthstones of Athens as spirits of beneficence (ll. 804–07) serves to reconcile the emotional understanding of these matriarchal Earth-spirits with the rational intelligence of the patriarchal Athene (ll. 848–69). In this transcendent union, both the catastrophic strivings of lower patriarchy ("the child of vanity is hybris"—ll. 533–34) and the undisciplined impulses of matriarchy are renounced (ll. 864–65 and 900).

The speeches of communion are voiced in comparable images; Athene invokes the gentle gardener's love as the model for the Eumenides' future care:

> Let it come out of the ground, out of the sea's water,
> and from the high air make the waft of gentle gales
> wash over the country in full sunlight, and the seed
> and stream of the soil's yield and of the grazing beasts
> be strong and never fail our people as time goes,
> and make the human seed be kept alive. Make more
> the issue of those who worship more your ways, for as
> the gardener works in love, so love I best of all
> the unblighted generation of these upright men.
> All such is yours for granting. In the speech and show
> and pride of battle, I myself shall not endure
> this city's eclipse in the estimation of mankind.
>
> [ll. 904–15]

And the Eumenides, in accepting a home, respond with gentle words, evocative of a pastoral scene of idealized serenity, words which, in their rejection of the Tyrtaean mode, recall once more Clytemnestra's pleas for peace at the end of the initial play:

Let there blow no wind that wrecks the trees.
I pronounce words of grace.
Nor blaze of heat blind the blossoms of grown plants, nor
cross the circles of its right
place. Let no barren deadly sickness creep and kill.
Flocks fatten. Earth be kind
to them, with double fold of fruit
in time appointed for its yielding. Secret child
of earth, her hidden wealth, bestow
blessing and surprise of gods. . . .

[ll. 938–48]

Death of manhood cut down
Before its prime I forbid:
girls' grace and glory find
men to live life with them. . . .

[ll. 956–60]

Let/not the dry dust that drinks
the black blood of citizens
through passion for revenge
and bloodshed for bloodshed
be given our state to prey upon.
Let them render grace for grace.
Let love be their common will;
Let them hate with single heart.
Much wrong in the world thereby is healed.

[ll. 980–87]

With the recognition on the part of the transformed
Erinyes of a unity which transcends both patriarchal and
matriarchal violence, Aeschylus presents a succession of
gentle fertility images, of the fruits of nature and of human
communion, each yielding a harvest of grace, charity, and
love. As the Chorus exits in blessing, Orestes is vindicated
through the triumph of justice, but, in one sense, Clytem-

nestra is also vindicated. The mystical transfiguration of the Erinyes into Eumenides announces the triumph of those aspects of her character which belong properly to the sphere of the Good Mother. Her hatred has been retransformed into love, and though she had to die to achieve such transformation, her death represents, symbolically at least, the death of the sacrificial mother who gives life to sustain life.

CHAPTER

III

Inceptions in Greek Tragedy II: Oedipus and Creon

To turn from the *Oresteia* to the Theban plays of Sophocles is to become aware of a new archetype, the hero of higher patriarchy, or Savior-Hero. As opposed to Agamemnon, whose lower phallic orientation centers about the satisfactions of his material appetites, we find embodied in the figure of Oedipus a quest which adds new meaning to the symbol of the Sacred Fire, a meaning to be sought in the realm of the ideal, in the symbolic "heavens" of all patriarchal purposiveness.[1] Whether this quest be wholly spiritual or not, the male who pursues it may be pictured as dissatisfied, striving ever for new goals, discontent with his present limitations, seeking through *change* to recapture or construct perfection. Even his "Naturalism" is a pursuit of the complex relationships which may yield him some pattern of permanence.

Ontology to him is the study of a reality which suggests the immutability of form. In his pursuit of "Light and Heaven," as exemplified most readily by the myths of Icarus and Phaethon, the overreaching of Marlowe's Tamburlaine, or the imagery of Milton's epics, he embraces a solar orientation expressed in the symbols of fire, flight, and ascent. All of his accomplishments are bulwarks against the tide of unconsciousness, the sea of undisciplined impulse which would wash him back into the Dragon-realm of darkness.

In these seeming tangibles, such a hero finds evidence of a permanence whose contents seem free from the organic dissolution to which matriarchal births are subject. In striving for these objectives, he believes that he can escape the infantile cradle of dependency and the Terrible Mother's coffin of death. The Hunter's game, the Warrior's enemy slung on the back of his horse, the Statesman's legal code, and the Priest's deity, all imply a pursuit of immutability. Despite the infinite gradations between the roles of destroyer and creator, between all the cultural and social factors which so differently shape the experiences of individual males, a pattern of quest emerges wherein, through the conquest of obstacles, the earthbound, organic matriarchate may be usurped and denied so as to achieve the transpersonal ideal, the entity which will survive the decaying flesh. All in all, it is the Hero's enduring persistence on this higher "road of trials" which characterizes the finest patriarchal endeavor:

> I am a part of all that I have met;
> Yet all experience is an arch wherethrough
> Gleams that untravel'd world, whose margin fades
> For ever and for ever when I move.
> How dull it is to pause, to make an end,
> To rust unburnish'd, not to shine in use!
> As though to breathe were life! Life piled on life
> Were all too little, and of one to me

Little remains; but every hour is saved
From that eternal silence, something more,
A bringer of new things; and vile it were
For some three suns to store and hoard myself,
And this gray spirit yearning in desire
To follow knowledge, like a sinking star,
Beyond the utmost bound of human thought.

[Tennyson, "Ulysses"]

Admittedly, the image of Odysseus is evoked, both in *The Odyssey* and in Tennyson's "Ulysses," to demonstrate quintessential *human* effort, but the constant application of the epithet "godlike" to him suggests a further ramification of patriarchal idealism deriving from the Sacred Fire. The patterning of myth insists that the making of the Hero, especially the Statesman-Hero, is initially the making of a god. As we have noted, after the dead ancestor has been deified by some particular Sacred Fire, certain clans agree to look upon him as the spirit of some deceased local hero, and thus he gains additional power as the god of a larger group. Eventually, as god of the State, he becomes the Good Father to his own worshipers, the conquering warrior to aliens. As an anthropomorphic embodiment of the very essence of patriarchy, this deified local hero gains wide cultural acceptance, and, as the founding father of an Ancestral House, demonstrates his capacity to give patriarchal birth. The Statesman-Hero, then, is cast initially in the image of a god, a guardian whose prime duty is to ensure the welfare of the communal group. His chief function is supposedly that of the wise lawgiver; his chief weapon, his primitive shrewdness become wisdom. In his earthly roles of priest, legislator, seer, and object of reverence, he is meant to demonstrate masculine intellectual capacity as a force infinitely superior to the biological capacity of the feminine. Thus it is that as god and father he obtains his right to rule.

One must emphasize the sacrificial aspects of such a heritage. Such a hero's authority is not due initially to his absolute power; it is based upon his "divine" actions, his capacity to bring rain, remove impurities from the soil, cure sick cattle, or, eventually, give of himself to death in some prescribed primitive ritual. Before his attainment of patriarchal priesthood, the Father as Elder was, undoubtedly, a primitive shaman, a medicine man dressed in a lion skin or bull mask exorcising with his borrowed *mana* the evil spirits which inhibited the fertility of field and tribe. His later differentiation into a visible aspect, or priestly King, and an invisible aspect, or god, has been explained as a rationalization for his many failures to achieve his ends on earth. For some mysterious reason, for some failure of observance, the divine force has been unwilling to accomplish what the shaman implored. But, despite his deficiencies, he remains of the utmost importance to the family and community because he alone possesses the power of magical contact with his counter-self, the anthropomorphic god:

> . . . the god is the hero as he appears in ritual, and the hero is the god as he appears in myth. . . . The myth describes the victories that the hero won over the forces inimical to his people, the laws and customs which he instituted for their benefit, and finally the apotheosis that enables him still to be their guardian and guide.[2]

Whether it be true that gods are projections of the reality of kingship and the theory of kings deriving their power from God is actually an inversion, is, however, relatively unimportant with regard to the archetypal symbolism of patriarchy. In lower patriarchy, the authoritarian ruler is for all practical purposes a god, and, in higher patriarchy, the god acts in a fashion quite similar to that of the solar Hero. The god and Hero are always perfected exemplifications of the ideal toward which man is striving at any one time. In his positive stage, the Father seeks to perceive, order, and understand for the sacrificial purposes of benevolism; the solar endeavors which lead him to approximate deity are meant always to result in some giving of a boon. In his study, *The Hero with a Thousand Faces*, Joseph Campbell presents the following version of the complete hero-quest:

> *The mythological hero, setting forth from his common-day hut or castle, is lured, carried away, or else voluntarily proceeds, to the threshold of adventure. There he encounters a shadow presence that guards the passage. The hero may defeat or conciliate this power and go alive into the kingdom of the dark (brother-battle, dragon-battle; offering, charm), or be slain by the opponent and descend in death (dismemberment, crucifixion). Beyond the threshold, then, the hero journeys through a world of unfamiliar yet strangely intimate forces, some of which severely threaten him (tests), some of which give magical aid (helpers). When he arrives at the nadir of the mythological round, he undergoes a supreme ordeal and gains his reward. The triumph may be represented as the hero's sexual union with the goddess-mother of the world (sacred marriage), his recognition by the father-creator (father atonement), his own divinization (apotheosis), or again—if the powers have remained unfriendly to him—his theft of the boon he came to gain (bride-theft, fire-theft); intrinsically it is an expansion of consciousness and therewith of being (illumination, transfiguration, freedom). The final work is that of the return. If the powers have blessed the hero, he now sets forth under their protection (emissary); if not, he flees and is pursued (transformation flight, obstacle flight). At the return threshold the transcendental powers must remain behind; the hero re-emerges from the kingdom of dread (return, resurrection). The boon that he brings restores the world (elixir).*[3]

Campbell places great emphasis upon the return of the hero with the communal boon for, in its social aspect, this return represents the achievement of solar consciousness by a Statesman-Hero who gives of himself in behalf of a group. This consciousness reflects full recognition of the world beyond the ego, and as wise lawgiver, the hero is to construct a stable, tolerant order which allows for individual expression without the threats of rejection and punishment. As such, the Statesman-Hero becomes also a form of the Savior-Hero for his achievement guarantees the most that man can hope for, an approximation of the "Heaven" of patriarchal idealism momentarily attained on earth. His chief attribute is his wisdom, a transformation of that intellectual quality which is, in its lower negative phase, mere cunning. In his most exalted form, he represents power and control over the self both in the Socratic sense of knowing oneself and in the "Christian" sense of giving of the strength of oneself in *caritas* to assist others. It is through his power over himself that the hero learns to be aware of the existence and rights of the world community, thus becoming better able to evaluate wisely, changing when need be, and resisting unwarranted change when necessary. Because his consciousness of others prevents self-absorption in actions which only gratify himself through the exercise of power, he becomes the source of that social and moral stability which is patriarchy's last hope against the onslaught of Spenser's proud *Titanesse*, MUTABILITIE, who seeks absolute sovereignty over men and their gods:

> Ne shee the lawes of Nature onely brake,
> But eke of Iustice, and of Policie;
> And wrong of right, and bad of good did make,
> And death for life exchanged foolishlie:
> Since which, all liuing wights haue learn'd to die,
> And all this world is woxen daily worse.
> O pittious worke of MVTABILITIE!
> By which, we all are subject to that curse,
> And death in stead of life haue sucked from our Nurse.[4]

The task of the Statesman-Hero as Savior, then, is to restore "Iustice and Policie" to those communities which have come under the social and political control of lower patriarchy. As the Healing Physician sustains the body and the good Father sustains the home, so the Statesman-Hero must sustain the State with the elixir of his enlightened wisdom, his knowledge of that true Justice and Policy which we find partially exemplified in a work such as the *Republic*. But such knowledge must not be limited to an intellectual "aristocracy," for the positive father represents more than intellectual quality; he represents also that emotional understanding of the goals of acceptance and unity which results in a transcendent vision. Thus, through this comprehensive wisdom, he will seek to create the tolerant, welcoming State which guarantees the welfare of all, even those who do not fully grasp its worth. Such a State will be truly modeled after the Physical Hearth rather than the Sacred Fire; its citizens, possessing communion, will be good children, and they will, as individuals, be afforded the opportunity of growth.[5]

As we know, Aristotle and modern psychological criticism join hands in a mutual concern with the Oedipus myth, demonstrating once again the possibility of uniting the intellectual and emotional components of basic human experience. Sophocles, himself, in imposing patriarchal form on such "matriarchal" matter, is praised for having achieved a remarkable aesthetic unity, for formulating emotion in such a way that these experiences reveal recurring dramatic patterns participated in by individuals who perform not only personal but archetypal roles. Thus, in the symbolic hero, Oedipus, Sophocles seeks to present a man capable of learning how to combine his recognition of a communal need for order with what Albert Schweitzer calls "reverence for life." The expense of this lesson involves his passage from greatness to misery in

Oedipus the King, but the knowledge gained also enables him, as solar hero, to pass from misery to greatness in the *Oedipus at Colonus*. As a protagonist, he is vastly different from Agamemnon and Jason, the representatives of lower patriarchal egoism and hatred; he is, by contrast, more the archetypal Statesman-Hero described above. Though somewhat rash, he is a man of intellect given to intense ratiocination; as a mirror of his creator, Sophocles, he exemplifies that tendency of the Greek mind to think in terms of a governing *logos* and a rational law which manifests itself not only in the physical universe but also "as a balance, rhythm, or pattern in human affairs."[6]

Yet Sophocles is not unaware of that primal substratum of passion which wreaks havoc in the ordered lives of men. Had he been, *Oedipus the King*, with its vast emotional reverberations, would never have become the fertile source it has as a referent for depth psychology. The basic conclusions of Freud concerning the child's incestuous desire for the parent of the opposite sex and his antagonism toward the parent of his own sex, with the concomitant factors of repression and ambivalence, have been greatly modified by later theorists,[7] yet each finds, in this drama, crucial exemplifications of the mother and father roles which act as formative influences on the developing personality. Likewise, the poets of Greek Tragedy seem to realize that nothing seems so to excite our sensibilities as a violation of the sanctity of the hearth, or a depiction of the success or failure on the part of a family to provide for the needs of one another. Not only Sophocles, but Aeschylus and Euripides also, recognize the value of such material as a means of reaching the profoundly unconscious responses of their audiences. Yet, despite such recognition, it is not only emotional response which these poets seek to elicit; they also wish to appeal to our moral sensibilities. The very ability to produce catharsis depends partially, at least, upon the poet's capacity to portray these scenes of family horror in a moral context, lest our visceral responses so muddy the larger human meaning that the portrayal lapses into mere sensationalism or sentimentality.

Confronting the text of *Oedipus the King*, we encounter two key passages; the final comment of the Chorus:

> You that live in my ancestral Thebes, behold this
>   Oedipus,—
> him who knew the famous riddles and was a man most
>   masterful;
> not a citizen who did not look with envy on his lot—
> see him now and see the breakers of misfortune swallow
>   him!
> Look upon that last day always. Count no mortal happy
>   till
> he has passed the final limit of his life secure from pain.[8]
>
> [ll. 1524–30]

—and the speech of the Second Messenger describing Oedipus' discovery of Jocasta:

> He burst upon us shouting and we looked
> to him as he paced frantically around,
> begging us always: Give me a sword, I say,
> to find this wife no wife, this mother's womb,
> this field of double sowing whence I sprang
> and where I sowed my children! As he raved
> some god showed him the way—none of us there.
> Bellowing terribly and led by some
> invisible guide he rushed on the two doors,—
> wrenching the hollow bolts out of their sockets,
> he charged inside. There, there, we saw his wife
> hanging, the twisted rope around her neck.
> When he saw her, he cried out fearfully
> and cut the dangling noose. Then, as she lay,
> poor woman, on the ground, what happened after,

was terrible to see. He tore the brooches—
the gold chased brooches fastening her robe—
away from her and lifting them up high
dashed them on his own eyeballs, shrieking out
such things as: they will never see the crime
I have committed or had done upon me!
Dark eyes, now in the days to come look on
forbidden faces, do not recognize
those whom you long for—with such imprecations
he struck his eyes again and yet again
with the brooches. And the bleeding eyeballs gushed
and stained his beard—no sluggish oozing drops
but a black rain and bloody hail poured down.
So it has broken—and not on one head
but troubles mixed for husband and for wife.
The fortune of the days gone by was true
good fortune—but today groans and destruction
and death and shame—of all ills can be named
not one is missing.

[ll. 1254–85]

The first passage voices once again the conclusion of the patriarchal intellect that wisdom can obtain no certain truth but the knowledge of suffering. Analysis eventually brings that frustration which can only be resolved through death. The second passage demonstrates the truth of the dictum that wisdom is suffering: even the preservation of Thebes itself seems a relatively minor issue as this man "of great soul" undergoes his agony, an agony to be intensified later when, banished into exile, he is forced to tear himself away from his small daughters.

The moral conflict may be stated thus: the responsibility-laden father, Oedipus (ll. 1460–75), must choose between his love for his now doomed Physical Hearth and his solar duty as the Savior-Hero of the State. Previously, he has cleansed the city through intellectual effort, answering the riddle of the Sphinx; now he must repeat his savior role by cleansing it once more through the removal of himself. The parallelism with the martyrdom of Christ has been often noted; thus it is possible that the revelation which comes to Oedipus in the Gethsemane of his self-blinding is more than a knowledge of factual truth, that it is, in actuality, a revelation of the value of self-sacrifice. Like the blind and rash Samson of Milton's drama, he must lose his sight to gain insight into a new dispensation that wisdom may inhere in love. How different he becomes after this agonizing moment of penitence and insight from the man who accused Teiresias of plotting against his authority. How different is the grieving father praying Creon to care for his accursed and forsaken daughters from the Oedipus who accused this same brother-in-law of treachery (ll. 618–21).

In the light of his progress toward insight, we gain substantiation of Erich Fromm's theory that Oedipus, in his concern for his daughters, and, later, for all mankind, represents symbolically the values of the older matriarchal cults.[9] The answering of the riddle was itself an act in behalf of humanity, removing disease and pain from the Theban victims; although basically an intellectual achievement, it is in no sense the act of an eponymous-hero—after all, Cadmus was the founder of Thebes. Throughout *Oedipus the King*, the Savior-Hero is primarily absorbed with removing the plague, and, although the two impurities are inextricably mixed, only incidentally is he concerned with the discovery of the murderer of the Old King. Though Jocasta is reported to have called on Laius at her death, there is little allusion by the son, Oedipus, to the defilement of the Sacred Fire of the House of Labdacus. In contrast to the *Agamemnon*, there is slight mourning for the dishonorably slain Ruler. Laius was proud and hot-tempered, thus he died. His character was his destiny, and in one sense his violent death was itself an instance of operative moral justice, for in seeking to perpetuate himself as the personal embodiment of his Ancestral House, he committed a terrible violation of the Physical Hearth. With the concurrence of the submissive Jocasta, he had taken his infant son, ankles staked together, from the warmth of his home to have him abandoned in the wilds of Cithaeron.

But the oracle must be fulfilled; Laius in his anger meets an angrier, stronger man, and unwittingly, Oedipus slays the patriarchal Elder. Thus, we have substantiation of Freud's use of this myth to depict the secret rivalry of son and father; but of even more importance, Oedipus through this action re-achieves the maternal womb, a symbolic act signifying his reacceptance by matriarchy.

This is much more than the fulfillment of a sexual dream; his re-entry also represents the further creation of a Family Covenant by Oedipus, Jocasta, and their children. The tragedy does not occur until, in the patriarchal quest for fact, the anagnorisis reveals the true relationship of Oedipus with his real parents, Laius and the younger Jocasta. Only then does the violation of patriarchal authority take its toll. Jocasta pleads with Oedipus not to pursue the investigation which will lead to the discovery of that incest which she knows and accepts with full willingness to minimize its importance, but Oedipus must *know*, and in finding out the truth, he discovers the extent of suffering which such knowledge is ever willing to reveal to those who pursue its challenge. In the final culmination of the tragedy, there is joy for the Sacred Fire: the plague has been lifted; the ghost of the dead patriarch, Laius, has been avenged, and we can assume that his spirit will now be at rest beneath the stone of his altar since the abrogation of his authority has been punished.

Yet, the first of our cited passages posits other problems. What of the suffering of the individual entailed in Oedipus' doom, the agony of the well-intentioned hero? What of

Laius' original sin of abandoning his helpless infant son—is it to go unpunished? What of the further violation demanded by an appeasement which will deprive the four children of Oedipus and Jocasta of the embracing tenderness of their Physical Hearth? Must all that is good and warm, nourishing and protective, be annihilated to propitiate a patriarchal ghost who, himself, initiated this train of tragic events? Reason would seem to provide little consolation, with no more sense of an operative moral justice in the cosmos than would a turning to the cryptic motivations of the Fates.

Before examining the mystical resolution to such questions in the *Oedipus at Colonus,* we may ask the significance of Oedipus' reaction to Jocasta's suicide. Since he cannot be sure who must bear the primary responsibility for his abandonment, and since Laius has been dead now for many years, Oedipus must confront Jocasta with this distant, but still traumatic, crime of rejection. Obsessed by an image of the Terrible Mother, he wrenches the bolts of the doors from their sockets and rushes into Jocasta's chamber on the very verge of matricide. But who is hanging there, "the twisted rope around her neck"?—not the mother who rejected him, but the wife of approximately twenty years of domestic happiness, the woman who had been Good Mother to his children. When he lets her slowly down, what a mixture of warring emotions must grip him. The complexities of his situation are unmanageable. He must blind himself, not only as a form of penance and remorse, but also, so that in this merciful darkness, he may at last think and feel and learn.

Learn what, though? The primary lesson of his contemplation would seem to involve a minimizing of patriarchal authority in favor of that tenderness which a loving father bears toward his own family, and, by extension, toward the human family. The seeds of this knowledge, we may assume, had been latent always in the mind of Oedipus seeking, as Statesman-Hero, to function as the Savior-Hero of the State; yet, without this tragic crisis, he could not obtain his epiphany. Preoccupied with the dictates which a Sacred Fire imposes upon a king, he failed to see that his early concern for status but aggravated the rashness which was blinding him to the truth.

Here we must interpolate again: the ramifications of this problem are actually most fully explored by Sophocles in the *Antigone*, a play in which Oedipus is not even present. In this tragedy, the conflict of Physical Hearth and Sacred Fire is elaborated in terms of a heroine (though the Greeks may not have regarded her as such) who seeks the ritual burial of her brother, Polyneices, a traitor, in the face of the opposition of her uncle, Creon, the patriarchal ruler. The importance of the burial lies not so much in the laying to rest of a departed spirit but in the display of loving fidelity by one member of a family toward another. Although she is partially depicted as the impulsive Gorgon rebelling against rightfully constituted authority, Antigone also represents certain matriarchal virtues derived, possibly, from an earlier association with her father. The figure of Creon in this play is not the virtuous brother-in-law of *Oedipus the King*, but the Claudius-like usurper, adamant in his defense of the prerogatives of the State over which he has gained control. He represents that concern for status and power which Oedipus must learn to reject. Obviously, he and Antigone as symbols may be regarded as archetypal proponents of the Sacred Fire and the Physical Hearth.

To add a further significant factor: Erich Fromm considers the entire Oedipus myth, in all its ramifications, as a prime example of "the rebellion of the son against the father in the patriarchal family."[10] In support of his thesis that this rebellion also mirrors the basic opposition of patriarchy and matriarchy, he points out, and rightly so, the lack of much evidence in these Theban plays of an explicit disparagement of incest, the lack of *eros* as a component in the marriage of Oedipus and Jocasta, and, finally, the justifiable plea made by Oedipus (*Oedipus at Colonus*, ll. 546–48, 982–94) that both his slaying of his father and his marriage with his mother were done in ignorance. Thus as Oedipus cries, "Before the law—before God—I am innocent," we recognize that his marriage with Jocasta was mostly an acquisition of the Queen as part of the property that belonged to the throne, and that their subsequent happy marital union, with its Family Covenant, was in no way defiled by the fact of incest. In other words, although the Freudian theory of Oedipal rivalry and attraction as a basis for future neurosis may be valid, critical investigation of the Theban plays has indicated that Freud but adapted the myth for his own purposes.

On the other hand, examining the text carefully, one discovers ample evidence of Fromm's interpretation:[11]

> *Haemon*
>> My father, I am yours. You keep me straight
>> with your good judgment, which I shall ever follow.
>> Nor shall a marriage count for more with me
>> than your kind leading.
>
> *Creon*
>> There's my good boy. So should you hold at heart
>> and stand behind your father all the way.
>> It is for this men pray they may beget
>> households of dutiful obedient sons,
>> who share alike in punishing enemies,
>> and give due honor to their father's friends.
>> Whoever breeds a child that will not help
>> what has he sown but trouble for himself,
>> and for his enemies laughter full and free?
>> Son, do not let your lust mislead your mind,
>> all for a woman's sake, for well you know
>> how cold the thing he takes into his arms
>> who has a wicked woman for his wife.
>> What deeper wounding than a friend no friend?

Oh spit her forth forever, as your foe.
Let the girl marry somebody in Hades.
Since I have caught her in the open act,
the only one in town who disobeyed,
I shall not now proclaim myself a liar,
but kill her. Let her sing her song of Zeus
who guards the kindred.
If I allow disorder in my house
I'd surely have to license it abroad.
A man who deals in fairness with his own,
he can make manifest justice in the state.
But he who crosses law, or forces it,
or hopes to bring the rulers under him,
shall never have a word of praise from me.
The man the state has put in place must have
obedient hearing to his least command
when it is right, and even when it's not.
He who accepts this teaching I can trust,
ruler, or ruled, to function in his place,
to stand his ground even in the storm of spears,
a mate to trust in battle at one's side.
There is no greater wrong than disobedience.
This ruins cities, this tears down our homes,
this breaks the battle-front in panic rout.
If men live decently it is because
discipline saves their very lives for them.
So I must guard the men who yield to order,
not let myself be beaten by a woman.
Better, if it must happen, that a man
should overset me.
I won't be called weaker than womankind. . . .

Haemon

Father, the gods have given men good sense,
the only sure possession that we have.
I couldn't find the words in which to claim
that there was error in your late remarks.
Yet someone else might bring some further light.

Because I am your son I must keep watch
on all men's doing where it touches you,
their speech, and most of all, their discontents.
Your presence frightens any common man
from saying things you would not care to hear.
But in dark corners I have heard them say
how the whole town is grieving for this girl,
unjustly doomed, if ever woman was,
to die in shame for glorious action done.
She would not leave her fallen, slaughtered brother
there, as he lay, unburied, for the birds
and hungry dogs to make an end of him.
Isn't her real desert a golden prize?
This is the undercover speech in town.
Father, your welfare is my greatest good.
What loveliness in life for any child
outweighs a father's fortune and good fame?
And so a father feels his children's faring.
Then, do not have one mind, and one alone
that only your opinion can be right.
Whoever thinks that he alone is wise,
his eloquence, his mind, above the rest,
come the unfolding, shows his emptiness.
A man, though wise, should never be ashamed
of learning more, and must unbend his mind.
Have you not seen the trees beside the torrent,
the ones that bend them saving every leaf,
while the resistant perish root and branch?
And so the ship that will not slacken sail,
the sheet drawn tight, unyielding, overturns.
She ends the voyage with her keel on top.
No, yield your wrath, allow a change of stand.
Young as I am, if I may give advice,
I'd say it would be best if men were born
perfect in wisdom, but that failing this
(which often fails) it can be no dishonor
to learn from others when they speak good sense.
                                    [ll. 635–723]

Once the conciliatory tone evaporates, Creon's initial speech voices all the traits of the authoritarian personality embodied in the patriarchal character:[12] a demand for unquestioning obedience to the father's will (ll. 639–44); the rejection of woman as the lustful temptress who dissuades youth from duty (ll. 648–53); the depicting of the Family as subordinate to the State (ll. 659–62); the insistence on the absolute powers of the appointed Ruler (ll. 663–71); and the belief in the necessity of imposing order as a means of preventing the social chaos which can come from the exercise of matriarchal emotion (ll. 672–80).

Haemon bases his rebuttal on that "good sense" which transcends mere authoritarian legality and rationalization. He cites the tendency of the Theban citizens to admire, if not wholly approve, the action of Antigone in her fidelity to the deceased brother of her Physical Hearth (ll. 690–700). He pleads with Creon to reverse his verdict, not only as evidence of his mercy but as witness of his adherence to those precepts of solar wisdom which should be the servants of justice (ll. 710–18). But obstinancy rather than flexibility is the chief characteristic of the authoritarian personality; as the debate continues, the Tyrant Father, Creon, refuses to be schooled by a boy (ll. 726–27); he refuses to have the town prescribe to him how he should rule (l. 734). Unlike Oedipus, who is truly concerned for the total communal welfare, Creon may be justly accused of ego-narcissism and a distorted notion that the State is but a mere projection of himself—in answer to Haemon's statement that "No city is the property of a single man" (l. 737), Creon asks, "Am I unjust, when I respect my office?" (l. 744). And so, adamant in the upholding of his authority and status, Creon renews the doom of Antigone even in the face of Haemon's threats. Fromm's interpretation of the meaning of Oedipal rivalry is neatly summarized by Haemon's parting rebuke, "You wish to speak but never wish to hear" (l. 757). This is precisely the desire of the patriarchal

Elder within both the Family and the State—to assert his views, right or wrong, to have them accepted with unquestioning obedience.

But this, of course, is what matriarchy cannot accept when the values of the Physical Hearth are threatened with destruction. In opposition to the cold births of law and order, Antigone offers the warm births of life and the tenderness of the Family Covenant. Thus she comes into conflict with Creon. In legally justifying the denial of burial rites to Polyneices, "the exile who came back and sought to burn / his fatherland" (ll. 200–01), Creon had asserted that only "The man who is well-minded to the state / from me in life and death shall have his honor" (ll. 209–10). As the heir of Laius and Oedipus, Creon is Zeus at Thebes and the rules of his administration constitute the only law, the only moral order (cf. ll. 162–91)—and his immediate will is punishment. When Antigone interferes in behalf of the Physical Hearth, she risks the judgment of the Sacred Fire.

The doomed Kore, Antigone, bases her defense on piety to the family:

> *Creon*
>   And you are not ashamed to think alone?
> *Antigone*
>   No, I am not ashamed. When was it shame
>   to serve the children of my mother's womb?
> *Creon*
>   It was not your brother who died against him, then?
> *Antigone*
>   Full brother, on both sides, my parents' child.
> *Creon*
>   Your act of grace, in his regard, is crime.
> *Antigone*
>   The corpse below would never say it was.
> *Creon*
>   When you honor him and the criminal just alike?

Antigone
It was a brother, not a slave, who died.
Creon
Died to destroy this land the other guarded.
Antigone
Death yearns for equal law for all the dead.
Creon
Not that the good and bad draw equal shares.
Antigone
Who knows that this is holiness below?
Creon
Never the enemy, even in death, a friend.
Antigone
I cannot share in hatred, but in love.
Creon
Then go down there, if you must love, and love
the dead. No woman rules me while I live.

[ll. 510–25]

It will be noted that Creon's reiterated harshness is in direct opposition to Antigone's upholding of matriarchal principle. In general, Antigone's words and actions reflect the symbolic orientation of the Physical Hearth: her very love for Haemon, embodying as it does the poignancy attached to all "star-crossed lovers," expresses the Kore's discipleship to Aphrodite (ll. 781–801); her intense loyalty to Polyneices reflects the Good Mother's willingness to sacrifice herself for the Family Covenant. But, as the Chorus, mistakenly confusing *agape* for *eros*, comments, she is basically in error—"Who has love within him is mad. / Love twists the minds of the just" (ll. 789–90). Thus, for the wrong she pursues, she must be entombed.

Still, though she falls, at last, victim to the *dike* of the Sacred Fire (ll. 853–82), Antigone, like her father, Oedipus, may be seen as representing "the humanistic principle of the matriarchal world with its emphasis on man's greatness and dignity."[13] A sense of unabrogated integrity, an insight into transpersonal obligations, and the strength (born of love) to meet death courageously, all seem manifest in Antigone's last long speech:

> O tomb, O marriage-chamber, hollowed out
> house that will watch forever, where I go.
> To my own people, who are mostly there;
> Persephone has taken them to her.
> Last of them all, ill-fated past the rest,
> shall I descend, before my course is run.
> Still when I get there I may hope to find
> I come as a dear friend to my dear father,
> to you, my mother, and my brother too.
> All three of you have known my hand in death.
> I washed your bodies, dressed them for the grave,
> poured out the last libation at the tomb.
> Last, Polyneices knows the price I pay
> for doing final service to his corpse.
> And yet the wise will know my choice was right.
> Had I had children or their father dead,
> I'd let them moulder. I should not have chosen
> in such a case to cross the state's decree.
> What is the law that lies behind these words?
> One husband gone, I might have found another,
> or a child from a new man in first child's place,
> but with my parents hid away in death,
> no brother, ever, could spring up for me.
> Such was the law by which I honored you.
> But Creon thought the doing was a crime,
> a dreadful daring, brother of my heart.
> So now he takes and leads me out by force.
> No marriage-bed, no marriage-song for me,
> and since no wedding, so no child to rear.
> I go, without a friend, struck down by fate,
> live to the hollow chambers of the dead.

What divine justice have I disobeyed?
Why, in my misery, look to the gods for help?
Can I call any of them my ally?
I stand convicted in impiety,
the evidence my pious duty done.
Should the gods think that this is righteousness,
in suffering I'll see my error clear.
But if it is the others who are wrong
I wish them no greater punishment than mine.

[ll. 891–928]

As in Sophocles' later plays, part of the cathartic effect of
the *Antigone* lies in a resolution affirming the necessity of
love. In this drama, we have a family reunion in Hades with
the imagined re-establishment of the solidarity of Oedipus'
stricken household. In contrast to the code of the Sacred Fire,
which insists upon adherence to precept as evidence of piety,
Antigone, as representative of the older matriarchate, justifies
her actions by asserting that piety towards one's Physical
Hearth is the supreme evidence of piety towards one's gods,
gods who are not mere anthropomorphic projections of the
needs of the State, but gods whose mercy enables them to
understand the loving "evidence [of her] pious duty done."
Though confronted with death and the mystery of what
divine evaluation might truly be, she willingly awaits final
justice.

That the gods may be partial to Antigone's viewpoint is
suggested by Sophocles' ironic conclusion to the affairs of
Creon, the proponent of the Sacred Fire, who receives his due
in the complete disruption of his own family. He is disavowed
by his son, Haemon, cursed by his wife, Eurydice, and
brought to the realization that he alone is responsible for their
suicides. In this discovery, he learns that patriarchal authority
is no fair exchange for the satisfactions to be derived from
intimate family relationships. The Messenger comments:

"Be very rich at home. Live as a king. / But once your joy has gone, though these are left / they are smoke's shadow to lost happiness" (ll. 1168–71). Teiresias' prophecy that Creon's violation of the Physical Hearth will be punished at home (ll. 1064–90) is fulfilled, and Creon, bowed with pain, can only admit his patriarchal frustration—"My life is warped past cure. My fate has struck me down" (ll. 1344–46). The Chorus concludes:

> Our happiness depends
> on wisdom all the way.
> The gods must have their due.
> Great words by men of pride
> bring greater blows upon them.
> So wisdom comes to the old.
>
> [ll. 1347–53]

This is an explicit statement of the principle that after great patriarchal endeavor, especially in lower pursuits, wisdom without love can tell us but of suffering. Intellectual analysis alone may give the Elder pride of accomplishment, but larger understanding must inevitably undermine this pride with its implications of mutability in human affairs. Because Creon has violated the Physical Hearth and preferred the State to his own family, his proud words return upon him as the blows of Fate. As often in Greek tragedy, when the gods wish to punish a person for his *hybris*, they do so by a disruption of his Family Covenant, by visiting disaster upon his home. The pattern is clear: (1) a sin is committed by one member of a family denying the rights or wishes of another; (2) in reaction, a counterdenial occurs as punishment for the original sin, often occurring as a retributive deed of violence; (3) this is followed by a repentance which occurs too late for the initial act to be reversed; and finally, (4) we have the demonstration by a protagonist of an excruciating admixture of guilt and grief over the original decision, which is compounded by the knowledge that the catastrophe is irrevocable.

It is this pattern which provides Sophocles his means of depicting the very substance of grief; yet, it is through understanding this pattern that Oedipus achieves his ability to transcend it. Like Creon, he has been punished at the end of *Oedipus the King* by the suicide of his wife and the disruption of his family; he, too, has learned that the maintenance of the welfare of the hearth transcends any rewards obtainable by patriarchal aspiration. But whereas Creon, the Tyrant Father, is left by Sophocles in frustration and despair, Oedipus, as the benevolent father,[14] is portrayed in the *Oedipus at Colonus* as worthy of a splendid acceptance, even of a resurrection.

The insight given Oedipus has been thought to derive, perhaps, from an egalitarian status within the family portrayed on some of the oldest Greek vases; unlike the "Victorian" father, surrounded by adoring, but subservient, wife and children, the father of these artifacts admits the mother to an equal position of privilege, both are seated, their heads are on a level. This democratic grouping supposedly represents a form of unity.[15] Although division of duties inevitably exists, we find here a pervasive sense of tenderness and mutual concern; the father is no longer the tyrannical Elder of the Tyrtaean fragments, but the persevering provider of food for the women and children of his responsibility. In burdening himself with years of effort to provide sustenance, the archetypal Adam devotes even the "sweat of [his] face" to care for those whose very existence would be threatened by his defection.

It is in this sense that Oedipus recognizes another basic masculine role, that of the Nurturing Father, who, in giving life in such terms, truly equals the mother's biological giving.

Although still accountable for proper guidance, the mentorship of this archetypal figure now comes to constitute an initiation into the more consciously realized meanings of the Physical Hearth; as the Good Mother's aid or surrogate, it is his protective strength which supports her in her own selfless offerings. As a symbol derivative of the Physical Hearth, then, such a father reflects a sharing of physical and emotional intimacy capable of inspiring not only a hope of protecting, loving arms, warm beds, and satisfying meals, but also the sustenance of a cohesive bond of tenderness.[16]

Such an insight borders upon revelation. Yet the poet can only depict its effect upon his protagonist dramatically; *agape* is not a subject easily rendered in lengthy soliloquies. Thus, like Aeschylus, Sophocles must turn, to the matter of mystical transformation; he must deal with the conception of *soul.* Though thought to inhere in many different parts of the organism, such an entity has been generally accepted by most cultures; it is usually associated with a transcendence of the body which contains it, and often it reflects a desire for ultimate communion with some force conceived of as its original cause. Thus the artist is compelled to fluctuate between two choices: whether this soul is to be attributed to a patriarchal *Logos,* the breath of life with all its intellectual connotations, or to some matriarchal source such as the bovine Audumla of Norse myth who licked material chaos into ordered form as a gesture of love; that is, is "soul" to be defined through *Geist* or *Seele?*

Sophocles actually avoids too explicit a commitment, resolving the question through a recognition that matriarchy and patriarchy each possesses its own spiritual orientations *and* transformation mysteries; each posits its own "heaven" or goal of aspiration; each prefigures its own ideals in its own images.[17]

Thus, in depicting the resurrection of Oedipus, that is, his salvation from his lower self, Sophocles begins as early as the concluding scene of *Oedipus the King* to present the results of that growing perception which culminates in the hero's final transfiguration. Once the tragedy of the persevering intellect has been demonstrated, and self-blinding has produced lucidity, the value of the Savior-Hero's sacrificial exile becomes apparent: Laius has been avenged, therefore the plague will be removed; Thebes has been preserved so that a city full of men, women, and children are grouped in serene solidarity about their hearths once more. Despite the individual tragedy, a union of matriarchal and patriarchal principles has been achieved (the State can now guarantee stability once more)—and it is Oedipus' love of his subjects as his children, as well as, or even more than, his pursuit of truth, which has provided the primary impetus for this reachievement of moral order. In contemplation, he has learned, and will learn further, the ramifications of those virtuous impulses which made him a good ruler and father to Thebes just as he had been good ruler and Nurturing Father to his family.

Thus it is that a father's concern for the welfare of his children manifests an epiphany gained from an act of sacrificial self-blinding. Imploring the kindly Creon of this earlier play, Oedipus pleads:

> Creon, you need not care
> about my sons; they're men and so wherever
> they are, they will not lack a livelihood.
> But my two girls—so sad and pitiful—
> whose table never stood apart from mine,
> and everything I touched they always shared—
> O Creon, have a thought for them! And most
> I wish that you might suffer me to touch them
> and sorrow with them.
>
> [ll. 1459–67]

In contrast to Agamemnon's ultimate rejection of Iphigenia from the communion table of his care, this request voices acceptance; Oedipus begs the privilege of actually embracing his daughters, demonstrating how tactile intimacy is to serve as a preliminary to emotional rapport, a conception reiterated in the *Oedipus at Colonus* when Antigone and Ismene bathe and dress their father anew as he is about to part from them in response to the voice calling him from the hill of Demeter.

At this time, Oedipus provides what may be designated as two "gospels," one directed to his daughters; the other to Theseus, lord of Athens, who has provided him with protection. To his daughters, he offers a single word as the boon of enlightenment:

> "Children, this day your father is gone from you.
> All that was mine is gone. You shall no longer
> Bear the burden of taking care of me—
> I know it was hard, my children.—And yet one word
> Makes all those difficulties disappear:
> That word is love. You never shall have more
> From any man than you have had from me.
> And now you must spend the rest of life without me."[18]
>   [ll. 1612–19]

And then of Theseus, he begs a covenant:

> . . . "O beloved one
> Give your right hand now as a binding pledge
> To my two daughters; children, give him your hands.
> Promise that you will never willingly
> Betray them, but will carry out in kindness
> Whatever is best for them in the days to come."
>   [ll. 1631–35]

Both "gospels" speak in terms of a matriarchal principle of love as the ultimate wisdom, a bond of such force that the hands of these girls will bind those of Theseus to enduring kindliness. Yet, patriarchal principles are upheld also as Oedipus turns, symbolically, from the now tyrannical Creon to the benevolent ruler, Theseus, to obtain for his children a new home. If the Hero-King will act as Nurturing Father in his stead, Oedipus, like the transformed Eumenides, will act eternally as a beneficent spirit toward the State, the "holy city" of Athens.

In recognizing the capacity of Athens to become mentor of Greece,[19] and, eventually, of the entire Western world, the play distinguishes the differing orientations of "higher and lower patriarchy" by contrasting the motivations of Oedipus and Theseus with those of Creon, who seeks to make of Thebes a mere extension of his personal Sacred Fire. Fromm believes that Creon (as a symbol of lower patriarchy) represented not only Theban aggressiveness (ll. 1534–39) but also the teachings of Sophocles' Sophist adversaries, especially those doctrines which justified "despotism [when] exercised by an intellectual elite [upholding] unrestricted selfishness as a moral principle." In opposition to such "amoral opportunism," Sophocles is said to offer, in the figures of Oedipus and Theseus, proponents of "the old religious traditions of the people with their emphasis on love, equality, and justice." These traditions may be considered as having roots in ancient matriarchal mores affirming the superior importance of man, the living creature, to the laws he formulates to govern his existence. This, as we know, constitutes the major distinction between the matriarchal and patriarchal viewpoints, but it represents also a dichotomy which clarifies the opposition of Oedipus and Creon. While Creon, like Agamemnon, once he achieves power, comes to represent all of lower patriarchy's striving for authority and status, Oedipus, from the very beginning, devotes himself to the solar pathways of higher patriarchy in seeking to bring the gift of life to his fellow men: to Fromm, the symbolic meaning of Oedipus' answer to the Sphinx is but a further affirmation that only "man himself can save mankind."[20]

But what of Theseus? The unusual, almost curious, stressing of the word "love" in these scenes suggests that the covenant between Oedipus and the city of Athens is based on something other than political or economic factors. In rebuffing Creon, Theseus rescues Antigone and Ismene from arrogant authoritarianism; in condemning Eteocles and Polyneices for their willingness to bargain their father for a throne, he recognizes Oedipus' essential innocence as worthy of a new hearth, a new family of citizens here by the sacred grove of Colonus. It is only natural, then, that Oedipus in his final revelation grant his mystical beneficence to a king who reveres peace, who is more concerned with the evaluation of the reasons for crime than he is with blind punishment or retaliation. As Oedipus undergoes his transfiguration, only Theseus, with shaded eyes, is allowed to watch:

> But in what manner
> Oedipus perished, no one of mortal men
> Could tell but Theseus. It was not lightning,
> Bearing its fire from God, that took him off;
> No hurricane was blowing.
> But some attendant from the train of Heaven
> Came for him; or else the underworld
> Opened in love the unlit door of earth.
> For he was taken without lamentation,
> Illness or suffering; indeed his end
> Was wonderful if mortal's ever was.
>
> [ll. 1656–65]

What, then, does Theseus see as a result of this covenant between Oedipus and the city of Athens? Perhaps, a revelation of his own, a vision of the possibility of embodying matriarchal principles within the ordered framework of a patriarchal political structure, of combining, in symbolic unity, the moral justice of the Court of the Areopagus with the mode of mercy found here at the shrine of these ancient goddesses.

That Aeschylus and Sophocles can come to somewhat similar conclusions suggests once more an archetypal pursuit of unity, man's universal need to justify rationally the promptings of his deepest emotions even as he seeks to feel dynamically valid those intellectual dictates he considers worthy enough to impose on himself and his fellows. In the infinite connotations of the term, *family*, in the recurrent crises wherein a man, a woman, and their children make the poignant effort to transcend their mutable flesh and attain a spiritual realm compatible with their highest needs, desires, and aspirations, these great dramatists find and express the possibility of such unity, and the horror resultant from a failure of this basic quest. Despite the shocking ironies necessitated by an individual's particular "road of trials," because such a spiritual realm has been achieved, Northrop Frye finds in the *Oedipus at Colonus* one of the finest exemplifications of a "paradox of victory within tragedy" as Oedipus achieves "a full rich serenity that goes far beyond a mere resignation to Fate."[21]

Thus, at Thebes, Oedipus, acting as both matriarchal Nurturing Father and patriarchal Statesman, sacrifices himself to restore health to the families of his community; at Athens, he is received into sainthood and a "heaven" which embraces both lunar and solar spirituality not because of any ascetic isolation, but because, as Savior-Hero, he has profited from his suffering in such a way that he has learned a great lesson, the efficacy of loving. Subjected to pain and death so that the forces which insist upon the necessity of human suffering may be propitiated, he transcends his destiny to bring the boon of stability to those who have turned to him for help, the message of *caritas* to those who see in his actions an anticipation of Christ.

CHAPTER

IV

A Shakespearean Corroboration I: Hamlet

SHAKESPEARE'S attempt "to hold as 'twere the mirror up to nature," to depict the infinite variety of passion, suggests that beneath much of his dramatic action we may find, as in Greek tragedy, the subtle interplay of family feelings, strivings for acceptance and communion, traumas of rejection and exile, the creation of a Family Covenant, and its abrogation. Kittredge has described *Hamlet* as "a family tragedy"; *Romeo and Juliet* certainly reflects parent-child antagonisms as well as "clan warfare"; both parts of *Henry IV* and *Henry V* are intimately concerned with the problem of the Ancestral House. Such instances could be multiplied ad infinitum, and all would substantiate the fact that Shakespeare, too, finds in the crises of the family situation a fertile source of those emotions having their genesis at the Hearth or Sacred Fire.

In his tragedies, especially, Shakespeare's power over language, both as rhetoric and image, enables him to transform the simple facts of observation into the creation of characters who are not only compelling personalities in themselves but also embodiments of those archetypal roles to which our own emotions inevitably respond. Through the poetry which so precisely "suits the action to the word, the word to the action," he evokes images pertinent to our own family experience, images which force us to undergo once more those crucial relationships which have molded our own emotional set. Thus we escape the confines of both fancy and form to achieve a reality which needs little clever intellectual manipulation, for most of us have experienced the shock of loss within the family circle and its subsequent repercussions, the sense of futility, depression, and emptiness which ensues as the survivors are faced with the demands of continuing life without the supporting strength of the deceased.

Then how doubly disastrous when such loss is compounded with murder and remarriage as in *Hamlet*. Again, we have experienced the dismay and insecurity which follows simple quarreling; how doubly catastrophic then, when, as in *King Lear*, the quarreling is compounded by outright dismissal and exile, a rejection, complete and seemingly irrevocable. It is through the poetic transfiguration of these situations, and the characters who participate in them, that Shakespeare achieves his capacity to exhibit, in Dr. Johnson's phrase, "the real state of sublunary nature."

But such skill does not always contribute to the best formal dramatic practice. The use of archetypal imagery, reflecting as it does the emotional predominance of the matriarchal unconscious, relying as it does on subtle associations, may result in structural imprecision. For example, Bradley, whose critical insight is always acknowledged even as he is rejected, insists that *as drama, King Lear* may even be inferior to

Shakespeare's other great tragedies—yet when he regards it as a product of the poetic imagination in all its intensity and sublimity, then he is compelled to rank it "with works like the *Prometheus Vinctus* . . . the *Divine Comedy* . . . the greatest symphonies of Beethoven, and the statues in the Medici Chapel." He continues by asserting that the limitations of the stage actually inhibit the overwhelming power latent in the text, that the theatre fails to convey "the peculiar greatness of [the play]—the immense scope of the work . . . the vastness of the convulsion both of nature and human passion [inherent in it] . . . the half-realised suggestions of vast universal powers working in the world of individual fates and passions."[1]

Bradley, then, has made the point of contrasting the dramatic defects of *King Lear*, its lack of structural order and its unsuitability for the stage, with its peculiar imaginative effects, the strangely poetic atmosphere which results in the widening "universal significance of the spectacle presented to the inward eye," the arousing of "sympathies and antipathies which we seem to be feeling not only for [the characters of the play] but for the whole race."[2] As he responds to what may be termed Shakespeare's "ur-patterns," he focuses our attention upon two significant motifs: variations on the theme of psychosis, and a recurrent imagery which likens the evil characters of the play to beasts. Applying this perspective to other texts, we see Shakespeare continually extending the correspondences common to the Elizabethan Chain of Being. In drawing pertinent analogies, he employs both a discrimination of madnesses and a subtle equating of personality with certain bestial images to convey (as in a medieval sermon) a quasi-moral commentary: those obsessed by a patriarchal ego-narcissism may be distinguished from those who learn the virtues of a matriarchal benevolism. In plays such as *Hamlet* and *Lear* (not to mention *Othello, Macbeth,* or *Measure for*

Measure), the quite unconscious intuitions of the poet's psyche function to provide profoundly moving insights which transcend any explicitly rational formulation.

Bradley, like Eliot, feels that we are not to seek in such work latent evidences of Thomism or snide slurs at contemporary Elizabethan-Jacobean figures, but rather a seer's revelation of the meaning of the human condition. To quote again that famous passage:

> The extremity of the disproportion between prosperity and goodness first shocks us, and then flashes on us the conviction that our whole attitude in asking or expecting that goodness should be prosperous is wrong; that, if only we could see things as they are, we should see that the outward is nothing and the inward is all.[3]

Whether Shakespeare was fully conscious of any such implications matters little; in his emphasis on the internal qualities of his characters' perception, he affords us an excellent parallel to that type of awareness demanded by Jehovah of Elijah and exemplified in the urgings of the great eighth-century prophets. That "the outward be nothing and the inward all" is not only the mode of Shakespeare, the poet, but also the mode of all spiritual revelation.

Thus we have manifested in *Hamlet* a distinction between inner and outer conflicts; in *King Lear*, a double exploration of inner states of mind—first, the growing awareness of both Lear and Gloucester that external trappings mirror no inward conditions; and second, a revelation of the poetic method of Shakespeare himself, who, in the play, communicates, through his use of the language of emotion, his own inward apprehension of archetypes.

To reiterate, the language of emotion depends for its effectiveness upon the utilization of reverberative imagery[4] functioning within a symbolism whose pertinence appeals to the most basic of human responses. Thus, the use of metaphor in Elizabethan-Jacobean literature as the figure of transport is employed to vary the level of meaning or to carry us beyond merely rational conviction in the same manner as other analogical devices have served in the texts previously examined to illuminate the opposition of our two primary symbol canons, the Physical Hearth with its dominant mode of tenderness, and the Sacred Fire with its dominant mode of authority.

HAMLET

When we first meet Hamlet, he is but newly removed from the psychological stage of the archetypal Child (note that Gertrude and Claudius persist in treating him as the rebellious adolescent); he seems to be confronting for the first time the questions of moral good and evil. In addition, he must seek the symbolic guiding father to make, like Prince Hal, a choice of imagos upon which to pattern his own identity; he must come to terms with the Archetypal Feminine represented both by the Kore, Ophelia, and the Mother, Gertrude; and above all, he must come to a decision as to the value of human existence. Is man like to a god, "noble in reason [and] infinite in faculties," or is he but the quintessence of dust, "only a beast in his sleeping and feeding, no more" (cf. II.ii, 304–24 and IV.iv, 33–39)? Which of these? The Child become Man must come to know.

Analytical psychology distinguishes between the quest of the "first half of life" during which the ego seeks to find itself in the sphere of personal achievement, and the quest of the "latter half of life" during which the center of consciousness shifts "to the self, the center of the total psyche."[5] As a sensitive young man aware of both spheres of selfhood, Hamlet, once he is enjoined to vengeance by the Ghost, is confronted with a myriad of choices: shall he be Orestes revenging his wrong according to a *lex talionis*—shall he be an avenging angel such as Samson—shall he be a Statesman-Hero such as Oedipus—shall he be a redeemer such as Antigone? His search for his father, his mother, and his own individuality in freedom from both, all seem to involve him in the delicate moral problem of taking cruel action to expunge evil. His Father's Word of Command is like to that of Tyrtaeus, yet his own feelings, as Goethe, Coleridge, and Bradley note, reflect reluctance—"O cursed spite / That ever I was born to set it right!" (I.v, 189–90). In undergoing his series of trials in an attempt to slay the Dragon, Claudius, the Youthful Hero is forced to decide whether, as the noble Hamlet of Wittenberg indoctrinated in "Christian" precepts, he should perhaps resist evil passively, or whether, as the royal heir of Denmark still suffused by paganism, he should act the brute to end his "troubles" with heroic slaughter.

In this sense, the entire play reflects a repetition of the Arunta puberty ritual, and in making his decision to risk that moral contamination involved in the shedding of blood, Hamlet speaks for all men forced to decide whether they should play the "passive" role of the matriarchal child or the "active" role of the patriarchal son.[6] Hence, Bradley can speak of *Hamlet* as "the tragedy of moral idealism," pointing out that the hero of such a drama becomes a fit subject for the demonstration of that central impression to be gained from Shakespearean tragedy, *waste.* Such an impression reflects the almost universal dilemma of the sensitive youth on the verge of maturity asking himself why should life, which is felt as a thing of infinite splendor, be suffused with such sadness and mystery; why, if man possesses such divine potentialities, must he devour and destroy himself as if this were the only end of living? Hamlet, tremendously aware of man's "greatness of soul" and incomparable dignity, sees all about him this being of inestimable worth torn by internal struggle, rendered helpless by chance, destroyed by his very virtues.[7]

Thus, like all youth, he must ask, if waste be the tragic fact, what sort of an ultimate power governs human life? In answer, Shakespeare portrays Hamlet as a young Job, an exceptional being, one who intensifies and heightens the common passions of humanity. In the second scene of Act I, we first encounter him seeking to free his "ego-consciousness" from its earlier dependence upon the mother who has "betrayed" him. He is a young man in the "inky cloak" of melancholia, suffering a common adolescent depression at the loss of his idealism—"How weary, flat, stale, and unprofitable/ Seem to me all the uses of this world!" (133–34) That he has become confused and upset by this hasty, almost incestuous, marriage, as approved by a compliant court, is obvious; to his mother's query at his particular grief, he speaks of not knowing "seems" (ll. 76 ff.), emphasizing his struggle to reconcile this gross reality with his earlier splendid fantasy. In his first soliloquy, he turns to "the Everlasting" for guidance, accepting the Christian injunction against self-slaughter even though this seems to be his deepest desire—escape from the "unweeded garden" of a naturally unnatural lust and its social acceptance. Why live in a world where woman herself abrogates the Physical Hearth, where mother and society embrace the evil man as the authority of their Sacred Fire—"it cannot come to good" (129–59).

While in the throes of this confusion, Hamlet is enjoined by the Ghost of his father to avenge his murder at the hands of his own brother, Claudius, the new king of the Old Law. Rottenness in Denmark, as at Thebes, is exemplified by disorder, the external threat of Norway and young Fortinbras, the excessive drinking and carousing at court, and the ominous signs of hovering evil which "bode some strange eruption to our State" (I.i, 69). Into this atmosphere of corruption, the Ghost appears as a spirit from the "Swamp of Mystery"; no one really knows whether he be true father or deluding demon; the guards only know that he must retire at dawn as an unwholesome vapor cast in opposition to "our Saviour's birth" (157–64). In responding to this injunction from a pagan Sacred Fire, Hamlet, in a sense quite other than that intended by Horatio, is deprived of his "sovereignty of reason / And drawn into madness" (I.iv, 69–78); that is, he loses his divine reason to adopt a primitive *lex talionis*. Turning to the Ghost rather than to "the Everlasting" for guidance, he receives the Word of Command, "If ever thou didst thy dear father love— / . . . Revenge his foul and most unnatural murther" (I.v, 23–25). Bound by a strange perversion of love, Hamlet answers:

> O all you host of heaven! O earth! What else?
> And shall I couple hell? Hold, hold, my heart!
> And you, my sinews, grow not instant old,
> But bear me stiffly up. Remember thee?
> Ay, thou poor ghost, while memory holds a seat
> In this distracted globe. Remember thee?
> Yea, from the table of my memory
> I'll wipe away all trivial fond records,
> All saws of books, all forms, all pressures past
> That youth and observation copied there,
> And thy commandment all alone shall live
> Within the book and volume of my brain,
> Unmix'd with baser matter. Yes, by heaven!
> [I.v, 92–104]

Even though he swears "by heaven," almost by habit, Hamlet vows to "wipe away" all the remnants of his previous teaching and idealism to adopt this pagan task.

But does he really want to perform this patriarchal duty? The first act ends upon a note of tragic regret that he, of all men, must be doomed to restore order to these disjointed times. Yet, because of his intense revulsion toward Claudius, he cannot bring himself to leave Denmark to its demise so that he may achieve his own fulfillment. Like Oedipus, he feels that he must be the Savior-Hero, and yet, like Orestes, he knows that he must kill to gain his goal. The situation is intolerable and practically irresoluble. However, once Hamlet takes the fatal step of embracing his patriarchal *lex talionis*, he, like Oedipus slaying Laius, is doomed. He becomes obsessed with the first stage of the Hero's "transformation process," the killing of the Dragon of Evil; and, despite moments of "Christian" reluctance, this compulsion to revenge drives all other considerations from his mind; his growth toward integration of self becomes arrested at an early stage of development. Thus he cannot accomplish the following important tasks of freeing the Kore-Captive, Ophelia, or of realizing himself as a potential Statesman-Hero.

Before these failures can be analyzed in more detail, we must recall the critical distinction which differentiates the ideal Hamlet of Ophelia's memory from the avenging Orestes of Act V. In Acts II and III, he is still the victim of a terrible shock to his sensibilities, a shock which leads him into indecision and profound despair. Certainly he is angered by Gertrude's and Claudius' violation of the Sacred Fire, yet this early anger is more that of a youth seeking the validity of some genuine sphere of morality than it is that of the child whose toy has been stolen; in other words, while he can still reflect upon these matters, Hamlet is not merely rebelling against usurping authority.

His first soliloquy, as we have noted, demonstrates his feelings of disillusionment and disgust at the ready acceptance by the court of a marriage considered by Hamlet to be a bestial abrogation of human dignity rather than the social duty claimed by his mother and uncle. It is this disgust which governs his feelings throughout these acts even while he is groping for his proof of Claudius' guilt, and yet this revulsion results from more than contempt for society, more even than the loss of his mother to a rival; it is, above all, the result of his reaction to Gertrude's failure to maintain the Family Covenant. In her abrogation of the bonds of tenderness and loyalty which he had felt were so strong, she has destroyed for Hamlet his Physical Hearth.

Thus, after the Players have read for him the tale of Priam's slaughter, when Hamlet exclaims so vehemently, "What's Hecuba to him, or he to Hecuba" (II.ii, 585), the answer, of course, is *nothing* to the First Player, but *everything* to Hamlet who sees in her the tenderness and grief which he has failed to find in Gertrude. Performance is nothing, it is illusion, but his own broken voice in this soliloquy results from more than a bitter perception of fact; it results from a painful recognition of the reality of his own loss; unconsciously, he feels that the tears of Hecuba represent the tears not being shed for himself or his father. Gertrude, like Hecuba, has been unable to prevent the murder of her husband, Nurturing Father and Ruler of the Sacred Fire both; but, unlike Hecuba, she will not weep—not because she is strong, but because she is weak, casual in her most intimate relationships, even to Hamlet, lustful. And because she is capable only of a negative lust rather than a constructive love (a factor seemingly much more significant than Hamlet's possible Oedipal attraction), she becomes for her son the Terrible Mother whose ineptitude and neglect deprive the Youthful Hero of the strength for growth.

The opposing images of Hecuba and Gertrude are most pertinent to an understanding of the failure of Hamlet's relationship with Ophelia. We have posited the necessity of the Youthful Hero's successful mastery of woman as a means of his achieving knowledge of his soul, or anima.[8] Communion with the Kore constitutes the key step not only to gaining moral strength but also to the incipient formation of a better family; thus successful communication with Ophelia may be considered as Hamlet's best means of achieving salvation, the best means of his rescue from the damnation of melancholy, confusion, and loss of perspective. Yet, Hamlet brings with him to his third-act interview with Ophelia (i, 88–169) two almost insuperable obstacles, the image of Gertrude as the violator of the Physical Hearth, and the cloak of madness which he can don at any time to forward his patriarchal vengeance. The poignancy of their opening interchange (88–102) indicates a tremulous awareness of their need for one another even as they play their little game of returning gifts. Even though Hamlet nobly rejects her ("I never gave you aught"), we sense that even yet they may fall into one another's arms and beg for a mutual forgiveness.

But dominated by the sordid image of woman bequeathed him by Gertrude, the moment that Hamlet suspects the spying of Claudius and Polonius, he casts the unwitting Ophelia in the role of the Archetypal Temptress. Convinced of her treachery, he immediately adopts his "antic disposition" and proceeds to berate her for employing her beauty for purposes of duplicity. Changing from verse to prose, and playing cleverly upon the double meaning of *honesty* as both sincerity and chastity, Hamlet banishes her to the nunnery of dismissal from his heart. Now, as the Young Son of the puberty ritual, or the Young Hero of Tyrtaeus, he will not submit to being made a fool of (142–46). All that the Elders have told him of woman's deceitfulness ("God hath given you one face, and you make yourselves another") is true; Ophelia is but another Gertrude to be scorned and rejected; he has said earlier to Polonius, "Let her not walk i' the sun;

conception is a blessing, but not as your daughter may conceive—friend, look to't" (II.ii, 185–86). Having lost the image
of the Good Mother as an integral part of his psyche, Hamlet
can only see woman as giving birth to lust and evil. Even the
Kore, Ophelia, must be banished to ascetic devotions (or to
the brothel she has come to represent) to preserve her virtue
and forestall the birth of more treachery.

Because of this initial loss of Gertrude, and the machina-
tions of the two Tyrant Fathers, Hamlet also loses Ophelia,
and in so doing, he loses any chance of understanding the
better nature of woman; he loses the chance of experiencing
salvation through love; he foregoes the opportunity of creating a genuine Family Covenant.

Thus we have a tremendous irony in Ophelia's comment on
Hamlet's madness; perhaps he is truly as mad as he would
have Ophelia think, for, in embracing vengeance above all, he
has lost everything, his "divine reason," his anima, and the
chance to fulfill his immense potential:

> O, what a noble mind is here o'erthrown!
> The courtier's, scholar's, soldier's, eye, tongue, sword,
> Th' expectancy and rose of the fair state,
> The glass of fashion and the mould of form,
> Th' observ'd of all observers—quite, quite down!
> [III.i, 158–62]

Throughout the play the transformation of Hamlet constitutes a process of degeneration: his feigned madness is itself
evidence of patriarchal deceit. He raves to Ophelia of being
"very proud, revengeful, [and] ambitious" (125), seeking to
cut her with his words, and yet, at the same time, does he not
display some sort of recognition of what he is to become?
Not that the Hamlet of Wittenberg ever wishes to be the son
of Claudius. Circumstance so entraps him that he cannot
achieve the ideal self voiced in his praise of Horatio:

> For thou hast been
> As one, in suff'ring all, that suffers nothing;
> A man that Fortune's buffets and rewards
> Hast ta'en with equal thanks; and blest are those
> Whose blood and judgment are so well commingled
> That they are not a pipe for Fortune's finger
> To sound what stop she please. Give me that man
> That is not passion's slave, and I will wear him
> In my heart's core, ay, in my heart of heart,
> As I do thee.
>
> [III.ii, 70–79]

It would seem that Hamlet is aware that unity of intellect and emotion results in the integration of personality, but, deprived of love through his father's death and his mother's defection, he is rendered incapable of such achievement. As a result, he again falls into his earlier state of depression. He rejects "this goodly frame, the earth [as] a sterile promontory," and man, in all his noble reason and angelic beauty, as "this quintessence of dust" (II.ii, 304–24).

Like Othello, victimized by confusion and a failure to control his emotions, Hamlet turns ironically to the extremes of patriarchal logic to solve his dilemma—"for there is nothing either good or bad but thinking makes it so" (II.ii, 255–56). His recourse to patriarchal analysis, or as termed by Coleridge, "an excess of ratiocinative meditativeness," leads him only to the frustration inherent in such relativism; and, like Edgar, to the discovery of the suffering of the human condition voiced in his fourth soliloquy (III.i, 56–89). Confronted by "the whips and scorns of time, / Th' oppressor's wrong, / the proud man's contumely, / The pangs of despis'd love, the law's delay, / The insolence of office, and the spurns / That patient merit of th' unworthy takes," what can logic do but plead for death and the reachieved peace of oblivion? Yet, to Hamlet, fear of the archetypal Swamp of Mystery "makes us rather bear those ills we have / Than fly to others that we know not of." He is forced to conclude that "conscience [reliance upon rational awareness] / does make cowards of us all," forcing man to lose what chance he has of accomplishing "enterprises of great pith and moment."

Yet Hamlet seems above being motivated by a mere hope of social success or a fear of social disapproval. In this central soliloquy, it is moral choice which concerns him:

> To be, or not to be—that is the question:
> Whether 'tis nobler in the mind to suffer
> The slings and arrows of outrageous fortune
> Or to take arms against a sea of troubles,
> And by opposing end them.

To live or not to live is but one facet of Hamlet's dilemma. In addition, he must ask whether being, that is, existence at its best, is to be found in the nobility of passive suffering or in heroic action? His teachings at Wittenberg, we may assume, have encouraged the former; his father's injunction, the latter. Further speculation has led him, up to now, to conclude with Ecclesiastes that all is vanity, life but a burden of suffering as it was to Job. Frustration, as expressed by indecision, has been the result. Thought alone, without the necessary mitigating influence of love (which has been denied him), has not served to validate Christian precept; it has led him only to confusion and despair, a recognition of the inadequacy of human effort when faced with ignorance and mutability.

Consequently, when Hamlet confronts Ophelia at the end of this soliloquy, he is still distraught, he has not reached a resolution; she might still have saved him had they been able to achieve some semblance of rapport. But the treachery of the Tyrant Fathers has prevented this; Hamlet can only turn to the revenge code of the Sacred Fire to give meaning to his life. His adoption of *lex talionis*, then, is not only an attempt to fulfill his father's Word of Command but intended also as a means of escape from the anxiety of an existence full of confusion. Does his action not suggest to some extent that the sensitive youth, after his pubertal initiation has proven spiritually unsatisfying, may turn to death, not merely as a means of fulfilling a Tyrtaean demand, but as a means of fleeing from a life without the coherence tenderness can give it? Does Shakespeare not suggest that lower patriarchal striving may be but an inadequate substitution for something more precious and less easily achieved?

After the failure of this interview with Ophelia, Hamlet abandons all moral reflection; he now uses the higher mode of rational speculation to convince himself of the necessity of the lower patriarchal mode of action. He realizes that he has not fully accepted the hero-challenge thrown down by his father; he sees himself, as in the third soliloquy, plucked by the beard and tweaked by the nose, the young warrior denounced by Tyrtaeus for his cowardice. Thus he makes up his mind to embrace death and exact his revenge regardless of the cost. "Conscience" (moral qualms) shall no longer hinder him. His first step is to use his intellect in a search for proof of Claudius' guilt, a proof gained by his uncle's reaction to the "mousetrap." The play scene is crucial on two scores: first, it provides Hamlet with some tangible evidence to support the Ghost's accusation and heighten his hatred; and second, it reinforces the emotional reality of his mother's desertion of their Physical Hearth. When Claudius calls for light, Hamlet begins to see. He sees that the King is guilty, but he also sees himself clearly now as the symbolic orphan, the lonely, abandoned child, the rejected one whose first-act melancholy was more than justified. Now that he has discovered these truths, the Tyrtaean logic of the Sacred Fire seems inexorable; his duty is to kill; justice demands the exercise of his aggressive feelings.

Allying himself with hell and "the witching time of night,"
Hamlet adopts the pagan orientation of the Ghost to swear,
"Now could I drink hot blood" (III.ii, 406–10). The imagery
suggests a denial of all "Christian" virtues in behalf of the
primitive ritual which will take place in Act V. Hamlet now
sets about to punish all those who have violated the Sacred
Fire of his father—but his immediate action is foiled by Claudius' attempt at repentance through prayer:

> *King.* O, my offence is rank, it smells to heaven;
> It hath the primal eldest curse upon't,
> A brother's murther! Pray can I not,
> Though inclination be as sharp as will.
> My stronger guilt defeats my strong intent,
> And, like a man to double business bound,
> I stand in pause where I shall first begin,
> And both neglect. What if this cursed hand
> Were thicker than itself with brother's blood,
> Is there not rain enough in the sweet heavens
> To wash it white as snow? Whereto serves mercy
> But to confront the visage of offence?
> And what's in prayer but this twofold force,
> To be forestalled ere we come to fall,
> Or pardon'd being down? . . . [*He kneels.*]

> [*Enter Hamlet.*]

> *Ham.* Now might I do it pat, now he is praying;
> And now I'll do't. And so he goes to heaven,
> And so am I reveng'd. That would be scann'd.
> A villain kills my father; and for that,
> I, his sole son, do this same villain send
> To heaven.
> Why, this is hire and salary, not revenge!
> He took my father grossly, full of bread,
> With all his crimes broad blown, as flush as May;
> And how his audit stands, who knows save heaven?
> But in our circumstance and course of thought,

'Tis heavy with him; and am I then reveng'd,
To take him in the purging of his soul,
When he is fit and seasoned for his passage?
No.
Up, sword, and know thou a more horrid hent.
When he is drunk asleep; or in his rage;
Or in th' incestuous pleasure of his bed;
At gaming, swearing, or about some act
That has no relish of salvation in't—
Then trip him, that his heels may kick at heaven,
And that his soul may be as damn'd and black
As hell, whereto it goes. . . . [*Exit*]
  King. [*rises*] My words fly up, my thoughts remain
              below.
Words without thoughts never to heaven go.
                                        [III.iii, 36–98]

The opposition of personalities, as with Othello and Iago, is superbly drawn. Surprisingly, we find Claudius seeking through penance the forgiveness of our Hopkins' poem; he confesses his re-enactment of the original sin of Cain, hopefully acknowledging the power of mercy to restore purity to the "cursed hand," the tainted soul. He knows all the proper terms and attitudes; grace is as real to him as it was to the Hamlet of Wittenberg; yet, as Elder, he cannot bring himself to lose his authority and its concomitant rewards. Consequently, he cannot obtain spiritual communication; ego subsumes self and he loses his soul. Without sincere repentance there is no transformation possible for the Tyrant Father, no way for the angels to whiten this "bosom black as death." Like Othello whose heart was turned to stone to bruise his hand, so Claudius sees his "heart," his feelings, made of "strings of steel," incapable of softening. And so, ironically, his "thoughts remain below" in the realm of lower patriarchy where "justice" permits the wicked prize itself to buy out the law. For Claudius, the tyrannical usurper, can never be more than the embodiment of worldly striving; he wants the women of the tribe for himself alone; he insists upon subduing all threats to his status by the threatening son and rival; and in so doing, he will deny to Hamlet and Gertrude any opportunity of preserving the values of the Physical Hearth. As Tyrant Father he will be satisfied only with complete authority.

In Hamlet's following speech, which so repelled Dr. Johnson, we meet the pagan "hero" at his worst, strangely enough untroubled by the contemplation of a deed fully equal to Claudius' own original violation of family ties. Because Gertrude as the Terrible Mother has provided him only with the image of love as lust, and the Ghost had enjoined him not to forgiveness but revenge, Hamlet has not been given the proper parental models for imitation. With his feelings distorted, how then does he employ his patriarchal intellect? He postpones his intended murder, not because of his earlier noble compunctions, but because a truly effective *lex talionis* demands a soul for a soul. He must wait until he can catch Claudius "about some act / That has no relish of salvation in't" so that, when tripped, his uncle will be irrevocably damned. Both speeches are suffused with the sort of medieval "Christian" imagery adapted by Renaissance authors to demonstrate the traditional opposition of purity and blackness of soul, the angelic role of mercy, and the problems of salvation. But the words for both Claudius and Hamlet are now but words without genuine feeling *or* "thought"; sharing in a similar type of motivation, ironically, and tragically, they become true father and son.

The indictment of Gertrude which follows immediately (III.iv, 8–217) is preceded by Hamlet's stabbing of Polonius, an unintentional murder perhaps, but one which actually results in the final separation of the Hero and the Kore, Ophelia. Hamlet's violation of her Physical Hearth prevents their ever creating a Family Covenant of their own; the Hero cannot free the Captive because his motivation in overcoming the Tyrant Fathers has not been morally valid. Though blighted himself by this act of murder, Hamlet proceeds to punish Gertrude, rebuking her as "the queen, your husband's brother's wife." This is her identity. Matriarchy is denied by the adolescent male—Gertrude is *not* his mother; she is the symbol of all the monstrous women who have ever destroyed and disillusioned men; she is the lustful temptress, the whore, the deceiver, and, worst of all, the absent mother who rejects her loving son.

The implications of an Oedipal "family romance," with its accompanying ambivalence in attitudes, have been fully elucidated by Dr. Ernest Jones.[9] That Hamlet in his revulsion toward Claudius may be betraying sexual jealousy as well as a guilt through identification which prevents his immediate slaying of his rival is a pertinent point to consider, but we would emphasize here an even stronger identification of the two men in their manifestation of lower patriarchal behavior. In seeking to punish his mother, Hamlet formulates his indictment in terms of Gertrude's apostasy from divine virtue; she has done

> Such an act
> That blurs the grace and blush of modesty;
> Calls virtue hypocrite; takes off the rose
> From the fair forehead of an innocent love,
> And sets a blister there; makes marriage vows
> As false as dicers' oaths. O, such a deed
> As from the body of contraction plucks
> The very soul, and sweet religion makes
> A rhapsody of words! Heaven's face doth glow;
> Yea, this solidity and compound mass,
> With tristful visage, as against the doom,
> Is thought-sick at the act.
>
> [40–51]

Gertrude has failed as the Good Mother through her sensuality, infidelity, and hypocrisy; she has blighted the innocent beauty of the Youthful Hero's image of the Kore through abrogating the "marriage vows" of the Physical Hearth; she has prohibited any possibility of achieving true spiritual communion because she has made of "sweet religion . . . a rhapsody of words." To enforce his point, Hamlet presents her with two pictures, one of Old Hamlet, a compendium of all virtues, a very god, the other of Claudius, her husband, a source of contamination and blight. Hamlet is contrasting the fertility of virtue with the sterility of vice, and, as is so frequent in Shakespearean tragedy, he equates love with divine order and lust with all the evils of both macrocosmos and microcosmos. That she should so refuse to exercise either valid passion or sound judgment as to choose this beast over this god can only be evidence of some sort of madness, cozening by the devil at "hoodman-blind"—even the unadulterated senses should not have led a matron to such folly (53–88).

So far, so good; perhaps the weakling Gertrude has deserved such a reprimand. But Hamlet, obsessed by the patriarchal need to punish (and perhaps by repressed guilt and desire), cannot leave her alone; he must hurt and hurt again— "Nay, but to live / In the rank sweat of an enseamed bed, / Stew'd in corruption, honeying and making love / Over the nasty sty" (91–94).

Gertrude is saved from further rebuke by the entrance of the Ghost who had previously enjoined Hamlet to "leave her to heaven" (I.v, 86), and although this "ecstasy" momentarily renews Gertrude's doubts as to Hamlet's sanity, it soon serves as a break in the tension which allows mother and son to reachieve some echo of their earliest communion. Hamlet, in what we must assume is full solicitude, prays her to repent:

Mother, for love of grace,
Lay not that flattering unction to your soul,
That not your trespass but my madness speaks.
It will but skin and film the ulcerous place,
Whiles rank corruption, mining all within,
Infects unseen. Confess yourself to heaven;
Repent what's past; avoid what is to come;
And do not spread the compost on the weeds
To make them ranker.

[144–50]

The disease imagery of the play combines with Shakespeare's even more frequent garden imagery to indicate here the subtly corrupting influence of evil habit which fertilizes vicious desires until they consume the entire personality (cf. ll. 156–70). Justifying his slaughter of Polonius, his cruelty to Gertrude, and his imminent killing of Claudius, Hamlet, like Othello, now sees himself as heaven's "scourge and minister," claiming that he "must be cruel, only to be kind" (172–79). Gertrude responds with a vow of secrecy (197–99), and in this momentary recommunion, Hamlet and Gertrude become like Hopkins' Mary and her sinful children; like Lear and Cordelia, they too exchange benedictions—Hamlet says, "Once more, good night; / And when you are desirous to be blest, / I'll beg of you" (170–72).

Employing most effectively the device of "the false dawn," Shakespeare perhaps would ask of us at this point to consider whether, in the future, this rather significant reversal of the roles of Madonna and Bambino will enable Hamlet, the son, to act as redeemer, agent of a spiritual intercession in behalf of mercy?

Many critics agree that *Hamlet* as a play falls off badly in the last two acts. One explanation, apart from Shakespeare's difficulty in amalgamating sources, may be that the hero becomes somewhat repugnant as he becomes more and more the avenger of the Sacred Fire, more and more the Warrior-Hero and narcissist seeking the recovery of his Ancestral House. Instead of progressing toward a mature realization of self, Hamlet becomes increasingly hostile, regressing toward a preoccupation with his wounded ego which can be salved only by the exercise of his lower patriarchal powers of strength and deceit. He loses that dignity which made him "Th' observ'd of all observers," and his "noble and most sovereign reason" becomes truly "out of tune and harsh." In these final acts, he seems incapable not only of love but also of the previous perception into the disparities of existence so characteristic of the ironist. He neither feels nor thinks with solar purpose any longer—how can we then identify with him or sympathize with his actions?

Of course, in one sense, Hamlet, like Clytemnestra, is avenging a violation of his Physical Hearth, but in doing so, he is now forced to use the cunning of Claudius to "beat him at his own game." Hamlet becomes the shrewd Odysseus who will use any means to gain his ends. The sensitive youth, "the courtier's, scholar's, soldier's, eye, tongue, sword," becomes a full participant in the arena of combat, sharing in the primal warfare of all males for status and authority (and perhaps the female prize that goes to the victor).

Hamlet's final soliloquy reveals the almost completely negative transformation of the Youthful Hero:

> How all occasions do inform against me
> And spur my dull revenge! What is a man,
> If his chief good and market of his time
> Be but to sleep and feed? A beast, no more.
> Sure he that made us with such large discourse,
> Looking before and after, gave us not
> That capability and godlike reason
> To fust in us unus'd. Now, whether it be
> Bestial oblivion, or some craven scruple
> Of thinking too precisely on th' event,—

> A thought which, quarter'd, hath but one part wisdom
> And ever three parts coward,—I do not know
> Why yet I live to say "This thing's to do,"
> Sith I have cause, and will, and strength, and means
> To do't. Examples gross as earth exhort me.
> Witness this army of such mass and charge,
> Led by a delicate and tender prince,
> Whose spirit, with divine ambition puff'd,
> Makes mouths at the invisible event,
> Exposing what is mortal and unsure
> To all that fortune, death, and danger dare,
> Even for an eggshell. Rightly to be great
> Is not to stir without great argument,
> But greatly to find quarrel in a straw
> When honour's at the stake. How stand I then,
> That have a father kill'd, a mother stain'd,
> Excitements of my reason and my blood,
> And let all sleep, while to my shame I see
> The imminent death of twenty thousand men
> That for a fantasy and trick of fame
> Go to their graves like beds, fight for a plot
> Whereon the numbers cannot try the cause,
> Which is not tomb enough and continent
> To hide the slain? O, from this time forth,
> My thoughts be bloody, or be nothing worth!
>
> [IV.iv, 32–66]

By now, Hamlet seems to have completely rejected any possibility of nobly suffering the "slings and arrows of outrageous fortune" with virtuous Christian (or Stoic) endurance; by opposing his strength to that of Claudius he will subdue his sea of troubles. Yet, like Job, Hamlet still possesses the inquiring mind which asks, "what is a man," what is the purpose of his existence. Certainly, he is not a beast. What, then, is the proper use of "that capability and godlike reason" with which he has been endowed? One possibility, as afforded the young Hero at Wittenberg, would be the scholastic answer that reason is to be used to assist man in achieving an

Imitatio Christi. But Hamlet can no longer think in these terms. As in the third soliloquy, he accuses himself again of that greatest of Tyrtaean crimes, cowardice, which he now persists in associating with "thinking too precisely on th' event." He admits "I do not know" why this deed of revenge remains undone; his earlier moral idealism no longer serves him even as a point of reference.

Consequently, he must turn to "examples gross as earth" to find his solution. In contrast to the ideal voiced previously in his praise of Horatio, Hamlet now turns to the model of Fortinbras, the Warrior-Hero, "whose spirit, with divine ambition puff'd" risks "all that fortune, death, and danger dare, / Even for an eggshell." The extent of the "scholarly" Hamlet's loss of perspective can be clearly seen as he now embraces the lower patriarchal mode of battle as proper heroic endeavor. Like the defensive Gulliver before the King of Brobdingnag, or Tyrtaeus exhorting his Spartan troops, Hamlet now justifies the quarreling and slaughter of war by the masculine criterion of "honour"—"The imminent death of twenty thousand men" that fight for nothing now seems to Hamlet evidence of right reason. Hence, the Youthful Hero, seeking his fulfillment, affirms his purpose and his patriarchal instrument, "O, from this time forth, / My thoughts be bloody, or be nothing worth!"

However, perhaps it is just because his thoughts have become bloodied that they are now "nothing worth." Hamlet's quest for vengeance has entirely supplanted his quest to free the Captive; as a result of this change, Ophelia is doomed to be childless and unloved. In her distracted state, she voices incoherences which reverberate with emotional meanings so subtly moving that she has become the very epitome of doomed and frustrated virginity. The prevailing flower imagery of her speeches in the fifth scene identify her immediately as the suffering Kore whose world of love has withered; the ambiguity of her song, "He is dead and gone, lady," indicates a natural mourning for Polonius, but it also hints at the loss of her soul (animus) as embodied in the departed Hamlet. That her lover should be the murderer of her father constitutes an intolerable dilemma; to escape she has sought refuge in madness. Still her basic identity manifests itself in her pathetic speech: she asks that God be at the King's table, she sings a pretty little song, ". . . By Gis and by Saint Charity . . . ," mirroring her matriarchal orientation; but, strangely enough, the little song ends on a bawdy note, "Young men will do't if they come to't. / By Cock, they are to blame."

We recall Hamlet's bawdy banter during the play scene (III.ii, 116–35), and the "fair thought [that lies] between maids' legs" becomes suggestive now of a suppressed desire for that physical intimacy which has been denied these young lovers. Ophelia, like Iphigenia, doomed to her barrenness by Hamlet's adherence to the code of the Sacred Fire, must depart from the play unfulfilled physically, deprived of any chance for spiritual communion or a Family Covenant. The violation of the Physical Hearth has stripped her of her senses and indirectly of her life; she exits as the chief external evidence of Hamlet's failure to ally himself with matriarchal spiritual values:

> He is gone, he is gone,
>   And we cast away moan.
> God 'a' mercy on his soul!
> And of all Christian souls, I pray God, God b' wi' you.
>   [197–200]

In seeking to avoid the "strong law" of Claudius, Hamlet had been forced to leave Denmark; now in Act V, he, like Odysseus, returns. The final act is introduced with further philosophizing on the meaning of a human experience which inevitably ends in the proving mutability of death. As the Politician, Polonius, was the eaten rather than the eater at his last supper (IV.iii, 17–41), so the rather casual speculations of Hamlet, Horatio, and the gravediggers but reinforce the irony that kings may take their progress through the guts of a beggar. Where be the compliant courtiers' kisses now, where the lawyer's legal quiddities, beloved Yorick's jests and smiles; where is "noble Alexander"? The answer of an archetypal patriarchal frustration is embodied in Hamlet's wry verse—they are all with "Imperious Caesar, dead and turn'd to clay," their destiny to "stop a hole to keep the wind away" (i, 236–37). Because of his failure to accomplish the preliminary transformation of the ego during the first half of life, the unfulfilled Youthful Hero has learned wisdom only as a knowledge of suffering. Hamlet becomes the early Job confronted by a vanity which denies both solar accomplishment and matriarchal love; thus, left with nothing to believe in, beset by remorse at his refusal of Ophelia and her subsequent ruination (*her* loss of full Christian burial may imply further *his* loss of values), he can act only from a despair even more intense than that suffered in Act I. His stoic resignation and decision to fight seem barely the result of a strong desire for vengeance; he speaks of honor and his right to kill the beast "who kill'd my king, and whor'd my mother" (ii, 64), but we feel almost as if he does not actually care. In contrast to Edgar's "ripeness is all" with its overtones of solar maturity, we detect in Hamlet's "readiness is all" a form of fatalism which finds in death the only solution to insuperable problems—

> Not a whit, we defy augury; there's a special
> providence in the fall of a sparrow. If it be now,
> 'tis not to come; if it be not to come, it will be
> now; if it be not now, yet it will come: the readiness
> is all. Since no man knows aught of what he leaves,
> what is't to leave betimes? Let be.
>   [V.ii, 230–35]

These are not the words of a young man who has found much meaning in life.

Thrown back, almost unwillingly, on revenge as the only course of action, Hamlet feels compelled to justify his intent to Horatio, ". . . is't not perfect conscience / To quit him [Claudius] with this arm? And is't not to be damn'd / To let this canker of our nature come / In further evil?" (ii, 68–70). This Tyrtaean logic, re-emphasizing the patriarchal mode of punishment as justice, is cast again in "Christian" terms, but, as in Act III, the words are meaningless; Hamlet has become a pagan under the aegis of his demon-father, the Ghost. When he meets Laertes in the arena of combat, Hamlet begs his forgiveness, but we wonder at his sincerity, his tongue is too sharp, his tone sarcastic; Laertes claims, "You mock me, sir" (ii, 237–69). We recall their previous meeting in Ophelia's grave as the two bloody avengers (i, 269–307) and Hamlet's boast, "Nay, an thou'lt mouth, / I'll rant as well as thou." As witnessed by his foiling of Rosencrantz and Guildenstern, we know already that Hamlet is extremely clever, and that, feeling himself "heaven's scourge and minister," he may be even more capable of falsification. By now he cares very little for human dignity—"And a man's life's no more than to say one" (ii, 74). It is difficult to believe his protestations of sorrow even to Horatio (75–79).

When Hamlet's suspicions are confirmed by Gertrude's cry of "I am poison'd" and Laertes' confession, his distorted quest reaches its climax. Does Hamlet, "th' expectancy and rose of the fair state," act nobly as a Galahad or Oedipus? Hardly. He stabs Claudius and forces the dying King to drink of the poison, the grail of a pagan ritual of blood. This is Claudius' "Last Supper," but the cup is offered him by the Revenge Hero, Hamlet, a creature of ungovernable passions, almost a beast in his frenzy. In a sense, this climax is a form of the symbolic Black Mass, for not only Gertrude and Claudius drink of the cup of evil communion, but Hamlet, also, as he had vowed earlier, now "drinks hot blood." He gains the mana of the tiger and with this strength he decimates the court and avenges his Sacred Fire. We recall the poignant grief of Lear holding the dead Cordelia in his arms, "No, no, no life! / Why should a dog, a horse, a rat, have life, / And thou no breath at all?" (V.iii, 305–07) The actions of Hamlet accomplish the same result as those of Edmund—here, too, there is no life at all.

In seeking a concluding, if not conclusive, interpretation of the problem of personality suggested by such action, we may turn to Jung's positing of another archetypal system designated as the "shadow," an element within the psyche which the Renaissance would have associated with man's capacity to sink to the bestial level of the Great Chain of Being.[10] Supposedly reflecting man's brute heritage in its equation of his lowest passions with animal instinct, the shadow is deemed responsible for those evil thoughts and actions known by the "soul" to be reprehensible, but either cloaked from view by the "persona" (a system capable of creating masks acceptable to the ego in its desire to adjust to society)[11] or confined to the unconscious to fester as neurosis-producing cathexes. Symbolically, the shadow reflects the medieval obsession with the Seven Deadly Sins or the inner guilt termed by theologians' "original sin"; outwardly, the shadow reflects man's fear of the external devil or enemy who threatens his destruction. Although, under certain circumstances, the shadow may contribute positive elements to the personality, in general it functions as a force inhibiting the achievement of self or the realization of spiritual potentialities.

The Hamlet of Act V may be considered the victim of this shadow component in his personality. In justifying his actions through perverse rationalization, in yielding to the emotion of hate and the instinct to kill for personal survival, Hamlet fails to discover a mode whereby maturity could be achieved. In the arena of combat, he found himself capable of strength and courage, but has he found more than that which the unthinking beast manifests quite naturally?

Were there no other solutions? Were there no other experiences which might have proven him as well or better? Certainly, the scholarly youth portrayed by Shakespeare in the soliloquies would have been aware of integrity in behalf of an unpopular principle, dire illness, the rack, the stake, and the Cross. But Hamlet, confronted, like Job, with the facts of inexplicable suffering, can turn at last for resolution only to the patriarchal Ghost, the Elder who wishes him to be satisfied with the formula of Eliphaz that those who sin must suffer—"What knowest thou, that we know not? what understandest thou, which is not in us?" (Job 15:9)

In seeking justification for the final actions of Hamlet, one might argue that he, like Oedipus, has acted as the Savior-Hero (the Warrior as Statesman), that his death, or crucifixion, at the hands of Claudius has removed the festering sores and rottenness from the body politic of Denmark, but our analysis hardly supports such a conclusion. The young Renaissance Prince, because of his early death, becomes incapable of profiting sufficiently from his experience to fulfill himself as the wise ruler; and although, with death imminent, Hamlet partially restores his earlier "Christian" beliefs by forgiving Laertes and Gertrude, his chief concern seems to be that his friend, Horatio, "absent [himself] from felicity awhile . . . to tell [his] story" (355–60), that is, preserve his reputation through justifying this slaughter. The patriarchal values of status, honor, and rightful punishment are to be upheld at all cost, even that of Horatio's continued drawing of his breath in pain.

Thus, we must question the loyal Horatio's final evaluation of his friend, "Now cracks a noble heart; good night, sweet prince, / And flights of angels sing thee to thy rest" (370–71). Does this moving farewell to his old friend of Wittenberg (not the avenger of Act V) actually eradicate, as Bradley claims, our sense of dismay at the Youthful Hero's death? Does this reintroduced religious tone heighten our hopes of an eternal reward for the "sweet" and just no matter what means they employ to accomplish their ends? Is there here a hint that, after all, the ultimate moral power of the universe carefully distinguishes between the final destinies of the good and evil? Is the resolution of Hamlet's world-weariness and fifth-act fatalism to be found in Bradley's sense of a pervasive divinity still manifest in the world as Hamlet exhibits again all the nobility of his nature in these last seconds of his life?[12]

Such an interpretation may be applicable to such as Oedipus, but it seems much less valid when applied to Hamlet who is at best only a cleansing Hercules. One hears in the final words of Fortinbras the hollowness of a patriarchally formulated rhetoric:

> Let four captains
> Bear Hamlet like a soldier to the stage;
> For he was likely, had he been put on,
> To have prov'd most royally; and for his passage
> The soldiers' music and the rites of war
> Speak loudly for him.
> Take up the bodies. Such a sight as this
> Becomes the field, but here shows much amiss.
> Go, bid the soldiers shoot.
> [V.ii, 406–14]

As the voice of the Tyrtaean mode, Fortinbras lauds the dead youth as one who has fought bravely in battle, one who would have borne the Elder's sceptre of authority well had he had the opportunity. But do we experience any renewed faith in moral order as Hamlet is carried off to the sound of martial

music and the peal of ordinance? Are we persuaded that the
preservation of the State at the expense of this Youthful
Hero's potentiality has been worth the denials involved?

The answer may be found in the sensing of Fortinbras that,
although such slaughter becomes the battlefield, here, within
the home, something "shows much amiss." "Take up the
bodies," he commands, and then we guess what may be
wrong. Hamlet's heroic quest had led him to the field of
slaughter where, forced to choose an image of the guiding
father as a pattern of proper behavior, he, like Gertrude,
chose the wrong picture. Perhaps, in fact, he has no choice at
all; the Ghost, fine man though he may have been when alive,
becomes, in death, much more the brother of Claudius than
either he or Hamlet can admit. The brutal injunction to
revenge does not truly befit the solar Hyperion; it is more the
mode of that "mildew'd ear," Claudius, and, ironically, in
observing a *lex talionis*, Hamlet becomes the son of his step-
father as well as of Old Hamlet. His noble personality becomes so warped that he can only find his identity as the
initiate offspring of a vengeful pagan demon. Thus, for the
archetypal Youthful Hero, Hamlet, there is no revelation of a
higher spiritual truth, no possibility of that synthesis of ego,
consciousness, and unconsciousness characteristic of the mature personality. Hamlet, arrested at an early stage on the
path of individuation, regresses, at the moment of crisis, to
ego-narcissism instead of proceeding through the transformation necessary for even a preliminary achievement of the
Jungian "True Self." At one time capable of sublimating his
ego, he fails to unite with the Kore in a bond of love, and
thus, losing his soul, he falls back into the embrace of the
"world dragon."[13] Like that other "soldier" Othello, Hamlet,
in abjuring an *Imitatio Christi*, fails to unite within his psyche
the two principles of tenderness and authority. "Great of

heart" but not "great of soul," there can be no flights of angels for him any more than for the Moor who was to be whipped by devils and washed "in steep-down gulfs of liquid fire."

CHAPTER

V

A Shakespearean Corroboration II: King Lear

IN ultimately achieving a patriarchal stature sufficient for dominance and control, Hamlet became his own Iago, convincing himself that passionate revenge was of more worth than love. Forcing himself to view human relationships in terms of a struggle of antagonisms rather than what he had first felt them to be, a mutual exchange of beneficences, he sacrificed his better self to propitiate the gods of the Sacred Fire; thus he could never, in the terms of Hopkins' poem, recover his feeling for the "live air [of] God's love, . . . patience, penance, [and] prayer." He could not become the Savior-Hero. Thus, as Hamlet's life concludes, we find him rather like the early Lear, a man devoid of *caritas*, unwilling, or unable, either to understand or forgive.

Little need be said here about the Old King's adherence to

the precepts of the Sacred Fire. We have but to keep in mind the authoritarian personality demonstrated in the first scene of the play. With regard to the informing images of the Physical Hearth, we may call to mind once more the psychological importance attached to the *nursing role* of the mother as the source of those emotions of warmth and tenderness which such nourishing and protection involve. But, one may object, there is no mother in *King Lear* to provide a basis for such a symbol. We know that Edmund's mother was fair and that there was good sport in the making of this "illegitimate," but of the mother of Goneril, Regan, and Cordelia, we have but one slight mention (II.iv, 132–34) and that a hint of her possible adultery. Certainly it would be difficult to attempt to recreate this missing figure from the natures and personalities displayed by her daughters—as Kent says, if it were not for "the stars, / The stars above us [that] govern our conditions; / . . . one self mate and mate could not beget / Such different issues" (IV.iii, 35–37). We might surmise that the favored, younger child, Cordelia, receiving genuine warmth and affection from her parents, was able to learn the meaning of love and how to reconvey it; and that Goneril and Regan, experiencing little love or regard after the usurping birth of Cordelia, thereby developed hostile tendencies toward their sister, their parents, and everyone else.

But this would be mere speculation. However, there is other evidence available in the imagery of the play of an overwhelming concern with the early relationships of a mother to her child. Images associated with the nursing mother are not peculiar to *King Lear*. In *Antony and Cleopatra*, the death of Cleopatra is couched in terms which evoke the very essence of the Madonna-Bambino relationship; as she applies the asp, Cleopatra speaks, "Peace, peace! / Dost thou not see my baby at my breast, / That sucks the nurse asleep?" (V.ii, 311–13) And in *Macbeth* when Lady Macbeth wishes "to screw [her husband's] courage to the sticking place" of murdering Duncan, she voices her injunction to be a "man" thus:

> I have given suck, and know
> How tender 'tis to love the babe that milks me.
> I would, while it was smiling in my face,
> Have pluck'd my nipple from his boneless gums
> And dash'd the brains out, had I so sworn as you
> Have done to this.
>
> [I.vii, 54–59]

And as the religious overtones of the Madonna-Bambino portrait strangely affect our emotions toward Cleopatra's suicide, so, in this passage, we are moved by this perversion of the nursing image. In subjecting her maternal feelings to the ends of attaining power and glorifying the Ancestral House of Macbeth, Lady Macbeth becomes the Terrible Mother. In the violence of her desire for these goals, Lady Macbeth employs a key image of the Physical Hearth, changing and distorting its usual context so that we are made suddenly aware of the magnitude and intensity of this contemplated deed of horror. Whereas Clytemnestra and Medea kill to avenge a wrong done their families, Lady Macbeth urges slaughter only as means of gaining status. Her patriarchal orientation is voiced explicitly in Macbeth's laudatory comment, "Bring forth men-children only; / For thy undaunted mettle should compose / Nothing but males" (72–74).

Shakespeare's preoccupation with this symbolic cluster of images is voiced immediately in the first act of *King Lear.* Foiled by Cordelia's failure to recognize his absolute authority and her refusal to make a verbal display of her love, Lear disclaims "all his paternal care, / Propinquity and property of blood" (I.i, 115–16) to banish her into exile. But whereas, now in his old age, he wished to disclaim his responsibility to the State, he did not expect to have to disclaim Cordelia also—"I lov'd her most, and thought to set my rest / On her kind nursery" (I.i, 125–26). In this poignant use of the nursing image we feel all of the old man's frustration and his heartfelt yearning for tenderness, a quality which, at the moment, is completely lacking in himself. But Cordelia will love her father only "according to [her] bond"; to the father who "begot [her], bred [her], and lov'd [her]," she can offer only half a loaf of obedience, love, and honor (95–106); thus, for opposing authority, she is rejected from Lear's Sacred Fire. As a consequence, she is forced to commit her aged, obstinate, father to the "professed bosoms" (125) of her elder sisters, and in this phrase which so contrasts with the previous "kind nursery" associated with Cordelia, we have our first hint of the true natures of Goneril and Regan, corruption behind a façade. They appear to be women, devotees of the Physical Hearth, but in reality, they, like Lady Macbeth, are "monsters," women who are willing to abandon the principles of matriarchy for their own selfish gratification. Thus, in contrast to the loving Cordelia, we have the Terrible Mother, Goneril, voicing an entirely different relationship of mother to child, "Old fools are babes again, and must be us'd / With checks as flatteries, when they are seen abus'd" (I.iii, 19–20). The idle old man "who still would manage those authorities / That he hath given away" (16–18) must be *treated as a child;* that is, he must be put in his place, he must be seen but not heard, he must cower submissively in his designated corner.

Yet Lear, for countless years, has been the Creon who has been heard and not questioned. Naturally, it is difficult for him to change. But the Terrible Mothers insist that the disrespected Elder must assume the role of child within their perverted family; in other words, they insist that Lear lose his identity, not only as King and father but also as a human being. As Lear repeats his tortured question, "Who am I," he receives the answer of Oswald, "You are my Lady's father" (I.iv, 86), the answer of the Fool, "Lear's shadow" (I.iv, 251).

This reversal of roles is expressively put in the Fool's rejoinder to Lear's question, "When were you wont to be so full of songs, sirrah?"

> I have us'd it, nuncle, ever since thou mad'st thy
> daughters thy mother; for when thou gav'st them the rod,
> and put'st down thine own breeches,
> [Sings]
>> Then they for sudden joy did weep,
>>   And I for sorrow sung,
>> That such a king should play bo-peep
>>   And go the fools among.
>
> [I.iv, 188–94]

The reduction of king to child is further elaborated in a debate over who possesses the right of whipping which only reëmphasizes that Lear has now become "An O without a figure" (210 ff.), but this bitter bantering ("I am a fool, thou art nothing") hardly compares with the verbal whipping which the senile child, Lear, receives in the following act from Regan:

> O, sir, you are old!
> Nature in you stands on the very verge
> Of her confine. You should be rul'd, and led
> By some discretion that discerns your state
> Better than you yourself. Therefore I pray you
> That to our sister you do make return;
> Say you have wrong'd her, sir.
>
> [II.iv, 148–54]

This speech is followed by the unsightly and embarrassing kneeling of Lear to Regan, where the reversal of order suggested by Regan is pointed up by Lear's mockery, " 'Dear daughter, I confess that I am old. / Age is unnecessary. On my knees I beg / That you'll vouchsafe me raiment, bed, and food' " (156–58). But of course, as Lear points out in his agony, such bare material necessity is insufficient:

> O, reason not the need! Our basest beggars
> Are in the poorest thing superfluous.
> Allow not nature more than nature needs,
> Man's life is cheap as beast's. Thou art a lady:
> If only to go warm were gorgeous,
> Why, nature needs not what thou gorgeous wear'st,
> Which scarcely keeps thee warm. But, for true need—
> You heavens, give me that patience, patience I need!
> You see me here, you gods, a poor old man,
> As full of grief as age; wretched in both.
> If it be you that stirs these daughters' hearts
> Against their father, fool me not so much
> To bear it tamely; touch me with noble anger,
> And let not women's weapons, water drops,
> Stain my man's cheeks! No, you unnatural hags!
> I will have such revenges on you both
> That all the world shall—I will do such things—
> What they are yet, I know not; but they shall be
> The terrors of the earth! You think I'll weep.
> No, I'll not weep.
> I have full cause of weeping, but this heart
> Shall break into a hundred thousand flaws
> Or ere I'll weep. O fool, I shall go mad!
>   [II.iv, 267–89]

Reason and need have little to do with one another. What Lear really *needs* is the understanding of a sympathetic heart, the acceptance of a tender mother; what he receives in its stead is the common sense, the good, sound logic of Goneril's and Regan's rather valid reasons for the dismissal of his "riotous" followers. But is such patriarchal reasoning the fit reward for the father who "gave [them] all"? Such reasonable needs as food and clothing may be had by some means even by such as Poor Tom. The stripping of a man to his essential self, the stripping of experience to its essential meaning, these are to be learned later; but here the façade of gorgeous raiment which cloaks the monstrous heart and the cold intellect begins to crumble before Lear's eyes. He has opened the door to his elder daughters' hearts to discover the shambles of their ingratitude, to find instead of loving children, "unnatural hags." What little reason he himself possessed had never led him to expect this—his need for acceptance cries out, but he is met only by their chastisement. But he will not weep. He will be a man. He mutters futile imprecations, but his railing reason tells him that these are but idle threats for he has made himself powerless by giving up his authority. In a terrible frustration, compounded by a mighty attempt to maintain restraint and "patience," he rushes out into the storm to meet his madness, and to seek once more his identity.

The storm in *Oedipus at Colonus* seems purposeful, the product of the gods. When Oedipus hears the thunder and lightning which call him to his "appointed end," the Chorus comments, "I fear it, for it never comes in vain, / But for man's luck or his despair. . . . / Ah, Zeus! Majestic heaven!" (ll. 1469–71) But, as is commonly accepted, the storm-scenes in *King Lear* minimize all cosmic referents, other than those of the usual correspondences between macrocosm and microcosm, to portray the powers raging in a tormented soul. According to the matriarchal mode of aesthetic expression with its emphasis on emotion and unconscious inner states, Lear himself *is* the storm. In Shakespeare's tragedy we have the very shivering of the flesh utilized to depict the sudden crack appearing on the wall of the mind.

And, as always, we must refer to the archetypically tremulous human organism which seems to find its sense of being alive only as it sits in the sunshine to feel the blowing of the wind. What, then, must Lear's response be as he is forced to wander on the brushless heath as "the night comes on" and the "bleak winds / do sorely ruffle" his old flesh (II.iv, 303–05)? "Unbonneted he runs," tearing his white hair, striving "in his little world of man to outscorn / The to-and-fro conflicting wind and rain" (III.i, 4–14). He has lost all, his daughters, his identity and sense of self, his dignity as a man, his dignity as a patriarchal King. With this loss of status there has come the complete loss of his authority and a resulting subjection to indignity—"Arraign her first. 'Tis Goneril. I here take my oath before this honourable assembly, she kicked the poor King her father" (III.vi, 48–50). "The little dogs and all, Tray, Blanch, and Sweetheart, see, they bark at me" (III.vi., 65–66). All, all in the mind, as Edgar later asserts, but the mind of Lear is no longer the mirror of daily reality. We have stepped behind this mirror just as we have stepped with Lear behind the façade of Goneril's and Regan's early affection. And in the realm of this old man's feelings, whether he be mad or but mad with grief, we find a crying need for love and the lack of a mother figure to provide for its satisfaction.[1]

Clearly, the only identity left to Lear after Act II is his new role of the unwanted child. Deprived of understanding and maternal care, he is sent from the family table out into the coldness of the heath, the swamp of exile where he is to encounter, in his Jobean quest to understand the reasons for his suffering, the archetypal Dragon of Mystery. At first, his remarkable physical stamina enables him to withstand the buffetings of the storm. He will not succumb to the "cataracts . . . hurricanoes . . . and oak-cleaving thunderbolts" (III.ii, 1–9) any more than he had previously succumbed to the degenerative diseases of old age. He throws into the face of the storm the Hero's counter-cry of challenge, "Pour on; I will endure" (III.iv, 18). But when an individual is subjected to such loss of love, one often finds mere endurance insufficient; one is apt to encounter the symptoms of emotionally induced illness, a common phenomenon with the aged—thus the disease of Lear's daughters' ingratitude takes on symbolic as well as physical repercussions.

As is evident in the rejection of Lear by Goneril and Regan, this play illustrates the revenge of the hostile child against the parent which takes the form of denying the aged mother or father either the love of the Physical Hearth or the status of the Sacred Fire or both. In their imposition of exile and great psychic insecurity on Lear, Goneril and Regan not only refuse to "honor their father" but they refuse even to endure his presence; thus the Family Covenant is shattered. As their previously repressed hostility comes into adult manifestation with their acquisition of authority, all the childhood slights, real or fancied, which they ascribed to Lear's sins as a parent, are revisited upon him in his helplessness. As a consequence, a deterioration of his mental health occurs which is fully as damaging to the personality of the old man as any denial of love, for which he might have been responsible, was damaging to his elder children. No matter whose the primary fault, the action of this tragedy persists in demonstrating the disastrous results of the weakening of those family bonds which encourage the growth and blossoming of emotional maturity. The crime on both sides is corruption through negligence.

Thus, in the counter-rejection of a parent by vengeful children we have a partial explanation of Lear's madness. The theme of this "unnatural" action is pointed out by Lear in one of his last moments of sanity and restraint:

> Thou think'st 'tis much that this contentious storm
> Invades us to the skin. So 'tis to thee;
> But where the greater malady is fix'd,

The lesser is scarce felt. Thou'dst shun a bear;
But if thy flight lay toward, the raging sea,
Thou'dst meet the bear i' th' mouth. When the mind's
    free,
The body's delicate. The tempest in my mind
Doth from my senses take all feeling else
Save what beats there. Filial ingratitude!
Is it not as this mouth should tear this hand
For lifting food to't? But I will punish home!
No, I will weep no more. In such a night
To shut me out! Pour on; I will endure.
In such a night as this! O Regan, Goneril!
Your old kind father, whose frank heart gave all!
O, that way madness lies; let me shun that!
No more of that.

                                              [III.iv, 6–22]

But there is more, much more. The pitiful remnants of his
sanity are blown away in the continuing storm. His unbeliev-
able rejection becomes an obsession, a screen through which
all natural and human action must be viewed. As earlier he
had indicted nature for being "servile ministers" to his "two
pernicious daughters" (III.ii, 21–24), so, when he meets Edgar
disguised as Poor Tom, he must ask, "Hast thou given all to
thy two daughters, and art thou come to this?" (III.iv, 49–
50); and so, when he meets the blinded Gloucester, he can
only see in this unrecognized stranger the embodiment of all
the threatening malice of humanity come to persecute him
further, "Ha! Goneril with a white beard?" (IV.vi, 97).

Filial ingratitude, then, becomes the criterion by which all
nature is to be judged. The microcosm, Lear, sees in the
abrogation of the Family Covenant a force capable of distorting "Nature" herself because this ultimate form of suffering
has taught him that the violation of the Physical Hearth is the
worst crime of which humanity is capable. When, through
madness, the flood gates of repression are open, a turbulent

stream of outraged feeling rushes from Lear's unconsciousness to mirror for us in his pain a traumatic shock to the universe itself. To break the cohesiveness of family emotional bonds with their psychobiological ties is to reverse all natural order —"Is it not as this mouth should tear this hand / For lifting food to't?"

But, we may ask, does Lear have any right to ally himself with the forces of a natural moral order? Do these macrocosmic referents, after all, serve only to demonstrate how Lear is deluding himself with a false sense of his own importance? Is he truly, like Job, representative of humanity, a matriarchal symbol of suffering mankind, or is he merely patriarchal King, top dog on a formulated social chain of being? Perhaps his pain is but the result of "poetic justice," a punishment to fit his earlier crime? After all, his was the original rejection. In exercising his authoritarian will, in foolishly asking for a ceremonial display of affection, in failing to understand the motives of the Kore, Cordelia, has he not demonstrated his incompatibility with "the good"? Has he not betrayed a consuming, patriarchal ego, jealous of its least prerogatives, and entirely willing to ignore and usurp the values of the Physical Hearth? Is he not culpable for his lack of tenderness and his failure to understand love?

We must admit the validity of the indictment implied in these questions, not only because Lear possessed a nurturing duty as father to his daughters, but also because, as King, Father to the State, it was his duty to maintain *order*, to see to it that everything functioned smoothly. As the controlling master who directs the family hierarchy, the father must see to it that the cat is put out and the windows locked; as Lear, he must see to it that the kingdom is divided among three responsible heirs, or better still, not divided at all. But Lear has not done this. Instead of realizing his potentialities as Savior-Hero in fulfilling his duties to others, as Nurturing

Father to his daughters, as Statesman-Hero to his people, he had sought, like Hamlet, his fulfillment in the pursuit of the goals of lower patriarchy; he had sought self-realization within the narrow limits of his personal ego; he had neglected the obligations demanded by the Sacred Fire in his concern with its privileges. Instead of laboring through enlightened benevolism to bring boons to the community, he had sought a public mouthing of his status, and the ease of retirement.

How then can we best examine this king who is no King, this figure who is obviously both the primal father of myth and the patriarchal father of legend, and yet no father at all? In terms of the text, parallelisms have often been drawn between Lear and the fall of a similar figure, the Duke of Gloucester, but, perhaps, even more rewarding comparisons may be drawn between the patriarchal manifestations of Lear and those of the two younger protagonists of the subplot, Edmund and Edgar.

Edmund, of course, is the very prototype of the egoist, but unlike the Lear of Act I, he is subtle and clever. After his initial voicing of his right to success (ironically couched in terms of an appeal to instinctual Nature and the principles of equality and acceptance), Edmund proceeds to use his reason in formulating a plan against Edgar (I.ii, 1–22). The law has denied Edmund his inheritance, so, to transcend the limitations of social ordering, he must achieve power, for he perceives that true authority inheres in status rather than law. At first glance, Edmund's soliloquies would seem to put him in the camp of primordial matriarchy, his impulses seem bestial, nonrational, and nihilistic, but on closer examination we see that his actions, until the very end of the play, reveal a patriarchal quest for prestige, an attempt to achieve identity through a status which will remove the stigma of "bastardy."

His means are ultimately and almost completely rational. The letter, so cleverly revealed with feigned reluctance, is an instrument to be justly compared with the handkerchief of the Machiavellian Iago. To grow and prosper, to attain his place in a patriarchal society, Edmund is more than willing to violate completely the ties of the Physical Hearth; he will turn father against son, drive brother into exile, and finally, with another letter (III.v), betray his father to the Duke of Cornwall on a false charge of treason—"The younger rises when the old doth fall" (III.iii, 26).

To lower patriarchy, this is just good common sense—a pragmatist will take full advantage of his opportunities; and if the law of Nature is to be interpreted in terms of the implications of a later "behavioristic" mode, he who possesses determination, he who "regards men and women, with their virtues and vices . . . merely as hindrances or helps to his end," will be the one who survives or attains his goal. Thus, as Bradley notes, Edmund is as indifferent to other human beings as if they were mere "mathematical quantities or mere physical agents."[2]

We think of Agamemnon, Jason, and Iago, but *their* completely mechanical approach to human relationships cannot be sustained by Edmund. For Edmund is not Iago. Undermining his cynically rational evaluation of "this . . . excellent foppery of the world" that makes the stars responsible for human misbehavior is a certain "goatish disposition" which he shares with his father and "whoremaster man." He may deny all superhuman influences, but he cannot deny or control the power of those elemental passions which govern his motives despite his protestations to the contrary. He seems so clever, so completely logical; he can speak of "these evil days" of universal corruption and bemoan the "unnaturalness between the child and the parent" in such a way that his own unnatural crimes are transferred to the head of Edgar (I.ii).

Later, he can speculate upon the advantages of taking either Goneril or Regan or neither in marriage according to the circumstances most beneficial to himself (V.i, 55–62); *yet* he does not seem to realize (until the very end of the play) that for him "neither" is no valid alternative. For Edmund, in addition to being burdened by a casual and credulous father, is also the victim of a deprivation of love. He, too, has a missing mother.

Thus, the thematic oppositions of lust and love which inform the play meet within the character of Edmund. He thinks he is consciously "using" the lusts of Goneril and Regan to further his own masculine purpose, but in reality, and most pathetically, even the perverted loves of these monstrous mothers possess subtly unconscious meanings for him. The reciprocal lust of the "illegitimate" and the Archetypal Temptresses is not for Edmund a mere means of sexual gratification—the life of the senses has little meaning for the purely enterprising opportunist—it is a disguised mode of obtaining love, the love which had been denied to him just as to the two sisters:

> Yet Edmund was belov'd.
> The one the other poisoned for my sake,
> And after slew herself.
>
> [V.iii, 238–40]

Knowing but a glimpse of love, even in this distorted form, Edmund is able to quit the stage "a better man" than Iago. Because of this momentary matriarchal recognition, he attempts to do some good, "despite of [his] own nature"— "Quickly send / (Be brief in't) to the castle; for my writ / Is on the life of Lear and on Cordelia. / Nay, send in time" (V.iii, 243–47).

On the other hand, the older man, Lear, is not clever. He does not have to be; he has achieved and consolidated his position; he is, in the first act, the man Edmund hopes to become. As we see Lear, clothed in the purple of his kingly repute, banishing Cordelia and Kent, we recall the later lines of Edmund at the height of his brief power, "for my state / Stands on me to defend, not to debate" (V.ii, 68–69). The primal father of myth is not to be questioned; the women of the tribe are his to do with as he wishes. Likewise, the patriarchal father of legend, like Creon, possesses complete authority; as the *roi soleil* of the Renaissance social chain, the State is his to rule or ruin. Thus, this play demonstrates both aspects of patriarchal authority, the Tyrant Father of the familial Sacred Fire seeking to impose his absolutism on recalcitrant children, and the Tyrtaean Elder of the State seeking to impose his own particularized form of civil order on the citizens under his control.

But because King Lear is not clever like Edmund, not capable of much reason, he does not realize that his powers are based solely upon his position. Egotistically, he believes that they are due to his own personal attributes, so he feels free to resign his position, assuming that his status will continue. In a sense, this is understandable, for Lear has been living the role of absolute monarch for many, many years; the patriarchal pattern of Western culture has become his pattern. Only in his unconscious could he possibly remember a time, the period of his matriarchally oriented childhood, when his authority was not complete. Thus, in believing that Lear is king rather than realizing that the king happens to be Lear, the old man suffers that delusion which so often leads to archetypal patriarchal frustration. Thus, when he loses that status of Elder for which Edmund yearns so desperately, the King must search on the heath and in his tortured mind for something else. What is he to find? Wisdom? Love? Or a final, despairing recognition of his own isolation and inadequacy?

If it is to be solar wisdom, we must compare Lear with the only solar Hero of the play, Gloucester's elder son, Edgar for, with the possible exception of Goneril, his brother, and the villainous Duke of Cornwall, he is the only really active figure of this tragedy. At first, however, Edgar is rather passive; his lesson of suffering begins with Gloucester's deception and his own subsequent flight; he becomes the Tyrtaean exile banished from home, and, like Cordelia, he suffers the pain of what he feels is a most unwarranted rejection. Both are perplexed children, victims of a parental wrath which they cannot comprehend. Like Cordelia, Edgar is also "the good child," one who follows the precepts which he later advances bitterly in his disguise of Poor Tom, ". . . obey thy parents; keep thy word justly; swear not . . ." (III.iv, 82–83). He is, as even Edmund admits, ". . . a brother noble, / Whose nature is so far from doing harms / That he suspects none" (I.ii, 195–97). Yet, it is his "foolish honesty," so similar to that of Cordelia's, which also leads to his being driven out on the heath, like Lear, defamed and "acold." His lesson in suffering continues as he learns in the "poorest shape / That ever penury, in contempt of man, / Brought near to beast" that it is to be his lot to suffer "the winds and persecutions of the sky," suffer the lot of the Bedlam beggar through no fault of his own (II.iii, 1–21). He, too, must face the Jobean problem whether the seemingly righteous can of necessity expect justice.

Edgar thus loses his identity also to become with Lear the epitome of suffering mankind, "Edgar I nothing am" (II.iii, 21); or as Lear puts it when he first sees him as Poor Tom, "Is man no more than this? . . . Thou art the thing itself; unaccommodated man is no more but such a poor, bare, forked animal as thou art" (III.iv, 105–13). This knowledge that the vagaries of circumstance can debase man to the level of beast, impugn the dignity of the human form, and reduce divine reason to incoherent babbling, itself becomes the very basis for Lear's growing awareness of the plight of others. Edgar's condition leads to Lear's epiphany; in a frenzy of sympathy, Lear tears off his own "lendings" (the robes of his previous status) to join Poor Tom in his nakedness, "Come, unbutton here" (113–14). It is through this display of sympathy by the mad Lear that Edgar learns a reciprocal wisdom, a knowledge of the communion possible for mankind as individuals face inevitable pain together:

> Who alone suffers suffers most i' th' mind,
> Leaving free things and happy shows behind:
> But then the mind much sufferance doth o'erskip
> When grief hath mates, and bearing fellowship.
>   [III.vi, 110–13]

Edgar, too, becomes more perceptive through suffering; he sees that "He [Lear] childed as I fathered." Stripped to their essential selves by the purgative force of the storm and the enforced contemplation of themselves which has resulted from their rejection by their families, both come to learn a new wisdom.

But, though ego-benevolism is involved in both cases, there is an essential difference. Edgar, in passing from child to man, learns the wisdom of suffering in and for itself—"Men must endure / Their going hence, even as their coming hither; / Ripeness is all" (V.ii, 9–11). After the defeat of the French forces by the British under Albany and Edmund, Gloucester says in despairing resignation, "No further, sir. A man may rot even here," but Edgar insists that he keep going—"Come on," he urges. The wisdom gained from *his* lesson of suffering on the heath has taught him the necessity of positive action as the only means of achieving virtuous goals and a properly mature orientation to experience. True endurance is not meant to be passive resignation in the face of disaster, but, as for all solar heroes, a spur to accomplish whatever good is possible despite the seeming triumph of evil. Edgar as the good man refuses to add even a thimbleful of evil to the already overflowing cup which threatens to engulf mankind. "Ripeness" is thus for him more than Stoic endurance; it also embodies the obligation of exercising Stoic virtue.

It is debatable, however, whether such philosophy implies the existence of an emotionally satisfying (fully *universal*) moral order. As in *Oedipus the King*, the preservation of the State, here, through the agency of Albany and Edmund, seems almost irrelevant when compared with the tragic individual catastrophes suffered by Lear and Cordelia. Despite his chivalric action, it is difficult to associate any sense of human dignity with the rather formal figure of Edgar; we cannot speak of him as we do of Oedipus, "To have been great of soul is everything." Just as a sense of a moral rhythm is lacking in the vast chaotic structure of *King Lear*, so there seems little sense of a real Sophoclean "piety" in the character of Edgar. Like Albany's, his piety seems to consist only in a superficial alliance with mere macrocosmic referents:

> The gods are just, and of our pleasant vices
> Make instruments to scourge us.
> The dark and vicious place where thee he got
> Cost him his eyes.
>
> [V.iii, 170–73]

This speech to Edmund about their father seems much more like Albany's "This judgment of the heavens, that makes us tremble, / Touches us not with pity" (V.iii, 231–32) than it does to Cordelia's forgiving (not merely tactical) "Shall we not see these daughters and these sisters?" (V.iii, 7) Edgar, as patriarchal hero, lives in this world, a world of retributive punishment and strict justice, where suffering is the natural lot of man, where the evil brother must be slain. In the final analysis, he seems more like Eliphaz than Job, for he seeks the fulfillment of the formula that "the sinful must suffer" rather than any matriarchal communion with spiritual forces.

Suffering, however, has taught Edgar a form of wisdom embodying the necessity of justice as well as punishment, and it is primarily through a recognition of this quest that he and Lear can communicate. In the harrowing mock-trial scene (III.vi), the stools are arranged and arraigned; Lear says to Poor Tom, "Come sit thou here, most learned justicer." The irony lies in the fact that only in the roles of madmen can Edgar and Lear even contemplate this topic together, for the limited patriarchal view of justice to which the real Edgar subscribes is not the justice sought by Lear in this strange episode. As judge at the mock indictment of Goneril and Regan, Lear is actually trying to achieve some form of transcendent justice beyond that of rationally formulated law. These are, after all, *his* daughters, and the emotional perspective of the Physical Hearth and Family Covenant strongly affect his point of view. Filial ingratitude, rejection, desertion, subjection to indignity, these are the crimes, and there are no legal precedents for an evaluation of such culpability. These are not the crimes of explicit treachery for which Edmund, and perhaps Gloucester, are guilty. These are crimes against the Physical Hearth, crimes against mankind's deepest nature, tenuous and difficult even for the prosecutor's accusation. How difficult, then, to determine a valid punishment when the crime itself can hardly be formulated in rational terms. Patience and restraint must dissipate before the onslaught of such frustration. Lear can only appeal in Joblike agony, "Is there any cause in nature that makes these hard hearts?" (III.vi, 81–82).

The patriarchal wisdom which may be gleaned from a knowledge of suffering is not in itself sufficient answer to Lear's probings; and the justice of his previous regal authority is totally inadequate for his present state because it was based on a complete delusion—"They flatter'd me like a dog. . . .

To say 'ay' and 'no' to everything I said! 'Ay' and 'no' too
was no good divinity." *But* "when the rain came to wet me
once, and the wind to make me chatter; when the thunder
would not peace at my bidding; there I found 'em, there I
smelt 'em out. Go to, they are not men o' their words! They
told me I was everything. 'Tis a lie—I am not ague-proof"
(IV.vi, 97–104). The old man has discovered one of the
truths about authority, the fact that "a dog's obeyed in office"
(IV.vi, 162; cf. I.iv, 125–26). But only in office—"Change
places, and handy-dandy, which is the justice, which is the
thief?" (157–58). Which is the dog, which is the beggar?
Who is the sinner, usurer or cozener, the judge who punishes
the poor whore with lashing, or the sensual man beneath the
robe who "hotly lusts to use her in that kind" for which he
whips her? The justice of the Sacred Fire is subject to the
vagaries of rationalization and personal desire; its secular
authority resides in the relativistic rather than the universal:

> Through tatter'd clothes small vices do appear;
> Robes and furr'd gowns hide all. Plate sin with gold,
> And the strong lance of justice hurtless breaks;
> Arm it in rags, a pygmy's straw does pierce it.
>   [IV.vi, 168–71]

Edgar exclaims, "O, matter and impertinency mix'd! /
Reason in madness!" (178–79). The entire play substantiates
Neumann's statement that "madness may be regarded as
sacred and taken positively as an inspirational initiation because, behind inundation by the spirit, the world of archetypes appears as the power that determines fate."[3] Through
his madness, Lear has perceived that true justice cannot be
found by the legal application of a formulated, authoritarian
code; his unconscious tells him he must seek it elsewhere.
Edgar, on the other hand, catches a momentary glimpse of
this archetypal truth, but he himself has not suffered enough

to wish to pursue it further. In the final analysis, Edgar cannot transcend the limitations of the Sacred Fire. At best, he remains the solar Warrior-Hero and Statesman-Hero of the patriarchal orientation.

But Lear has suffered with an intensity beyond Edgar's comprehension; the madness born of his grief and frustration is a real, not, like Hamlet's, a feigned madness, and thus he attains to a greater perception, a greater revelation, a greater "matriarchal" understanding. When Lear says to Gloucester, "If thou wilt weep my fortunes, take my eyes" (IV.vi, 180), we are meant to understand that although this is a perception shaped by Lear's individual suffering, still it is capable of conveying insight into that world of meaning which inheres in the unconscious. The implication is, that, despite his own suffering, Gloucester is really too feeble in intellect and too weak in character ever really to understand much, to be any more than a passive victim. Unlike Kent, Gloucester had been voiceless in protesting the banishments of the first act; we gather that he has always been a compromiser and a submissive underling rather than "a good counselor" to his prince. Only in the face of terrible cruelty did his loyalty reassert itself, and then surreptitiously. His own suffering has been entirely passive; his recognition of Edmund's villainy and his final reconciliation with his elder son are both achieved under Edgar's direction. But the fortuitous patterns of experience insist that the weak suffer equally, if not more so, than the strong. Matriarchy accepts and offers pity for Gloucester too, but all in all, he is an old man whose beard is to be plucked by those stronger than himself; his eyes must be gouged out so that he can see his mistake, but even then, unlike Oedipus and Lear, he sees but darkly.

How then is Lear's greatness of perception to be expressed and understood? Whence comes its "universality"?

One way of finding out would be to note how the earlier birth and nursing imagery are utilized again toward the end of the play to elicit a meaning which incorporates the wisdom of the unconscious learned by Lear in his tremendous struggle on the heath. At first (before Cordelia's re-entrance), Lear shares with Edgar the philosophy that wisdom is but the knowledge of suffering. In a moment of lucidity, during which he seeks to console Gloucester, he cites a universal axiom in the popular sermonizing style of the day:

> Thou must be patient. We came crying hither;
> Thou know'st, the first time that we smell the air
> We wawl and cry. I will preach to thee. Mark. . . .
>
> When we were born, we cry that we are come
> To this great stage of fools. . . .
>
> [IV.vi, 182–87]

This is quite similar to Edgar's Stoic doctrine that to suffer is the natural state of man.

Yet, the imagery employed in the above passage substantiates somewhat the Rankian theory of the birth trauma with its suggestion that the physiological difficulties of birth are compounded by an instinctual recognition that a paradisal state of warmth and security has been exchanged for a "stage of fools," or, in Platonic terms, that the knowledgeable soul has been contaminated by the acquisition of a body. We need not speculate to any great extent how this trauma may have contributed to the formation of a primal anxiety in Lear, but the action of the play does suggest that his problems may possibly be better interpreted in the light of this basic rejection with its corollary view of man's attempt to regain original bliss. Both Rank and Freud maintain that the pleasurable experience of nursing partially alleviates the pain of the birth trauma, that the euphoric state of the infant's relationship with the nursing mother imposes upon the psyche a lifelong memory of the exaltation of receiving love. In theory, then, man seeks to avoid repetitions of these traumatic rejections during his lifetime in favor of achieving states similar to the intra-uterine or nursing stages of development. To reiterate, we have the importance of the symbolic figure of the "missing mother" in the tragedy of *King Lear.*

It is quite obvious that the behavior of Goneril and Regan constitutes for Lear a repetition of this psychical state of rejection, and that, for him, his daughters perform the role of the Terrible Mother. They are not only evil children, but they also represent all the harshness and callousness of a world lacking in the qualities of the Physical Hearth. We have sought a preliminary explanation for their cruel exile of their father in the possibility that once they have acquired his patriarchal authority, they are exercising a form of counter-rejection, that they are gaining vengeance for some earlier mistreatment on his part.

Whatever the explanation, the fact remains that they have become "monsters," and that they offer Lear in the place of the missing mother only the "professed bosoms" of a duplicity which hides hateful hearts. *They are monsters as children:* Lear, bidding farewell to Goneril once and for all, calls her, not his daughter, but "rather a disease that's in my flesh . . . a boil, / A plague sore, an embossed carbuncle / In my corrupted blood" (II.iv, 223–28); *they are monsters as wives:* Albany, made recently aware of Goneril's cruelty, berates her for "bemonster[ing her] feature," i.e., hiding her devil's self in "a woman's shape" (IV.ii, 59–67); and finally, and most crucially, *they are monsters as mothers or mother surrogates:* we recall that when Lear made "his daughters [his] mother," the Fool noted that "they for sudden joy did weep" that he should be so foolish.

This clever masking, and shocking reversal of natural family roles, enables them to accomplish what they had never expected to be able to do, "their purpose of unkindness" (I.iv, 75). The extent of the indictment is made as early as the first act when Lear thunderingly rebukes Goneril as a "degenerate bastard" (I.iv, 275), a repository for the "marble-hearted fiend, Ingratitude" (281), and a "detested kite" (284). In his denunciation of this "sea-monster" who is his own child, Lear becomes the Old Testament fertility-god, Jehovah, visiting a sterility curse upon the disobedient and impure:

> Hear, Nature, hear! dear goddess, hear!
> Suspend thy purpose, if thou didst intend
> To make this creature fruitful,
> Into her womb convey sterility;
> Dry up in her the organs of increase;
> And from her derogate body never spring
> A babe to honour her! If she must teem,
> Create her child of spleen, that it may live
> And be a thwart disnatur'd torment to her.
> Let it stamp wrinkles in her brow of youth,
> With cadent tears fret channels in her cheeks,
> Turn all her mother's pains and benefits
> To laughter and contempt, that she may feel
> How sharper than a serpent's tooth it is
> To have a thankless child!
>
> [I.iv, 297–311]

In such a curse, we discover the key configuration of Goneril. Again, the fiend feared by patriarchy? Without doubt. But more—she is denounced as unfit for motherhood, not only because of her usurpation of authority but also because she has failed to understand love. What sort of child could she possibly produce for the Ancestral House but "a thwart disnatur'd torment," since she, herself, is entirely incapable of communicating tenderness? Certainly, she would destroy a child just as she seeks to destroy her old father.

This ruinous lack of matriarchal virtue is expressed not only by Goneril's and Regan's exile of Lear but also substantiated by their association with Edmund in the entangling web of lust. Such lust becomes the only means they have of communication, and, as symbolic of the unnatural perversions dominating the play, love become lust serves as the symbol of all human potentiality for good deformed by man's strange penchant for evil. In his inspired madness, Lear perceives, "The wren goes to't, and the small gilded fly / Does lecher in my sight" (IV.vi, 114–15). In his despair, lust (evil) seems natural, the essence of human experience; thus, unwittingly, and ironically, he cries, "Let copulation thrive; for Glouces-ter's bastard son / Was kinder to his father than my daugh-ters / Got 'tween the lawful sheets" (116–18). His elabora-tion of this theme reflects the tendency of patriarchy, in its frustration at the seeming indestructibility of evil, to attribute this evil to the chthonic powers of matriarchy:

> Behold yond simp'ring dame,
> Whose face between her forks presageth snow,
> That minces virtue, and does shake the head
> To hear of pleasure's name.
> The fitchew nor the soiled horse goes to't
> With a more riotous appetite.
> Down from the waist they are Centaurs,
> Though women all above.
> But to the girdle do the gods inherit,
> Beneath is all the fiend's.
>
>   [IV.vi, 120–29][4]

Certainly Lear's personal situation justifies his denial of the feminine, and, although he may not be aware of his daughters' lust for Edmund, he has intuitively grasped the proper sym-bolism which expresses most succinctly this perversion of good to evil. In so far as Goneril and Regan are "Centaur-monsters" who can only express themselves carnally, they represent the bestial side of human nature which, to the Renaissance, suggested a tendency toward emotional chaos (the prudish face which pretends to virtue is but a delusive façade for the rioting flesh below). It is no wonder, then, that Lear must pray for "civet . . . to sweeten [his] imagination" for he has now become aware of "the sulphurous pit" of bestial impulse in mankind, an impulse made infinitely more destructive when combined with an accompanying perversion of man's "divine" reason. The supplanting of a loving filial gratitude toward their father by a selfish lust for Edmund serves as an admirable device for depicting the malformed natures of the two evil sisters. As the 3rd Servant says of Regan, "If she live long, / And in the end meet the old course of death, / Women will all turn monsters" (III.vii, 100–02).

In substantiation, Albany, like Edgar a figure of solar patriarchy in the play, speaks as the voice of outraged moral order. After Goneril's pledge to Edmund, Albany enters to rebuke her, at last, for her treatment of her father, not knowing that even then she is contemplating the violation of their own Physical Hearth (IV.vi, 267–77):

> O Goneril,
> You are not worth the dust which the rude wind
> Blows in your face! I fear your disposition.
> That nature which contemns it[s] origin
> Cannot be bordered certain in itself.
> She that herself will sliver and disbranch
> From her material sap, perforce must wither
> And come to deadly use. . . .
>
> Wisdom and goodness to the vile seem vile;
> Filths savour but themselves. What have you done?
> Tigers, not daughters, what have you perform'd?
> A father, and a gracious aged man,
> Whose reverence even the head-lugg'd bear would lick,
> Most barbarous, most degenerate, have you madded.
>   [IV.ii, 29–43]

Appealing as a righteous character to the moral justice of the "heavens," Albany sees clearly that if divine punishment is not visited upon such "vile offences," then "Humanity must perforce prey on itself, / Like monsters of the deep" (IV.ii, 46–50).

But these daughters' "mouths" *have* torn the aged hand that fed them, and Goneril's final actions will but further display the extent of evil of which humanity is capable. To have Edmund for herself, she plots Albany's death and eventually poisons Regan. Defeated in this attempt through Edgar's conquest of Edmund, she appeals to legality in her mistaken sense of her own authority, ". . . the laws are mine, not thine. / Who can arraign me for't?" (V.iii, 158–59) Arraigned and convicted by the letter taken from Oswald, she exits, silent as Iago, to die like a man, a Cassius, not a Brutus. Incapable of human love, capable only of lust and a horrible perversion of reason for her own ends, Goneril, as the beast, the "dog-hearted daughter," becomes the very image of the monstrous Terrible Mother (not only the matriarchal figure of impulse whom man fears but also the malformed "masculine" woman of his own social creation).

Were the play to end here, the triumph of Albany and Edgar with their patriarchally formulated codes of morality would hardly suffice to convince us of the worth of human existence and the value of Stoic endurance. For although the State is preserved, what are the deaths of Goneril, Regan, and Edmund compared to our picture of that "ruined piece of nature" (IV.vi, 137), the maddened Lear with his faith in humanity torn to shreds by his "pelican daughters"?

In her discussion of the "splitting of a type figure," Maud Bodkin applies the Freudian theory of ambivalence to *King Lear* in most illuminating fashion:

As to the feeling of the child, the parent may be both loved protector and unjustly obstructing tyrant, and these two aspects find their emotional symbolism in separate figures in the play; so, to the feeling of the parent, the child may be both loving support of age and ruthless usurper and rival, and these two aspects find expression in separate figures, such as the tender and the wicked daughters of Lear.[5]

We have noted that the rejecting actions of Goneril and Regan have proven them more than adequate "rivals"; as successful usurpers, they have acquired their father's throne, they have driven him to madness and the complete loss of his identity both as King and human personality. The destructive Terrible Mothers, victims of a lust for authority which fully parallels their sensuality, take full advantage, coldly and rationally, of their father's inability to understand the meaning of love in Act I. This ignorance on Lear's part marks the beginning of his downfall as a patriarchal King, yet it also serves to mark the beginning of his development as a "matriarchal human being." In the first scene, France counters Lear's arrogance by stating a key principle of the play which is to be given later dramatic manifestation, "Love's not love / When it is mingled with regards that stands / Aloof from th' entire point" (I.i, 241–43). Lear's inability to understand this, emotionally, leads him to banish his truly "tender daughter," Cordelia, for failing to love him as much as she should, and then later to base his hopes for affection on what he thinks is the "tender-hefted nature" of his wicked daughter, Regan:

> Thou better know'st
> The offices of nature, bond of childhood,
> Effects of courtesy, dues of gratitude.
> Thy half o' th' kingdom hast thou not forgot,
> Wherein I thee endow'd.
>
> [II.iv, 180–84]

Lear has been completely deceived by Goneril's and Regan's verbalizations of "love," the superficial counters for which he exchanges two larger counters, the halves of a kingdom. But the verbal displays and the two kingdoms are both false coins; neither represents the true value of genuine affection. The meaning of love may only be learned on the heath.

Abjuring all roofs, subjecting himself to the purgative terror of the storm, Lear finds that his initial stupidity is to be punished a thousandfold, "I am a man / More sinn'd against than sinning" (III.ii, 59–60). As sinner he has been "foolish," he has been childish in the sense that he has been incapable of perception into the motives of others; as a child he has been brash and willful; as a child he has identified those who yield to his wishes with those who love him. It may be truly said of Lear that when he was a child (a childish King, an authoritarian personality), he spoke, felt, and thought as a child; but now that he has been forced to enter the "adult" world of suffering, the heath, he must become a man.

The heath is obviously symbolic of Lear's road of trials, where, confronted by the traditional dark night of the soul, probing desperately for the meanings of justice, love, and virtue, he finds a correspondence to his own internal agony in the "dreadful pudder" of the tempest (III.ii, 49–59). But more important, he also discovers through this experience that there is within himself a latent empathy, a capacity for pity, and an ability to perceive the quality and existence of other human beings. As they all seek shelter from the storm in the miserable hovel, Lear, recognizing that his companions are also cold and wet, speaks thus:

> [*To the disguised Kent*]—
> Prithee go in thyself; seek thine own ease.
> This tempest will not give me leave to ponder
> On things would hurt me more. . . .
> [*To the Fool*] In, boy; go first.—You houseless poverty—
> Nay, get thee in. I'll pray, and then I'll sleep.
>   [*Exit Fool*].
> Poor naked wretches, wheresoe'er you are,
> That bide the pelting of this pitiless storm,

> How shall your houseless heads and unfed sides,
> Your loop'd and window'd raggedness, defend you
> From seasons such as these? O, I have ta'en
> Too little care of this! Take physic, pomp;
> Expose thyself to feel what wretches feel,
> That thou mayst shake the superflux to them
> And show the heavens more just.
>
> [III.iv, 23–36]

Thus his own distress takes him on the first step toward a greater wisdom, to an initial recognition that justice involves more than a mere exercise of authority, that it must be also an instrument to protect the poor and oppressed. Once more, we may note parallelisms to the development of the concept of "righteousness" in the Old Testament: the good man, the King as Savior-Hero, must take care of others; practical ethics is his chief concern. Lear escapes his childishness, his narcissism, through suffering himself and seeing others suffer; thus he gains the wisdom that suffering teaches, that man is momentarily subject to intense physical or psychical pain and that, in Edgar's terms, "Ripeness is all."

But is this second step toward knowledge, this recognition of Stoic endurance and virtue, sufficient to save Lear from his madness? Apparently not, for it is immediately after the perception quoted above that his mind disintegrates, and he is confronted again with the frustration and obsessive dilemma noted earlier—"Is there any cause in nature that makes these hard hearts?" The wisdom of suffering will not provide him with an answer. Having attained to manhood, even a Job-like stature, Lear, like Job, is still confronted with the intolerable problems of theodicy, and the human reasoning power which he has gained at such cost seems of little avail. Is this, then, for Lear the dead end of human understanding, a complete frustration in his recognition of personal isolation and inadequacy?

In the fourth act we have the return of Cordelia, the missing mother who symbolizes the accepting forces of the Physical Hearth. She is to be the Good Mother whose task it is to restore to Lear his identity, to make of him again Lear instead of "Lear's shadow." But what are to be the means of his salvation, the source of the transforming wisdom that he is to discover in renewed communion? In the surpassingly lovely reconciliation scene (IV.vii), Lear becomes himself again, becomes sane once more, by becoming as a little child.

This theme of transformation is introduced by Cordelia, who, in her great pity, believes that Lear's madness is the only cause of his illness. Like Mary, in Hopkins' poem, she prays, "O you kind gods, / Cure this great breach in his abused nature! / Th' untuned and jarring senses, O, wind up / Of this child-changed father!" (IV.vii, 14–17) Lear's loss of strength is manifest as he is carried in upon a chair by servants, newly clothed, fast asleep, helpless as a child in its crib. When he awakens, all madness gone, in the simplest, most moving, language he admits:

> I am a very foolish fond old man,
> Fourscore and upward, not an hour more nor less;
> And, to deal plainly,
> I fear I am not in my perfect mind.
> Methinks I should know you, and know this man;
> Yet I am doubtful; for I am mainly ignorant
> What place this is; and all the skill I have
> Remembers not these garments; nor I know not
> Where I did lodge last night.
>
> [IV.vii, 60–68]

And as he recognizes Cordelia, he reaches out to touch her cheek:

> Be your tears wet? Yes, faith. I pray weep not.
> If you have poison for me, I will drink it.
> I know you do not love me; for your sisters

Have, as I do remember, done me wrong.
You have some cause, they have not.

[71–75]

Thus when Cordelia tearfully extends her complete forgiveness, "No cause, no cause," this aged, "child-changed" father
can only accept and plead, "You must bear with me. / Pray
you now, forget and forgive. I am old and foolish" (84–85).
Here, Shakespeare presents a truly perceptive paradox: when
in Act I Lear thought himself fully a man in the Tyrtaean
sense, when he could not admit the possibility of his being
"old" and "foolish," when his actions proved him so, then he
was as the scribes loving "the chief seats in the synagogues,
and the uppermost rooms at feasts." Covetous and overright-
eous, he sought the highest place and the exaltation belonging
to a king. Relying on the "reason" of lawyers and elders, he
thought his authority absolute and his status unquestionable.
But "truth's a dog must to kennel," and, as the Fool perceived, Lear was then the fool.

Now in Act V, Lear sees himself clearly for the first time,
and what he sees is a "very foolish fond old man," a child. But
this is not a despairing recognition of mere inadequacy and
helplessness, it is a revelation. As Christ rejoiced, ". . . that
[God] hast hid these things from the wise and prudent, and
hast revealed them unto babes," so, in becoming as a child,
Lear gains the wisdom of the knowledge of love similar to
that conceivably possessed by the child at his mother's breast.
And, in so far as the Renaissance may be considered still, to
some extent, an age of faith, the voicing of such revelation can
only be equated with the traditional "peace . . . which pass-
eth all understanding." Supposedly transcending the patriarchal necessity of making analytical discriminations, it rejects
rational judgment as the only means of ascertaining truth, it
devotes itself to the acceptance of all, the sinful woman and
the prodigal son, the Fool and Poor Tom.

Thus, as Lear gains the wisdom of Fromm's tender mother for whom all men are the children of an all-embracing "Heavenly Father," we see him symbolically as representative of enlightened mankind, one capable of responding to the orientation enjoined in Hopkins' poem. Yet, despite this epiphany, Lear himself remains largely passive; it is Cordelia who, in this "great religious drama,"[6] plays the role of the Redeemer ("Thou hast one daughter / Who redeems nature from the general curse / Which twain have brought her to"—IV.vi, 209–11). In her matriarchal role of the Good Mother, she it is who performs the *Imitatio Christi,* suffering herself that love may be obtained, yet offering the hurt child, Lear, the "kind nursery" of her tenderness. She is the one who cares not only for the poor and oppressed, as does Lear, but also for "the broken-hearted."

Lear, on the other hand, can only be viewed as victimized by his world of pain; even the patriarchal wisdom acquired, and the generosity and pity displayed for the "houseless poverty" of humanity, are hardly more than empathy and recognition, important as they may be. His suffering, like that of Job and Oedipus, would seem almost purposeless if the ultimate action of the play did not result in a sense of the revelation of love and the meaning of communion. Without the restoration of the missing mother, Cordelia, the final impression left by this tragedy would be but that we experience at the moment of Oedipus' self-blinding with the brooches of Jocasta—not that man is evil, but that he can be unbelievably unfortunate.[7]

Thus in exploring how this final relationship of Lear and Cordelia illuminates the human condition, one must stress the possibility that man has within him the capacity to respond to love. Whether such capacity be called, in accordance with Renaissance theory, angelic understanding, the divine remnant which urges man to reunite with his Creator, whether it be called, in more modern terms, the ability of the psyche to learn such response and reconvey it once experienced, such giving of the self can only be designated as good when contrasted with those forms of narcissim which, as evil, inhibit man's realization of this capacity.

However, the Cordelia of Act I is herself hardly aware of these transcendent powers; she is not yet the Redeemer for she herself has not yet suffered—thus, because of her bluntness, she cannot save her father from his folly. Still, even here, she represents the image of the fruitful Kore on the verge of a transformation into the creative Good Mother and the pitying Demeter. Although her father's rejection is her Gethesemane, just as the exile to the heath is Lear's, she leaves the scene about to be happily married to France, perhaps to have children and establish a Physical Hearth of her own.

But this is not to be, and the frustration of her opportunity to fulfill herself as a real mother constitutes the beginning of her real agony. In Acts IV and V, her pain is compounded by the necessary return home of France to meet another crisis, her sisters' violation of their Family Covenant, her discovery of Lear's exile and madness, and, finally, the failure of the crusade itself which, in the older sources, restored Lear to his throne ("No blown ambition doth our arms incite, / But love, dear love, and our ag'd father's right"—IV.iv, 27–28). Cordelia herself must be crucified before she can become capable of offering Lear redemption: she must undergo a suffering similar to that of giving birth before she can produce the child who is the object and medium of love, before she can become capable of understanding and offering tenderness to her father who strangely enough has become this child.

It may be justly asked what evidence the play itself presents for equating Cordelia with such a force of redemption. Again, the imagery provides grounds for the interpretation: we find, first of all, a succession of religious terms applied to her person—". . . she shook / The holy water from her heavenly eyes" (IV.iii, 31–32); "[she] redeems nature" (IV.vi, 210); she is to the awakening Lear, ". . . a soul in bliss" (IV.vii, 46), an angelic "spirit" (49). The communication of Lear and Cordelia is constantly referred to as an exchange of "benedictions" (IV.iii, 45; IV.vii, 58; V.iii, 10–11). Lear feels obligated to pray to her for forgiveness (IV.vii, 84).

But there is more. As the tender mother figure of the Physical Hearth, Cordelia manifests many of the attributes associated with the Virgin Mary or the Jesus of the Gospels. Even in the rather formal eulogy by the courtly messenger who describes her reaction to Kent's letters, we see the equanimity of an almost spiritual figure whose calm is torn by an angelic pity:

> Patience and sorrow strove
> Who should express her goodliest. You have seen
> Sunshine and rain at once: her smiles and tears
> Were like a better way. Those happy smilets
> That play'd on her ripe lip seem'd not to know
> What guests were in her eyes, which parted thence
> As pearls from diamonds dropp'd. In brief,
> Sorrow would be a rarity most belov'd,
> If all could so become it.
>   [IV.iii, 18–26; cf. also 27–34]

The rainbow imagery delicately conveys the mixture of grief and pity which makes her tears "heavenly," pointing forward to Lear's final eulogy, "Her voice was ever soft, / Gentle, and low—an excellent thing in woman" (V.iii, 272–73). Hers is the universal crooning voice of the nursing mother as heard by the child. Her latter speeches are full of concern for others, not only for her father, but for Kent whom she so values for his goodness, to whom she is so grateful (IV.vii, 1–3). As the Good Mother, as the agent of redemption, as Madonna and Redeemer both, it is her loving kiss which is to restore to Lear his sanity and identity and remove him from the world of pain and illness:

> O my dear father, restoration hang
> Thy medicine on my lips, and let this kiss
> Repair those violent harms that my two sisters
> Have in thy reverence made!
>
> [IV.vii, 26–29]

Thus Lear's reconciliation with Cordelia represents more than a family reunion; it represents the re-establishment of a broken Family Covenant. Lear's exile to the heath, with its psychological repercussions, has constituted a symbolic violation of both the Sacred Fire and the Physical Hearth, and the intensity of the suffering undergone there has made him obsessively aware of the "hard hearts" and "naked wretches" of the world, the two categories into which, for him, all mankind may be placed. At first, the patriarchal wisdom of suffering so controls his thought that he can only respond in terms of its retributive justice of punishment—awakening to find Cordelia, he can only say, "If you have poison for me, I will drink it" (IV.vii, 72). He has sinned and he must suffer. But when Cordelia, who has learned a much different wisdom from her suffering, responds with complete forgiveness, then Lear, too, learns of that higher spiritual truth which has received voicing in I John 4:7–12:

> Beloved, let us love one another; for love is of God, and he who loves is born of God and knows God. He who does not love does not know God; for God is love. In this the love of God was made manifest among us, that God sent his only son

into the world, so that we might live through him. . . . Beloved, if God so loved us, we also ought to love one another.

Thus, through contemplation of Cordelia's act of mercy, so characteristic of the matriarchal mode, Lear is finally redeemed from the restricting narcissism of his patriarchal kingship; disavowing the value of authority and status, he seeks to help her in turn:

> No, no, no, no! Come, let's away to prison,
> We two alone will sing like birds i' th' cage.
> When thou dost ask me blessing, I'll kneel down
> And ask of thee forgiveness. So we'll live,
> And pray, and sing, and tell old tales, and laugh
> At gilded butterflies, and hear poor rogues
> Talk of court news; and we'll talk with them too—
> Who loses and who wins; who's in, who's out—
> And take upon 's the mystery of things,
> As if we were God's spies; and we'll wear out,
> In a wall'd prison, packs and sects of great ones
> That ebb and flow by th' moon.
>   [V.iii, 8–19]

Such an attitude represents more than a symbolic reachievement of the womb of serenity; Lear has become transfigured himself through the grace of Cordelia, and, as a child, he is now able to perceive the essence of spiritual love—"Whosoever shall not receive the kingdom of God as a little child shall in no wise enter therein."

In this aspect of the play, we have suggested that part of the humanist tradition which emphasizes the Platonic concept of the child's superior innocence, the process whereby *eros* develops into *agape*, the Pauline implications of *caritas*, and, as in Spenser, the frequent identification of love with divine virtue. Thus, in her role of the Redeemer, Cordelia may be likened not only to such as Oedipus, but also to the Savior-

Heroes of the Judaeo-Christian tradition: she willingly accepts pain to accomplish her quest as does the Suffering Servant of Deutero-Isaiah; she displays mercy toward her enemies; she disregards her personal welfare, even the preservation of her own life, to ensure the welfare of another; and, above all, she displays a willingness to forgive those whose ignorance of the power of evil has led them to become its agents and its victims. Add to this that her redeeming function possesses validity as an expression of an archetypal role: in the image of the Good Mother, she gives birth to the holy child, for the "child-changed father," Lear, under her aegis has become much more of a "spiritual" figure by the end of the play.[8]

Still, as we have noted, Lear represents mankind, the recipient; thus he cannot himself be a Savior-Hero such as Mary's Jesus. With the single exception of his final slaying of the "slave that was a-hanging" Cordelia, once he has lost his patriarchal authority, Lear is *acted upon* and the shock of her death and his own quick demise prevent his exercise of even a Statesman-Hero's role (". . . these same crosses spoil me"— V.iii, 278). Unlike Oedipus, Lear can bring no boon to his community. Therefore, the saving attributes of spiritual matriarchy, love, tenderness, and *caritas*, must be demonstrated by some other source, Cordelia. The woman who supplies the resurrection of the missing Good Mother becomes not merely the fount from which the holy child arises, but, as occurs through an emotional mergence of identity in Hopkins' poem, she becomes an intercessory agent with spiritual essence, not only the Mother of Christ but, almost, Christ Himself.

Yet, we must ask as Kent asks soon in such a different context, "Is this the promis'd end?" (V.iii, 263) Tragically, the play does not conclude on the above note of reconciliation; Lear and Cordelia cannot live out their lives "like birds i' th' cage" exchanging mutual benedictions. They cannot so easily reject patriarchal concerns, for the worldly-oriented do not "wear out" so readily; vanity and evil must intrude upon any prison an individual seeks for shelter. At the very moment of Lear's speech, the "great one," Edmund is preparing their deaths, lighting the "brand from heaven" which shall "fire [them] hence like foxes" (22–23), part them perhaps forever. The dramatic device of the "false dawn" is employed with consummate skill by Shakespeare here at the beginning of the third scene, for with the momentary restoration of this version of the Family Covenant, we experience a deep sense of relief and a feeling that everything may yet conclude happily; we are tempted into believing that the Physical Hearth has been preserved.

Thus the appearance of Lear with the dead Cordelia in his arms fulfills the eschatological image of horror voiced by Kent and Edgar (263–64). With the shock of this reversal, what are we to think? The Captain has accomplished his "man's work," he has not been "tender-minded" (V.iii, 26–39), and now Lear's "poor fool" has been hanged. And when the missing mother is gone again, "dead as earth," and "gone for ever" (V.iii, 257–63), why should not "heaven's vault" completely crack, nature go mad as Lear on the heath, and the Last Judgment end in a final renewal of chaos? We are forced to ask whether the Dragon of Mystery has not triumphed once again. For with the death of the Good Mother, what hope can there be of love and redemption? Sorrow only must prevail. What can we know from this play but a world "cheerless, dark, and deadly" (290), a world in which all the good are "dead and rotten" (285)?

"Is this the promis'd end?" If it were, then we should derive from *King Lear* only the dark side of the coin that tells us to be wise is to suffer; in a sense, we should even be deprived of the virtuous endurance connoted by the Stoic "Ripeness is all." For Cordelia's death has not been that of Oedipus; her death has benefited no one; she has been killed offstage and we are not even shown the greatness of her heart demonstrated, as with Hamlet or Othello in their last moments. But all the loveliness associated with the Kore, the tenderness epitomized by the Good Mother, and the greatness of soul which made her capable of a redemption *do* receive ultimate manifestation in the final words of her grief-stricken father. The image patterning of the matriarchal symbolism of this play culminates in the memorable, "Pray you undo this button. Thank you, sir" (V.iii, 309).

This is the voice of the small child asking for assistance from the tender mother he knows will help him. In this quiet request, the subtle, reverberative power of an image of poetry to appeal to a universally human response is superbly realized. The voice of the archetypal Child embodies the emotional essence of the Family Covenant, and, as Lear speaks in this voice, we recall his earlier "Come, unbutton here" when he tore off his patriarchal identity to join Poor Tom as a common member of humanity. Though mad, this was the moment in which Lear first learned sympathy, a knowledge of compassion brought to its spiritual peak in his final communion with Cordelia. And now at the moment of this little gesture of kindness, Lear finds again the missing mother and her love— "Look on her! look! her lips! / Look there, look there!" Whether the feather stirs in a hand trembling with emotion, whether this be delusion or truth matters little—Lear dies, as Bradley asserts, from "unbearable joy."[9]

The greatness of the Savior-Hero, Cordelia, then, is manifest primarily in the "child-changed" person of her father, for she has taught him an ultimate wisdom. As has been often noted, that she and Lear, too, are dead when the play ends is, in one sense, also little more than "a trifle," for like Oedipus and Christ, the meaning of her existence is only to be found in her living. This imaged father and his daughter have demonstrated the gift of understanding which is to be received at the Physical Hearth—at its simplest: to have had the opportunity to live; to have known and understood love; that is enough. All else is superfluous. "This tough world" may be a "rack" upon which man must endure the agonizing "stretching" of his strength, but, with the gift of life, the Good Mother offers man an even greater gift, the opportunity to know of an all-enveloping tenderness, the sustaining "air" of love.

CHAPTER

VI

The Subjective Response

IN his essay, "On the Relation of Analytical Psychology to Poetic Art," Jung emphasizes that even psychology can only deal with "that aspect of art which consists in the process of artistic form . . . whereas that which constitutes the essential nature of art must always lie outside its province." If psychology is thus limited, direct sociological investigation must be regarded as even more peripheral to this "innermost nature"; all such approaches can only be considered "powerless . . . as is the capacity of the intellect to present or even apprehend the nature of feeling." Yet, despite such basic restrictions, Jung still feels justified in asserting that "the determinants of the artistic creation, the material and its individual treatment, . . . can be traced back to the personal relations of the poet with his parents." Despite variables, he believes that certain "psychic preconditions are universally present" which remain constant for all human beings due to "the relative similarity of the human conditions of life," and that these preconditions (whether "one poet is influenced more by the . . . father and another . . . by the mother") constitute formative influences in any aesthetic expression.[1]

As we have noted, for the poet it is the symbol which provides a means of exploring both the individual and collective unconscious so as to transcend what Jung terms "contemporary consciousness, . . . the symbol being the possibility and intimation of a meaning higher and wider than our present powers of comprehension can seize."[2] Yet, symbolic meaning must in no sense be equated with lack of clarity or the chaos of impulse. All art must be understood; it must be meaningful even though it does not possess a scientific precision of meaning. Perhaps, this is where the family as a source of those images affording poetry with dynamic emotional symbols proves most useful. The family, as we experience it, very definitely and concretely *is;* as a specific point of reference, as that part of our daily existence which embodies procreation, nutrition, affection, or the lack of these, it dominates our psychical energy, functioning like the earth under our feet as the very foundation of feeling. To ground the artwork in the basic images associated with the family gives it a transpersonal concreteness beyond the restricted consciousness of the individual artist and the personal aberrations which may arise from his unique impressions. Thus, we may use the term, *family*, here in two meaningful senses, that of the family of our immediate experience, and that of the family of mankind sharing a common heritage of similar emotional experience. The manifestation of either (or their combination) in mythological figures or primordial images is said to arouse in us awareness of an archetype.

With regard to such archetypes, Jung maintains:

If we subject these images to a closer investigation, we discover them to be the formulated resultants of countless typical experiences of our ancestors. They are, as it were, the psychic residua of numberless experiences of the same type. They depict millions of individual experiences in the average, presenting a kind of picture of the psychic life distributed and projected into the manifold shapes of the mythological pandemonium. These mythological forms, however, are in themselves themes of creative phantasy that still await their translation into conceptual language, of which there exist as yet only laborious beginnings. These concepts, for the most part still to be created, could provide us with an abstract scientific understanding of the unconscious processes that are the roots of the primordial images. Each of these images contains a piece of human psychology and human destiny, a relic of suffering or delight that has happened countless times in our ancestral story, and on the average follows ever the same course. It is like a deeply graven river-bed in the soul, in which the waters of life, that had spread hitherto with groping and uncertain course over wide but shallow surfaces, suddenly become a mighty river. This happens when that particular chain of circumstances is encountered which from immemorial time has contributed to the laying down of the primordial image. The moment when the mythological situation appears is always characterized by a peculiar emotional intensity; it is as though chords in us were touched that had never resounded before, or as though forces were unloosed of the existence of which we had never even dreamed. The struggle of adaptation is laborious, because we have constantly to be dealing with individual, i.e., atypical conditions. No wonder then, that at the moment when a typical situation occurs, we feel suddenly aware of an extraordinary release, as though transported, or caught up as by an overwhelming power. At such moments we are no longer individuals, but the race; the voice of all mankind resounds in us.[3]

Aristotle in the *Poetics* is much concerned with such "typical situations," with the nature of universals, and the role played by the mimetic function in their representation. To him, the very seriousness and magnitude of tragedy depend upon this breadth of perception, and yet, he, too, suggests that it is the successful evocation of personal pity, fear, and like emotions which truly implement the psychotherapeutic office of catharsis. Not until the poet has probed the innermost reaches of the psyche can the more or less extraneous problem of the moral order of the universe, the factor which transcends individual human destiny, be contemplated, revealed, and understood. Formulated *meaning* can only be built upon a pertinent emotional substructure.

To consider these aesthetic implications further: we see in Greek and Shakespearean tragedy that certain feelings (bred within the family) often manifest themselves spontaneously in a fashion quite similar to the intuitive seizing of the exact metaphor or symbol by the creative artist. Miraculously, both expressions spring from unconscious sources to which the participant was unaware that he had access. Hidden responses and associations, truly universal in nature, communicate themselves, in an almost automatic revelation, to both the persona and his maker, to both the trained and untrained reader. The experiential truth of the smallest human gesture is often as valid in ascertaining meaning as the greatest issue—"Pray you, undo this button."

In so far as such emotion produces a recognizably universal image, it may be termed an archetype, a force of energy capable of moving its perceiver and changing him. Poetry, for example, in using the archetype to make the perfected intensity of an experience available to the reason for analysis, has always been accepted as a sort of transformation mystery. Just as in early vegetation mysteries, raw food was roasted and transmuted to a higher edible state, so poetry transforms the *felt* significance of a human action into a source of higher understanding, a totality of wisdom beyond the exclusively rational. Thus, though formal discipline be mandatory for precise communication, the poet as seer, as the eminently keen instrument of human perception, would seem obligated also to achieve some form of emotional revelation, that knowledge which is vision, epiphany, and insight. Greek myth and legend *must* become *Oedipus Rex;* the chronicles of Holinshed *must* become *King Lear.* Only then do we obtain those inspired recreations of circumstance, those revelations of import, which enable us to understand the full complexity of such terms as authority and tenderness without sentimental distortion.

In one of Hardy's poems, an aged thrush carols forth such ecstatic sound in a world of "growing gloom" that the despairing poet thinks "there trembled through / His happy good-night air / Some blessed hope, whereof he knew / And I was unaware." Similarly, responses associated with the archetypal father and mother, however evoked aesthetically, can only be confronted as perceptions of the human psyche, felt, vaguely understood, and with a dismaying sense of inadequacy, consciously expressed. The darkling thrush sees but faintly, yet he sings. The conscious mind, voicing the feeling of the poet, sings also after the fashion of the thrush, but, in terms of Ernst Cassirer's essay on *Language and Myth,* it uses the song as a mode of "its own self-revelation":

. . . What poetry expresses is neither the mythic word-picture of gods and daemons, nor the logical truth of abstract determinations and relations. The world of poetry stands apart from both, as a world of illusion and fantasy—but it is just in this mode of illusion that the realm of pure feeling can find utterance, and can therewith attain its full and concrete actualization. Word and mythic image, which once confronted the human mind as hard realistic powers, have now cast off all reality and effectuality; they have become a light, bright ether in which the spirit can move without let or hindrance. This liberation is achieved not because the mind throws aside the sensuous forms of word and image, but in that it uses them both as *organs* of its own, and thereby recognizes them for what they really are: forms of its own self-revelation.[4]

In the simultaneity of such perception of disparate realities, we encounter the opposition and interplay of authority and tenderness once more as psychological orientations breeding the very modes of awareness whereby each may be seen and differentiated. As Hardy sees the objective reality of darkness *and* the subjective reality of hope, so we see demonstrated in the family both a mode of analytical logic and a form of understanding best described as intuitive (Father concludes this must be done: Mother feels it right to do so).

In speaking further of such modes of expression, Cassirer makes a most pertinent distinction between two powers of language, the power of logic in which "words are reduced more and more to the status of mere conceptual signs," and the power of the mythical (or archetypal) image deriving from an earlier stage of artistic representation where, "especially in the magical realm, word magic [was] everywhere accompanied by picture magic." According to such theory, the original unity of myth, language, and art "gradually resolved into a triad of independent modes of spiritual creativity," and though "the same mythic animation and hypostatization . . . originally accorded to images" was still bestowed on human speech, for "language . . . to grow into a vehicle of thought, an expression of concepts and judgments, . . . the wealth and fullness of immediate experience" had to be foregone. Once the magic circle of mythical consciousness was broken and the image became but a counter available for analysis, "in the end, what [was] left of the concrete sense and feeling content it once possessed [was] little more than a bare skeleton.[5]

To restore the possibility of "pure feeling," despite "the

emancipation of language and art . . . from their native soil
of mythical thinking," is the role of the poet. He must reassert
the "ideal spiritual unity" of the two powers of language on
"a higher level":

> . . . there is one intellectual realm in which the word not only
> preserves its original creative power, but is ever renewing it;
> in which it undergoes a sort of constant palingenesis, at once a
> sensuous and a spiritual reincarnation. This regeneration is
> achieved as language becomes an avenue of artistic expression.
> Here it recovers the fullness of life; but it is no longer a life
> mythically bound and fettered, but an aesthetically liberated
> life.[6]

Such aesthetic liberation is demonstrated most clearly in the
"mythic power of insight" which informs, with little argu-
ment, the texts of such as Aeschylus, Sophocles, and Shakespeare, an insight which, in Cassirer's terms, "discards all
material constraints to live as a spirit in the word of language
and in the mythical image without falling under the control
of either." The poet, in addition to such "spiritual life" and
flights of imagination, has an obligation to translate melody
into meaning, to invest the song of the thrush with Hardy's
response. To achieve that transcendent spirit in word and
image of which Cassirer speaks, he must verbalize his insight.

But this is difficult for many reasons. Song spawned by
emotion does not fall readily into the syntax of common
denotation; nor, unless the interplay of attitude which distinguishes the Hearth from the Sacred Fire be recognized, will
the perception of paradox in language suffice for much more
than a mere demonstration of wit[7] and an ironic comment on
irony itself, how we mean one thing and say another (even
when the semantic intention is purposeful).

To escape the logical inadequacies of speech and convey
profound, or "pure," feeling is quite another matter. Hardy's

thrush does not *know* what he voices in his song, nor does Hardy, yet we all know that the mere existence of song is itself evidence of natural vitality, of a desire to voice emotion. In this sense, the analogical platitude which associates bird and poet is true. Thus, in seeking escape from the restrictions of denotation and abstraction, the self-imposed deceptions of a Tyrtaean logic, or the confusion of paradox, the poet can only turn to certain subtleties of verbalization to achieve his insight.

In doing so, he must naturally be aware of Brooks's distinction between word as word and word as image so that, contextually, he may create the proper aesthetic arrangement of these tools. He must employ that "principle of rich indirection" of which Brooks speaks so that the individual image may become "a symbol heavily charged with meanings which no dictionary can be expected to give."[8] Applying such comment to the texts hitherto explored, we see in the ramified symbolisms of the Hearth and Sacred Fire suggested meanings which transcend by far the actual dramatic situations which compose the scenes themselves. Even in prose, unconscious voicings of these dominant psychological orientations may be said to affect our manner of expression: appositional inferences such as "it seems to me" or the patronizing "after all" would seem to indicate a position of adopted authority which could be termed, loosely, patriarchal. By contrast, certain adverbial usages such as "ineffably" or "unfathomably" suggest a limitation of finite comprehension, a groping for the *felt* as real, which can only be termed, though even more loosely, matriarchal.

This is, of course, even more true of poetry. It is the precisely evocative rather than the precisely denotative word which "works" during the processes of association. Without doubt, it is the motion and form of cradling we recall when we seek an image of the Physical Hearth, the arc of line in line which the painter's eye sees as beauty when the Madonna holds the Bambino, but, we must note, in addition, that such form possesses also a "thermodynamic" component associated with some early sense of warmth, with feelings of tenderness, love, and protection. As in Hopkins' "The Blessed Virgin Compared to the Air We Breathe," the connotations often associated with a daily physical life are used by poetry to extend meanings, in this case, the possibility of spiritual life. As with Hardy's thrush, the "blessed hope" is not seen, but revealed.

Frustrated, perhaps, by its attempt to define such subtle feelings categorically, the verbal mode of the Sacred Fire rejects their validity by insisting upon strict denotation. Embracing this hope of revelation, the verbal mode of the Physical Hearth accepts the reality of feelings, seeking to suggest them through the infinite varieties of meaning embodied in connotation. Each, to some extent, through its own particular language informs and illuminates the other.[9]

Examining, for example, Tyrtaeus' fragment #7 once more, we note little, if any, connotation except what was not intended, the duplicity of the Elders; the poem relies upon direct injunction and threat, rhetoric employed for the practical purpose of exhortation—"Young men, stand firm and fight." Not to do so is to risk exile. On the other hand, Hopkins, though lauding the virtues of the intercessory Mary, feels that the only way to depict her subtle *spiritual* essence is to use a connotative analogy with the "world-mothering air." He knows no measurable way of proving either her immortal existence or her divine capacities; "the logical truth of abstract determinations and relations" is an inadequate instrument for his creative purpose.

Is Hopkins presenting us, then, with a "mythic word-picture of [a] god," a fragment of rationalized desire based upon the doctrinal assumptions of his Sacred Fire? If one can appeal to the honest dubiety of the "Terrible Sonnets" as evidence of a willingness to explore the sincerity of his own feelings, one would have to say no. Although the world of "The Blessed Virgin . . ." may be designated as one of "illusion and fantasy," the poet substantiates the reality of this world by finding in it the images of a natural world of primordial experience, the "charged, steepèd sky," the cradling arms of the air, and the all-embracing sea of the womb. Through such images and their reverberative associations, Hopkins invokes what is for him, and for those who share his perception, a "pure feeling" of merciful love. Through the liberation of poetry, Mary ceases to be mere mythic word-picture to become herself a spirit of this ethereal world which, for the moment of insight, has its own reality. As Cassirer states, this "freeing of the spirit" from its material restrictions is achieved through the structural use of the sensuous forms of word and image employed as "*organs*" of the mind seeking its own liberation, its freedom from the inhibiting world of the word, the flesh, and the devil of analytical introspection.

The significance, the singularity, then, of the two image groups discussed under the headings of Physical Hearth ("If I have understood, / She holds high motherhood / Toward all our ghostly good . . .") and Sacred Fire ("Be high of heart, be strong in pride of combat") resides in their capacity to function within texts not only as controlling factors in the formal integrity of the work but also, because of their essential pertinence to any individual experience, as factors in what might be termed its "moral integrity," its attempt to answer the Jobean questions posed by the feelings when the mind fails its function. Greek and Shakespearean tragedy deal with, but are hardly subject to, relativistic determinism, skepticism about ethical standards, or a consuming critical demand for "wit." Beneath all seeming complexity, one usually finds, as a key to understanding, the archetype, demonstrating through such figures as the Good and Terrible Mothers, the Kore, King, and Tyrant Father, the archetypal patterns of "the way," the hero-quest, and the search for home. As Maud Bodkin puts it, such drama illustrates "the manner in which forces of emotion may, through shapes created by imagination, become palpable to sense."[10]

Consider, for instance, *Hamlet.* The ambivalent attitude of the child toward his parents in such a work receives its clarification in terms of our previous perception of a conflict of demand and attachment. Subjected to an injunction to revenge from the ancestral spirit of his Sacred Fire, frustrated by a need for love not forthcoming from the mother of his Physical Hearth, the Youthful Hero fails to find "the way," achieve his hero-quest in valid moral terms, fails also to find home, reachieve a lasting communion with Gertrude, or found a Family Covenant with Ophelia. Despite Bradley's attempt to reassure us of Hamlet's heroism and heavenly acceptance, we may doubt, at the end of the play, the accomplishment of a catharsis; atonement would seem to have been achieved in no terms other than that of a patriarchal *lex talionis,* the ultimate abrogation of the Physical Hearth for which Orestes was also culpable. If this is the only insight to be gained from such tragedy, what have we left but further shared despair?

But what of the drama's verbalization? Certainly, our insight into Hamlet's moral failure must be sought in more than his initial lack of adherence to the proscriptions of the Sacred Fire—or in more than his later resigned fulfillment of its demands. Perhaps, in so far as form impresses content, it is to be sought in the structure of the play itself. H. D. F. Kitto sees in Sophocles' introduction of a third actor to create intensely dramatic "cross-scenes," his subtle use of irony in language and plot, and his clever interweaving of choral odes to illuminate the plight of his tragic hero, the possibility of an informing order in all life. He believes that Sophocles, in demonstrating "the idea of a universal rhythm ruling in the physical world and in human affairs alike," has afforded us a conscious rational demonstration of some form of transcendent justice actually operative in our lives.[11] Similarly, Aristotle, in elucidating the marvelously coherent structure of *Oedipus Rex*, insists upon the imposition of patriarchal form upon matriarchal matter as a mimetic function before the magnitude of the archetypal experience can be successfully expressed. The primordial chaos of emotion and family crisis through which Oedipus wanders achieves import only when it is made clear that aesthetic order reflects moral order, and that the emotional dynamism of the drama is directed toward a solar understanding. We may ask whether Hamlet's wanderings are similarly directed?

At first, it would seem not. As a play, *Hamlet*, as we have noted, suffers from structural flaws; there is almost universal agreement that it is not "well-made." Does this, then, inhibit the communication of its emotional meaning? Can the psychotherapeutic and moral function of catharsis be still realized without a completely lucid structuring? In terms of our intuitive response to the experience portrayed, our very finding of ourselves (in Hazlitt's phrase) in the character of the protagonist, there is again almost universal agreement that the play succeeds. One way of explaining this would be to note how Shakespeare, in his genius, transcends the denotative limitations of language by using these very limitations as a means of portraying the tragic inadequacies of his chief characters. They seek to use words to explain their emotions, to provide for motivation, to excuse their behavior. But they fail. Their words, like the rich gifts given by Hamlet to Ophelia, "wax poor when [the] givers prove unkind." "Their perfume [sincerity] lost," they have no meaning.

It is this attempt to reconcile speech and behavior upon

which the tragedy dwells, almost to the exclusion of all else. Language is the instrument employed by both Claudius and Hamlet in their attempts to interpret their own and others' performance. Both are tremendously preoccupied with the efficacy of words: Claudius seeks help from heaven to alleviate his sense of guilt, but to no avail. His brother-slaughter, his lust-spawned marriage, and his Machiavellian pursuit of the maintenance of status cause his "words [to] fly up, [his] thoughts [to] remain below," damned to confinement in a lower patriarchal world where his actions possess their only authority. Feeling wills grace; words are conceived of as quite rational means of persuasion—the rhetoric of prayer will obtain for him his salvation—but Claudius cannot reason himself into a valid repentance, and thus, by recognizing within himself his material greeds, he renders the angels helpless: "words without [emotionally motivated] thoughts never to heaven go" (III.iii).

In quite similar fashion, Hamlet in his soliloquies has sought meaning in words, differentiating between what seems and what is, probing the motivation behind the speech of Rosencrantz and Guildenstern, seeking always a rational answer to the "sea of troubles" confronting him. But when recognition comes, not through logical analysis, but through Claudius' emotional outburst, "Give me some light," Hamlet himself turns from "thinking too precisely on th' event" to something else—in the troublesome fourth and fifth acts, to bloody action and despairing speculation, yes, but, more meaningfully, at the end of Act III, to what might be termed the emotional mode of communication characteristic of the Physical Hearth, to a complete venting of his feelings, both good and bad. In a scene reminiscent of Oedipus' discovery of Jocasta's earlier abandonment of his infant self, Hamlet, despite his self-administered warning, rushes into Gertrude's closet intent, perhaps, on outrage—she is, after all, in Ernest Jones' interpretation, the unfaithful beloved. But, as with Oedipus, his feelings find here a woman for whom he has a profound affection. Unlike Oedipus, he is granted the opportunity of saving her.

This entire scene revolves about reason's pandering to will (III.iv, 88), rationalization providing excuses for various forms of selfish action—the mind is a devil which "hath cozened [Gertrude] at hoodman-blind, / Eyes without feeling, feeling without sight. . . ." Because of this blindness to the proper guidance of her maternal feelings, Hamlet accuses her of acting in such a way as to "make of sweet religion . . . a rhapsody of words." There is no harmony to her morality. Yet, in seeking some explanation for this defection, Hamlet can but come to the conclusion that it cannot be love in such a "matron's bones," but warped judgment, which has so "apoplexed" her senses that she can choose a Claudius over Old Hamlet.

Hamlet can use such phrasing because he, too, knows of the capacity of words to deceive, to provide seeming answers. But he knows also the fallacy of "seems" which he had denied in Act I's pomp and circumstance; beneath all reality, beneath all show of words, there is "that within which passes show," the sincerity of emotion. Thus, to save her, in a strange reversal of the Madonna-Bambino relationship, he enjoins her not to deceive herself with false appearances: "Mother, for love of grace / Lay not that flattering unction to your soul, / That not your trespass but my madness speaks." Let the emotion of guilt be voiced, he urges her, let no rationalization inhibit that heartfelt confession of sins whereby purgation and forgiveness are to be achieved. For the moment of this interview, employing the same tradition to which Hopkins adhered, Hamlet ceases to use words to convince his mother of her moral guilt; in their stead, he seeks to re-establish a feeling between them, a bond of communion which will lead her to the virtues of prayer and penance voiced in "The Blessed Virgin. . . ."

That Hamlet does not follow his own advice, that he yields instead to the patriarchal frustration to which the failure of logic has led him, that he substitutes for prayer and benevolism the Tyrtaean patterns of honor, pride, and punishment, these are but the superficial motivations provided for the bloody denouement expected from an Elizabethan Revenge Play. That the Hamlet who truly loves Ophelia and who seeks to save Gertrude is a poor choice of hero for this type of play has been often pointed out in any exploration of Shakespeare's sources—thus the structural flawing of the drama. Moral inadequacy has produced dramatic inadequacy. Neither Horatio nor Shakespeare can save Hamlet, the master of words, from "silence."

As has been noted, *King Lear* too is sadly lacking in structure; it is, after all, but a series of episodes illuminating a growth of awareness *within* the protagonist rather than a careful construct demonstrating the sort of character development we might expect from a well-formed novel; it even lacks that inexorable patterning of situation which leads to an *anagnorisis* as in *Oedipus the King*. Yet, though such a statement may seem somewhat heretical in the light of the *Poetics*, even the *Oedipus* seemingly derives its primary impact from the insights we receive of a violation of the Physical Hearth rather than from its splendidly conceived structure. In both plays, it is the relationship of a king, burdened by the anxieties of authority, to his family which moves our feelings, which involves us in actions and the interpretation of action to the point of personal concern. It is in this sense that we may renew the validity of Dr. Johnson's comment that Shakespeare reflects nature itself, or, in more modern terminology, that he represents the spontaneous, intuitive voice of the unconscious, both in a simple statement such as Falstaff's "I would 'twere bed-time, Hal, and all well," or in an evocative image such as Ophelia's "and I . . . That sucked the honey of his music vows."

The moment we compare Shakespeare with his sources we are reminded once again that the prime function of literature is to recreate experience rather than merely comment upon it. In the older versions of this play, the restoration of Leir to his throne by Corde(i)lla and her husband Aganippus, is but a chronicle of sentiment, a tale of the fall and rise of a British monarch told only for the entertainment and edification of a youthful prince. Such versions are but a legendary formulation of doctrine; they possess no more pertinence for human experience than Lydgate's *Fall of Princes*. Certainly, the re-telling of such a narrative would not seem capable of evoking a eulogy such as that of Johnson's:

> *Shakespeare* is above all writers . . . the poet of nature; the poet that holds up to his readers a faithful mirrour of manners and of life. His characters are not modified by the customs of particular places, unpractised by the rest of the world; by the peculiarities of studies or professions, which can operate but upon small numbers; or by the accidents of transient fashions or temporary opinions: they are the genuine progeny of common humanity, such as the world will always supply, and observation will always find. His persons act and speak by the influence of those general passions and principles by which all minds are agitated, and the whole system of life is continued in motion. In the writings of other poets a character is too often an individual; in those of *Shakespeare* it is commonly a species.[12]

Why this universality? Johnson finds the answer in Shakespeare's recognition of the role of the "passions" in human life; not only the universal agency of love, but also "any other passion, [which] as it [is] regular or exorbitant, [constitutes] a cause of happiness or calamity." Since Shakespeare's drama is "the mirrour of life," he who wishes to know life may find here "human sentiments in human language" and "scenes from which a hermit may estimate the transactions of the world, and a confessor predict the progress of the passions." Appealing from criticism to nature, Johnson finds exhibited in these plays

> . . . the real state of sublunary nature, which partakes of good and evil, joy and sorrow, mingled with endless variety of proportion and innumerable modes of combination . . . expressing the course of the world, in which the loss of one is the gain of another; in which, at the same time, the reveller is hasting to his wine, and the mourner burying his friend; in which the malignity of one is sometimes defeated by the frolick of another; and many mischiefs and many benefits are done and hindered without design.[13]

It is this very lack of design which so differentiates the world of daily reality from the aesthetically conceived world of formal art; and, as we have noted, it is also this very lack of design which distinguishes the matriarchal mode of expression from the patriarchal. If we take *King Lear* as an example of the matriarchal mode and compare it, even briefly, with Sophocles' *Oedipus the King*, we readily perceive the distinctions. Patriarchal consciousness, in its aesthetic manifestations, formulates; it perceives structure; it tends to order and organize. Since it carefully distinguishes similarities and dissimilarities, it perceives paradox and is capable of irony. Thus, despite his sharing of that capacity for evoking emotion which makes Aeschylus so much a figure of the primordial unconsciousness of the Physical Hearth, Sophocles must be designated primarily as a proponent of the Sacred Fire. Plot, pattern, and clarity of presentation, as revealed in his tragedies, demonstrate for us that his primary search is for that solar ideal which grounds *arete* in rationalism. To Sophocles, the good man is he who thinks soundly and well, who meets the challenge echoing out of the Swamp of Mystery with a keen mind. Thus the actions and expectations of the characters of his plays are usually carefully manipulated, and their hopes and fears gain their success or frustration because what might have been, in reality, spontaneous human impulse is carefully controlled by the masterful fingers of the ultimately rational creator. Despite Fromm's notation of those matriarchal overtones which give Sophoclean drama its richness, the dominance of form in a work such as *Oedipus the King* makes it, to a great extent, a work of judgment, and in it Aristotle can find categories which obey certain laws and procedures.

Such is hardly the case with *King Lear*. As stated previously, the matriarchal mode is supposedly incapable of discrimination; it tends to picture human experience as a chaos. Is the problem of the play, then, one of aesthetic failure, or just a matter of a differing approach to the portrayal and interpretation of life? In his *Mimesis*, wherein he discusses "the literary representation of reality in European culture," Erich Auerbach makes a preliminary distinction between two kinds of style:

> The two styles, in their opposition, represent basic types: on the one hand fully externalized description, uniform illumination, uninterrupted connection, free expression, all events in the foreground, displaying unmistakable meanings, few elements of historical development and of psychological perspective; on the other hand, certain parts brought into high relief, others left obscure, abruptness, suggestive influence of the unexpressed, "background" quality, multiplicity of meanings and the need for interpretation, universal-historical claims, development of the concept of the historically becoming, and preoccupation with the problematic.[14]

That Auerbach chooses the *Odyssey* to depict the style of "uniform illumination" does not necessarily associate it immediately in spirit and tone with *Oedipus the King*. Despite similar backgrounds in Greek antiquity, *Oedipus the King* is far from being completely externalized; its "psychological perspective" matches that of *King Lear;* its ironic subtleties and philosophical import far transcend the limitations of perspective found in the epic's reflection of an Heroic Age. However, both texts, despite their differences in age and perspective, do mirror for us facets of a strongly patriarchal consciousness. If the *Odyssey* consciously depicts the father as Warrior-Hero, *Oedipus the King* similarly presents him as the Statesman–Hero. If the *Odyssey* insists upon "externalizing" its action with the utmost clarity of description and connection, the *Oedipus*, despite its matriarchal concerns and psychological penetration, insists just as fully upon a similar lucidity of presentation—its irony is perfectly clear to the discerning audience, its recognitions and reversals may be plotted on a graph, its mechanics are precisely designed.

On the other hand, despite some similarities in patriarchal orientation, the Old Testament narrative of the sacrifice of Isaac seems much closer stylistically to *King Lear* than it does to the *Odyssey* or *Oedipus the King*. The chiaroscuro effects noted by Bradley, the suggestive haziness of the "background quality," the necessity for interpretation, and the "universal-historical claims" (or archetypicality) attached to the Old Testament style by Auerbach, all these seem most pertinent to an analysis of *King Lear* as a "matriarchal" play whose coherence must be sought in its emotional reverberations rather than in its formulated structure. When Gloucester says to the mad Lear (IV.vi, 152), "I see it feelingly," we have a key to what may be termed the whole instinctual style of the play; perhaps, even an explanation of the dramatically difficult scene of Gloucester's earlier "fall" from the cliff at Dover (IV.vi, 11–24, 49–74). In the images of ascent and descent which Edgar in his double role describes for the blinded

Gloucester, we see how the human psyche responds emotionally to images which create their own reality. This reality, so similar to that experienced by Abraham but denied the unwitting Isaac, is a reality which springs only incidentally from the actual situation; its primary quality inheres in the response aroused, perhaps unconsciously, by the emotional reaction to the situation, an emotion which can be aroused by poetic images in a reader who is not even present at all.

Does this mean that literature which relies on stressing the emotional rather than the rational components in art is philosophically inadequate? Not really. The work in question may be antilogical, but it is not therefore anti-intellectual as long as it is concerned with the meaning of human experience and the acquisition of that understanding which can come from contemplating such meaning. At its best, such literature harmonizes (matriarchal) feeling and (patriarchal) thought. To quote T. S. Eliot:

> We say, in a vague way, that Shakespeare, or Dante, or Lucretius, is a poet who thinks, and that Swinburne is a poet who does not think, even that Tennyson is a poet who does not think. But what we really mean is not a difference in quality of thought, but a difference in quality of emotion. The poet who "thinks" is merely the poet who can express the emotional equivalent of thought. But he is not necessarily interested in the thought itself. We talk as if thought was precise and emotion was vague. In reality there is precise emotion and there is vague emotion. To express precise emotion requires as great intellectual power as to express precise thought. . . .
>
> I would suggest that none of the plays of Shakespeare has a "meaning," although it would be equally false to say that a play of Shakespeare is meaningless. All great poetry gives the illusion of a view of life. When we enter into the world of Homer, or Sophocles, or Virgil, or Dante, or Shakespeare, we incline to believe that we are apprehending something that can be

expressed intellectually; for every precise emotion tends towards intellectual formulation.[15]

Eliot further insists that Shakespeare is not to be "interpreted according to some dominant scheme derived by the individual critic's examination of chance references in the plays"; on the contrary, Eliot feels that it was Shakespeare's "business to express the greatest emotional intensity of his time, based on whatever his time happened to think."[16] It seems wise to emphasize the word, *happened*, for Eliot, in asserting that the poet makes poetry just as "the bee makes honey, the spider secretes a filament," is agreeing with Dr. Johnson that even while he may become its spokesman, the great poet transcends the cultural determinants of his age. Whereas Dante lived in a period when "one coherent system of thought" was dominant, Shakespeare, like the other English dramatists of the late sixteenth and early seventeenth centuries, lived in "an epoch when it [became] particularly difficult to associate poetry with systems of thought or reasoned views of life.[17] The loss of coherence mourned by Donne may in itself serve as a partial explanation for Shakespeare's, or Webster's, power to rise above particulars to universals, to arouse archetypal emotional responses in the reader as a human being whether he be acquainted with the many contemporary references or not.

Eliot's emphasis on "emotional intensity," the matriarchal mode of expression, is undoubtedly most subtly manifested in Shakespeare's portrayal of Cordelia. Noting that she appears in only four of the twenty-six scenes of the play, and that she speaks scarcely more than a hundred lines, Bradley seeks to explain why she has become one of the most beloved figures of Shakespeare's entire canon:

> There is a harmony, strange but perhaps the result of intention, between the character itself and this reserved or parsimonious method of depicting it. An expressiveness almost inex-

haustible gained through paucity of expression; the suggestion of infinite wealth and beauty conveyed by the very refusal to reveal this beauty in expansive speech—this is at once the nature of Cordelia herself and the chief characteristic of Shakespeare's art in representing it.[18]

The capacity to suggest "infinite wealth and beauty" without resorting to lengthy discourse is itself the very mode of the truly poetic image which evokes ever-widening reverberations from the unconsciousness. Bradley associates with Cordelia what he calls a "dumbness of love," an inability to voice so profound and tender an emotion ("What shall Cordelia speak? Love, and be silent"—I.i, 63); yet, in the speeches devoted to her, both her own and those descriptive of her, we find the means to an intuitive understanding of her role as the epitome of matriarchal benevolism. She, herself, breaks silence in her informing asides only to assure us that this silence is to be equated with love, that it is *because of* her love that she must be silent ("I am sure my love's / More richer than my tongue"—ll. 79–80).

Why, then, must such a voice be rendered eternally mute? Why must she die? To answer this demands more than an emotional apprehension of her character; it demands at least a modicum of rational analysis. Bradley responds with an application of his own familiar theory. According to this view, in Shakespearean tragedy the chief source of the convulsion which produces suffering and catastrophe is always moral evil. This evil, exhibited always as negative and a principle of death, "isolates, disunites, and in destroying others, destroys itself"; that is, it functions primarily (and loudly) as a force inhibiting human communication and communion. Thus, with the death of Cordelia, the tragedy of *Lear* ends, as it began, in silence. But the silence, itself, has a different quality, different echoes, almost different gestures. There are no words to express the intangibles of human feeling summoned up by the crucifixion of the redeemer, or the ironic momentary hope of her resurrection voiced by Lear. The speeches of Albany, Edgar, and Kent but renew a recognition of a material world of pain. Listening to them, we hear but the silence of frustration with which Hamlet is drummed from the stage at Fortinbras' command.

However, Bradley posits, by contrast, a corollary view, equally cogent: there seems to be implied in the resolutions of Shakespearean tragedy, as a counterbalance to this rampant force of evil, a basically *good* moral order, a demonstration of the possibility that the inner soul of the universe cannot abide brute viciousness or the distortion of reason, and thus acts, from the moral necessity of its own nature, to expel the poison of such evil. Unfortunately, since both elements constitute inextricable parts of a whole, such expulsion necessitates some *waste* of virtue; thus, the irreconcilable facts which leave man speechless before the archetypal Swamp, frustrated by the inevitable conflict of a good and evil which can only be overcome by self-torture and self-waste.[19]

In the light of such a tragic mode, Cordelia *must* be wasted for the purgation of evil, yet Bradley "feels" (his own usage) that the reader, caught up in Shakespeare's larger aesthetic (the moral implications of his artful recreation of life), may also come to recognize that ". . . the heroic being, though in one sense and outwardly [a failure], is yet in another sense superior to the world in which he (she) appears; is, in some way which we do not seek to define, untouched by the doom that overtakes him; and is rather set free from life than deprived of it."[20] Thus, in Lear's simple, "Pray you, undo this button," its echoing of Cordelia's compassion, we hear a renewal of the voice of tenderness, an awareness of the possibility of release and, then, spiritual communication. Just as when, at the conclusion of the *Oedipus at Colonus*, the messenger relates how "some attendant from the train of

Heaven" came to open "in love the unlit door of earth" (ll. 1655–1665) for one aged man, so we recognize, in the silence which follows Lear's passing cry of joy, more than despair, we perceive the possibility that he, too, has been accepted by heavenly forces, rescued from his blindness, because he has learned how to weigh and value his experience with some understanding—an understanding, perhaps inexpressible, but embodying a silence comprehensive enough to quell his own earlier pain, comprehensive enough to allay the weeping of even such as Antigone and Ismene. We recall the Chorus assuring these living (alive in their virtue as opposed to the *dead* Goneril and Regan) daughters that Oedipus' "last hour was free and blessed" (l. 1721), and that "these things are in the hands of God" (l. 1779).

This is not to imply that Sophocles does any more than anticipate the later connotations embodied in the term, *agape*, but this poet of great insight, in returning his hero to the sacred grove by the Hill of Demeter, is certainly affirming more than the just rewards of heroic endurance. That Oedipus suffers with a splendid dignity is of supreme importance to Sophocles, the solar intellect, but that the quality of his perception is such that he can learn matriarchal values from his suffering seems implicit in all the poignant family scenes which Sophocles does so well, implicit in the blessing which the Savior-Hero bequeaths to Theseus and the families of Athens.

Perhaps even the finest of intellects must turn at last from reason to take one step further, to find a suprarational truth which comes from a knowledge of tenderness and the meaning of *caritas*. Shakespeare has Lear, like Hardy's thrush, feel compelled to sing even though he knows he and Cordelia are caged by darkness, imprisoned by evil, shut off from the world—but not from each other. At Colonus, Sophocles portrays all of Oedipus' anguish as worthwhile in that he can give of himself one more time for the salvation of Athens, the "holy city." When Socrates, too, gives of his last hours for a similar purpose, spending his last minutes to reassure his friends of the immortality of the soul, he is giving of himself in death as he had given in life to assist those who needed him. His final hours make his entire dialectic and his stinging of his fellow citizens meaningful in an example which transcends his best logic. When he goes to his death, no reader of Plato doubts but that his is a better path than that of his accusers or his jury, not because he has proven for us that man is immutable, but because he has demonstrated that the examined life can lead a man to the knowledge of love.

He does not know whether he goes to the best night of sleep a man can ever have or to the realm where blessed spirits converse and communicate in perfect understanding with absolute Goodness, but Plato has convinced us that his life, unlike that of Agamemnon or Jason, has been significant.

All this has been but implied by these texts. The structuring of dramatic situation, even the images which have illumined the characters' inner selves, are but preparation for what has *not* been said, for what must be felt—that how and why one dies matters as a fulfillment of how and why one lived. As R. P. Blackmur put it in a wonderfully apt title, *Language as Gesture*, words but grope toward meaning, clumsily, hopefully, seeking a way through regions of confusion. An actor like John Gielgud can translate Shakespeare's poetry into pertinent gesture through facial expression, tone of voice, the movement of a hand, but, in doing so, he is but calling up associations, functioning within a life provided him by the dramatist's capacity to return us to personal experience.

In demonstrating how Shakespeare has transcended scene to create reverberative rhetoric and imagery, we have sought to follow the suppositions of analytical psychology which equate the masculine elements of the psyche with consciousness or logic, the feminine with unconsciousness or feeling;[21] in discussing the Hearth and Sacred Fire, we have sought to extend these equations, suggesting how the use of such archetypes may inform not only an author's mode of expression but the mode employed by him in differentiating his characters, their attitudes, their particular ideologies. Thus, any examination of texts in this light is meant to clarify the meaning of emotional response, and, if possible, evaluate *dramatis personae* in terms of their capacity to transform mere material circumstance into spiritual life. For example, the action of *King Lear,* as opposed to that of *Hamlet,* posits a differing aesthetic as a prelude to the elucidation of its moral meaning. In a sense, the very last words of Hamlet, the word-monger, reflect a form of logical positivism which itself suggests a vanity in the manipulation of verbal counters leading ultimately only to complete silence. Hamlet, like Hotspur, rejects the mode of poetry which makes him alive; he becomes an apostate from his creator, Shakespeare. He does not recognize, to use Richards' terms, that poetry (feeling rendered thought) has a creative, indigenous language of its own inaccessible to science; that there are words (and images) which *can* distinguish appearance from reality, ". . . the actions that a man might play, / [from] that within which passes show" (I.ii, 76–86). Paradoxically, just as Gertrude's credulity leads her to accept "the trappings and the suits of woe" for truth, so Hamlet's belief in the power of logic leads him to think that rational analysis will solve his dilemma. Overwrought by warring feelings, he wishes only to be *"denoted* truly" (italics mine).

The art of *King Lear,* on the other hand, as manifested in the portrayal of, and attitudes held by, Cordelia and Lear, admits the possible validity of the creative word after the fashion of the spiritual *Logos* of St. John. But it does not limit this word to the agency of a Sacred Fire; it adds to patriarchal logic, a note of matriarchal feeling with a strong emphasis on love (cf. John, 13:34). Instead of having the protagonist, as in *Hamlet,* take ultimate refuge in the inadequacies of reason, thought, and speech (and a fatalistic resignation to oblivion), Shakespeare portrays Lear as coming to song, gesture, and meaningful silence for purposes of ascertaining a transcendent truth through the exploration and discovery of primordial response. Here, Shakespeare uses his symbols as instruments of transformation, his archetypal images as catalytic agents whereby certain organic (objective) and spiritual (subjective) realities can be fused. Thus he correlates conscious and unconscious meaning in such a way that the resultant birth of understanding is freed not only from the limitations of its age, but from the frustration of mere denotation.

If one looks at Bradley's now-dated pages, one may lament the failure of a perspective which projects personal attitudes upon the figures of conventional Elizabethan drama, but one can still be impressed by his effort to find a moral meaning, a moral philosophy, in the world of Shakespeare, which, as Johnson assures us, is the world of man. This world is also the world of poetic insight without which we would have but measured mechanical response, and, eventually, only silence in the realm of human understanding, man rendered beast (though more subtly) as on the commonly accepted Elizabethan Chain of Being.

Such a "Fall," Bradley, as humanist, would reject. Human communication cannot be thus measured; the "scientific" study of vocal reflexes and language will not resurrect the abandoned *logos* of Eliot's *Ash Wednesday:*

> If the lost word is lost, if the spent word is spent
> If the unheard, unspoken
> Word is unspoken, unheard;
> Still is the unspoken word, the Word unheard,

The Word without a word, the Word within
The world and for the world. . . .

Bradley's discussion of Cordelia's "dumbness of love" as revealing a capacity for tenderness suggests, as in Eliot, the still
valid existence of a spiritual "Word" echoing Jung's assertion
that "the capacity of the intellect [is powerless] to present or
even apprehend the nature of feeling." Only Poetry will
suffice to evoke from silence, the barrier, the silence of understood communion.

Extending this notion of connotative speech one step further, Bradley states that the implied themes of sacrifice and
salvation embraced by Cordelia's actions lead to a quite different conception of tragedy (from that of the Greeks):

> It implies that the tragic world, if taken as it is presented, with
> all its error, guilt, failure, woe and waste, is no final reality, but
> only a part of reality taken for the whole, and when so taken,
> illusive; and that if we could see the whole, and the tragic
> facts in their true place in it, we should find them, not
> abolished, of course, but so transmuted that they had ceased to
> be strictly tragic,—find, perhaps, the suffering and death count-
> ing for little or nothing, the greatness of the soul for much or
> all, and the heroic spirit, in spite of failure, nearer to the heart
> of things than the smaller, more circumspect, and perhaps even
> "better" beings who survived the catastrophe.[22]

Such an interpretation of tragedy, though it embodies the
necessity of the tragic hero being "great of soul" like Oedipus, emphasizes even more fully the beneficial effects of
emotion on the life of man. When patriarchal intellect reaches
its dead end of frustration, then, within the human psyche,
there may be found resources which give not only strength
but pertinence to life. It is a strange paradox of existence that
the emotions, which give rise to undisciplined hatred and

chaos, can also give rise to nobility and hope for a transcendent spiritual order. From the perspective of "the whole" which is the perspective of unity, Cordelia's giving of love, intangible a factor as it may be, negates the seeming triumph of the patriarchal mode—"Whosoever shall seek to save his life [in Hamlet's terms] shall lose it; and whosoever shall lose his life [in the manner of Cordelia] shall preserve it."

Hamlet has obeyed the Elder's injunction to take physical revenge. Acting, eventually, as a "young man . . . strong in pride of combat," he "stands firm and fights," gaining the abstract reward of honor, fulfilling himself in terms of the questionable logic of Tyrtaeus—only to find himself deceived and damned (the angels may be but in Horatio's wish). Cordelia, on the other hand, has fulfilled herself in the image of Hopkins' Blessed Virgin. In exercising matriarchal compassion, she enables her father to grow beyond his role of Elder, feel for the "loop'd and window'd raggedness" of mankind in such a way that he obtains maturity and spiritual fulfillment through loving—thus, despite all tragic circumstance, he is saved—and so is she.

If the theme of sacrifice, then, is an essential aspect of tragedy, it must often exist, as many critics have pointed out, as that moral element in the action which prevents tragedy from becoming ultimately tragic. In *Oedipus the King*, social and religious justice are achieved through the sacrifice of the individual, and a vague sense of triumph modifies our pity at the hero's destruction—our fear is partially allayed. But only partially, for this is action in the secular world, and our identification with the sufferer may lead us to the verge of a personal despair. However, in the *Oedipus at Colonus*, or the Gospel stories of the Crucifixion, the extended mercy of a figure of redemption leads us to a sense of exaltation. We are led to an insight, a revelation of the glory of exercised human potential for good. We perceive the function of the Jungian idea of transformation, the possibility of spiritual transcendence achieved through mastery and subjugation of the ego on behalf of the Self.[23]

So with the main plot of *King Lear*: in one sense, the violation of justice and the reality of death portrayed are brutally tragic, forestalling any sense of fulfillment; yet, in another, the formal narration of such events results in a revelation similar to that manifest in St. John, a knowledge of moral virtue surpassing even that to be gleaned from Shakespeare's more precise voicing of concern for the preservation of the moral order of the State. Undoubtedly, the ending of this play, like that of *Oedipus the King*, leaves no one very content—the possibility that all may yet be only vanity clouds the perspective of the remaining living characters ("Our present business / Is general woe"—*Albany*. V.iii, 318–19). We have been confronted with the death of the rightful King; we have seen the unjust hanging of the Kore who rose to fulfill the matriarchal role of the missing Good Mother. How much comfort can be derived from the purging of the evil characters who have met their just ends? Can any comfort be derived from considering the possibility that the second loss of Cordelia by Lear is, after all, only his just punishment for an initial violation of both the Physical Hearth and Sacred Fire? Is this not the ultimate destiny of all those who, like Clytemnestra, Agamemnon, Jason, and Creon, disfigure love?

The answer, as we have seen, is negative, but in a very strange way, for in those tenuous terms which admit the possibility of "soul," or even in terms which exalt the fulfillment of the finest capacities of the human psyche, *King Lear* is no tragedy at all. Cordelia (through Shakespeare) has revealed to Lear (and to us) that love and mercy transcend all; she has demonstrated how to give and forgive. The cathartic experience of this play inheres not in its conclusion but in those poignant scenes of reconciliation which manifest the possibility of harmony. Reconciliation and reacceptance after strife and suffering, serenity and peace after storm, this is the harmony which blends in unity the matriarchal and patriarchal modes. *King Lear* achieves this sense of harmony, aesthetically as well as experientially, not because of its precise, intellectual ordering—we have noted that the play is deficient in dramatic structure—but because it speaks "what we feel, not what we ought to say" (V.iii, 326).

A study of this nature need come to no conclusion, for the issues posed by Tyrtaeus, Hopkins, the Greek tragic dramatists, and Shakespeare are the issues of life—and life persists.

Explication de texte, as is obvious, involves two fundamental concerns: the perception of structure and the perception of insight. In this study, the aim has been to explore the achievements of a few arbitrarily selected dramatists who have found in the poetic utterance of "concrete truths" Cassirer's "realm of pure feeling"; to find, in addition, a continuing humanistic concern for essential meaning.

In doing so, it has been assumed that the family, as a source of emotion, often provides the mind with those "sensuous forms of word and image" which are most characteristic of poetry, that the analogies spawned by the modes of authority and tenderness can be expressed in language through the polarities of logic and intuition and the polar tones of fact and fantasy. Through such means, through the capacity of familial response to transform sensual response into emotional response, we have sought to demonstrate how two dominant psychological orientations may inform certain texts; how, through the agency of connotative language, the silent words voiced by gesture in drama, and the subliminal meanings, voiced, but not spoken, by poetry, suggest certain pertinent symbolisms, or even the possibility that poetic imagination can transform such response into a means of revelation evocative of communion with a world of spirit.

Admittedly, this could not be done without the formal ordering of emotion in its proper context. And though the insight rather than its infinitely varied verbalization would appear to be of prime importance, without the latter, the former could not exist; without the discipline of art, we might have only the grunt of pain, the vague crooning of the nursing mother, forced as air through the larynx, rather than the tuneful insight of song.

Much more might be said; we have probably said enough. That the analytical psychology of Jung and Neumann can only be considered a valuable tool in the elucidation of insights based on emotional response, that "archetypal criticism" has limitations leading to the possibility of false interpretation, that the texts must speak for themselves, all this is obvious. Literary criticism of this sort cannot be confined by the more rigorous approaches apposite to the consideration of more precisely defined scholarly topics. Thus, to summarize: out of biological urgency life appears to be nourished and protected at a Physical Hearth which to some extent regards the Hunting Father as an alien. In a later counterdenial of natural affection as a cohesive force, patriarchy usurps matriarchal dominance to construct the Sacred Fire. Because of the biological evidence of his inferiority as creator, man advances the proposition that only through the accomplishments of masculine strength, reason, and consciousness can social progress occur. Further, intellectual procreation is advanced as the original creative force of the universe; the divine Word of Command is asserted as precedent to the genetic principle which constitutes the basic power of matriarchy. Thus the rites of the Sacred Fire gain added validity because its flame supposedly partakes of the spiritual while the flame of the Physical Hearth is merely corporeal. The Priest who lights its eternal coals represents not only the force of discipline and intellect, that which evaluates rationally the experiential situations of the group, but he becomes also the boon-giver of immortality to those whom he considers worthy. The elaborate codes of this new creation assume the role of shaping the emotions and needs of men as the children of society, thus making the State a culminating, conditioning agency of infinite power.

However, though the Sacred Fire is meant to serve as a symbol of all patriarchal striving for the ideal, its pragmatic uses, especially with regard to the State, all too often come to demonstrate the mere imposition of authority. In rejecting the Physical Hearth (with its conception of spirituality as compassion) as an embodiment of chaos and a source of undiscriminating acceptance, patriarchy denies the real warmth of natural affection in favor of an attempt to attain similar security within its own masculine world. And this, as Ecclesiastes asserts, is one of the ultimate roots of tragedy, for the world of perfection is not intended to be part of human destiny—"Then I looked on all the works that my hands had wrought, and on the labour that I had laboured to do: and behold, all was vanity and vexation of spirit, and there was no profit under the sun."

As an extension of the Sacred Fire, the State as fatherland seems often incapable of becoming a true home. The emotional bond is weak, and the tension between "natural feelings" and indoctrinated duties becomes a source of conflict. To deny the State in behalf of the family is a crime against the patriarchal gods and their social and moral codes; to deny the family is to accomplish the almost impossible task of suppressing those emotions which lend human existence a significance beyond vanity. Thus, by extension, the incompleteness of works which seek to present rationally the theoretical values of the Sacred Fire, the State, and patriarchal authority without embodying and accounting for the tender emotional intimacies of family life. In such works, the depictions of human experience constitute social, or even political, representation rather than emotionally evocative realities. Without including the matriarchal component, they remain ideational rather than fully experiential—perhaps, sterile.

Notes

Chapter I. Two Poems, Two Flames

1. Sir Baldwin Spencer and F. J. Gillen, *The Arunta* (London: Macmillan & Co., 1927), I, 201–03, cited by Joseph Campbell, *The Hero with a Thousand Faces* (New York: Meridian Books, 1956), pp. 138–39.

2. Erich Neumann, *The Origins and History of Consciousness*, trans. R. F. C. Hull ("Bollingen Series XLII" [New York, 1954]), pp. 143–44 (to be referred to hereafter as Neumann, *Origins*).

3. E. Diehl, ed., *Anthologia Lyrica Graeca* (Greek edition), Nos. 6–7. T. F. Higham and C. M. Bowra edit the English version in *The Oxford Book of Greek Verse in Translation* (Oxford, 1938), No. 97, pp. 181–82.

4. Carleton Brown, ed., *Religious Lyrics of the Fifteenth Century* (Oxford, 1939), p. 119.

5. Erich Neumann, *The Great Mother*, trans. Ralph Manheim; see chap. vii, "The Phenomenon of Reversal and the Dynamic of the Archetype" ("Bollingen Series XLVII" [New York, 1955]), pp. 75–83.

6. Gerard Manley Hopkins, "The Blessed Virgin Compared to the Air We Breathe," in *Poems of Gerard Manley Hopkins*, ed. W. H. Gardner (New York: Oxford University Press, 1948), pp. 99–103.

7. See Johan Huizinga, "Religious Sensibility and Religious Imagination," in *The Waning of the Middle Ages*, trans. F. Hopman (New York: Doubleday Anchor, 1954), pp. 190–200.

8. Cf. Margaret Mead, *Male and Female* (New York: Mentor Books, 1955), pp. 56–66.

9. Cf. Hopkins' poem, "That Nature Is a Heraclitaean Fire and of the Comfort of the Resurrection," *Poems*, pp. 111–12.

10. W. H. Gardner, *Gerard Manley Hopkins, a Study of Poetic Idiosyncrasy in Relation to Poetic Tradition* (New Haven: Yale University Press, 1948), I, 188.

11. See pp. 320–21 and 324–35. See also Neumann, *The Great Mother*, pp. 3–17, where, in describing this tool, Neumann distinguishes four aspects of the archetype: its emotional-dynamic component which is the effect it has in producing both positive and negative emotions on the personality; its symbolic component which is its aforementioned capacity to manifest itself in specific psychic images; its material component which is its sense content as apprehended by consciousness; and its structure which includes the other three components in a "complex network of psychic organization." Perhaps the most significant distinction drawn is that between the elementary and transformative characters of such key archetypes. See pp. 24–38.

12. The term *archetype* is employed in this study as used by Drs. Jung and Neumann according to the discipline of analytical psychology. I have not cited Jung expressly except in a few pertinent instances; reference should be made to the completed volumes of the Bollingen Foundation Series (XX), *The Collected Works of C. G. Jung*, and to earlier editions of pertinent texts as cited in my Selected Bibliography.

Jung himself carefully distinguishes four basic psychological functions: thinking, feeling, sensing, and intuiting. To Jung, thinking is the intellectual process whereby man seeks to discover the "logic" of things; feeling is the function which ascribes value to the thing in terms of our subjective experience of it (whether it gives us pleasure or pain, whether we love it or hate it, embrace it or fear it, and so forth); sensing is the means whereby we derive knowledge of the "objects" we encounter; and intuiting is the function which enables us to go beyond all the others in achieving an understanding of the essences of experience. See C. G. Jung, *Psychological Types*, trans. H. G. Baynes (New York, London, 1953), pp. 9–14, a text which offers succinct explanations of many of the terms employed here (chap. xi, "Definitions," pp. 518–617).

We need not be concerned at any length with the validity of Jung's theory of the collective unconscious except to note that the human mind seems to function not only as a personal force but also at the behest of forces external to itself. Despite the variety of individual cerebrospinal systems, mythological and other analogues reveal a common ground of response and creative expression signifying some sort of constantly recurring perception which itself hints at least of a common membership in the human family. Whether these be actually structured in the brain or not is beyond the scope of this study. Nor is it significant whether a phylogenetic or an ontogenetic approach be taken. Phylogenetic explanations, it is true, are not susceptible to proof or disproof, because any notion of origins, whether cultural or individual, cannot be put to an adequate test. Ontogenetic explanations, however, are probably somewhat more susceptible to such investigation. Explaining recurrent patterns in human behavior through certain characteristics of the organism, they presuppose a universal unconscious fashioned by common psychophysiological conditions which can be put to a test. For our purposes, it is sufficient to note that imagery in literature persists in demonstrating certain recurrent prototypes of attitudes towards the family.

13. Neumann offers a pertinent word of caution:

. . . When we say masculine or feminine dominants obtrude themselves at certain stages, or in certain cultures or types of person,
this is a psychological statement which must not be reduced to
biological or sociological terms. The symbolism of "masculine" and
"feminine" is archetypal and therefore transpersonal; in the various
cultures concerned, it is erroneously projected upon persons as
though they carried its qualities. In reality every individual is a
psychological hybrid. Even sexual symbolism cannot be derived
from the person, because it is prior to the person. Conversely, it is
one of the complications of individual psychology that in all cultures the integrity of the personality is violated when it is identified
with either the masculine or the feminine side of the symbolic
principle of opposites [*Origins*, fn. 7, p. xxii].

See also pp. 104–08, 125, and fn. 15, p. 340; and Jung, *Two Essays
on Analytical Psychology*, Vol. VII, *Collected Works* ("Bollingen Series XX" [New York, London, 1953]), pp. 186–88.

To avoid confusion, one should be aware that the terms
"masculine" and "feminine" and their derivatives, "matriarchy"
and "patriarchy," are used throughout this study, as in Neumann's work, not to indicate "personal sex-linked characteristics,
but as symbolic expressions" (*The Great Mother*, pp. 320–21 and
325 ff.). "Matriarchy" and "patriarchy," then, are not meant to
designate, as in common anthropological and sociological usage,
social structures, but, as in depth psychology, those opposing
forces which conflict or unite within the psyche as the basic
sources of dramatic (literary) action.

One special usage must be emphasized: that elaborated upon by
Neumann in his *Origins* that "matriarchy and its symbol canons
must be equated with the unconscious, patriarchy with relatively
full consciousness," the former mirroring an extension of a
prenatal embryonic state of instinct, the latter concerned with
the progress from our first infantile ego-consciousness to the
relatively mature freedom of adult mastery of the world (p.
xxii). Thus, risking oversimplification, we may equate the patriarchal mode of knowledge with the supposedly more "masculine" processes of logical analysis and rational formulation, the
matriarchal with the supposedly more "feminine" functions of

feeling and intuition. However, there is no doubt that the Archetypal Masculine and Feminine share in both.

14. Neumann, *The Great Mother*, p. 16. See also C. G. Jung and C. Kerenyi, *Essays on a Science of Mythology*, trans. R. F. C. Hull ("Bollingen Series XXII" [New York, 1949]), pp. 101–03.

That the idea of archetypes is to be established by an appeal to a notion of origins is now considered of doubtful value. However, it is for anthropologists to ascertain the differences between the most advanced primates and the lowest forms of *homo sapiens*, to determine how varying brain size contributes to the increasing complexity of tool-making and tool-saving methods, to tell us how early stone weapons turned into intercontinental missiles. Cf. Ruth Benedict, *Patterns of Culture* (New York: Mentor Books, 1948), pp. 17–18.

15. *Das Mutterrecht: Eine Untersuchung über die Gynaikokratie der alten Welt nach ihrer religiösen und rechtlichen Natur* (Basel, 1948). (*"Das Mutterrecht ist das Recht des stofflichen Lebens, das Recht der Erde, aus welcher jenes seinen Ursprung herleitet. Im Gegensatz dazu ist das Vaterrecht das Recht unserer unstofflichen, unkörperlichen Natur"*—II, 199.)

See Neumann, *The Great Mother*, pp. 90–92 and 94–119, where he adapts Briffault's thesis that the forms of the social instincts which govern society are "related to the functions of the female" (Preface to Vol. I of *The Mothers*, pp. v–vi, and I, 447–90). See also Fromm's discussion of the rejection of such theories, "The Oedipus Complex and the Oedipus Myth," in Ruth Nanda Anshen, ed., *The Family: Its Function and Destiny* (New York, 1949), pp. 342–43. Bachofen and Briffault are seldom if ever cited in the behavioral sciences these days because of their excessive concern for origins and their tendency to "discover" them by speculation, but, in interpreting mythology and ancient custom, their work remains pertinent to the literary investigation of certain dramatic conflicts and poetic symbolisms.

The behavioral sciences from the early thirties to the present have looked upon such matters (sexual role differences) as cultural and therefore relative, differing from society to society about as much as logical possibilities would indicate. However, more recently a possible beginning of a reversal in this attitude has been detected. This new note suggests substantiation for this study in the possibility that there may well be physiologically engendered differences in the two sexes as indicated by Talcott Parsons' view that in almost all societies the male is directive leader while the female is the expressive leader of the family (see Talcott Parsons and Robert Bales, *Family: Socialization and Interaction Process* [Glencoe, Ill.: The Free Press, 1955]). Robert Winch takes the view that successful marriage is one involving a complementary relationship of mates rather than an identity of personality characteristics in the two (see *Mate-Selection* [New York: Harper, 1958]). The difficulties of precise demonstration, however, are vast.

For the above note, as well as for his kindness in pointing out to me certain differences in approach employed by social psychologists and other behavioral scientists, I am indebted to the late Professor Manford Kuhn of the Department of Sociology and Anthropology at the University of Iowa.

16. Neumann, *The Great Mother*, p. 91. For a discussion of the myth of the Dragon Fight and its meaning, see his *Origins*, pp. 154–55.

17. *The Great Mother*, pp. 269–70. Reference may be made to all of Part II, section B, "The Transformative Character," especially pp. 211–305. See also Neumann's summary of the mythic priority of the "Feminine Life Force" as presented by J. J. Bachofen, *Urreligion und Antike Symbole*, II, 356–59, in *Origins*, pp. 47–48.

18. *The Great Mother*, pp. 279–80 and 281 ff.

19. In *Der Mythus von Orient und Okzident* (München: Beck, 1926) Bachofen elaborates with some hint of idealization:

> The motherly love is not only more tender but also more general and universal. . . . Its principle is that of universality, whereas the patriarchal principle is that of restrictions. . . . The idea of the universal brotherhood of man is rooted in the principle of motherhood, and this very idea vanishes with the development of patri-

archal society. The patriarchal family is a closed and restricted organism. The matriarchal family, on the other hand, has that universal character with which all evolution begins and which is characteristic of maternal life in contrast to the spiritual, the image of Mother Earth, Demeter. Each woman's womb will give brothers and sisters to every human being until, with the development of the patriarchal principle, this unity is dissolved and superseded by the principle of hierarchy. In matriarchal societies, this principle has found frequent and even legally formulated expressions. It is the basis of the principle of universal freedom and equality which we find as one of the basic traits in matriarchal cultures. . . . Absence of inner disharmony, a longing for peace . . . a tender humaneness which one can still see in the facial expression of Egyptian statues penetrates the matriarchal world.

Pages 214 ff. as cited by Fromm, "The Oedipus Complex and the Oedipus Myth," in Anshen, *The Family*, pp. 341–42.

20. Pages 293–94. See also his Schema III following p. 82 and his discussion on pp. 24–39, 46, and 47–48. Neumann distinguishes between the elementary and the transformative characters of this archetype demonstrating how each possesses both a positive and negative pole. In his discussion of the symbology inhering in each aspect, he presents us with a variety of archetypal feminine figures ranging from primordial fertility goddesses of the earliest paleolithic periods, goddesses with accentuated bulbous breasts, large buttocks, and sensuously tight-skinned bellies reminiscent of all seed-filled melon fruits, to the transformed goddesses of the spiritual axis, the Sophia of transcendent wisdom and the Virgin Mary of divine intercession. Reference to the whole series of plates (1–185) at the conclusion of this text is particularly useful in visually illuminating the matriarchal principle.

21. Cf. C. S. Lewis, *The Allegory of Love* (London: Oxford University Press, 1938), pp. 297–360. In line with tradition, Spenser suggests other negative roles than that of the Archetypal Temptress who uses her natural beauty and sexual power for self-aggrandizing purposes.

It would seem that Western woman's subjection as private property has led to her being cast in a variety of images emphasizing her subjection to the gratification of masculine desire. One would note in addition to the possible debasement of woman as the household servant of the Sacred Fire, her preliminary submission in the role of erotic slave. The debasing of the maiden, the defiling of innocence with no thought of a permanent relationship or permanent responsibility, prostitutes the Kore. In a significant reversal of roles, the male becomes the archetypal tempter and it is the Kore who fails to realize her identity as creative woman (witness the defiling of Gretchen by Faust). Elaine and Guinevere, Malbecco's mistress, Dame Hellenore (*The Faerie Queene*, Book III, cantos ix–x), Pope's Belinda, and the neurotic "fine lady" of Eliot's *The Waste Land* would seemingly reflect this subtle patriarchal usurpation of a woman's right to achieve valid communion.

22. C. G. Jung, *Two Essays on Analytical Psychology* (Vol. VII, *Collected Works*), pp. 186–209. See also Neumann, *The Great Mother*, pp. 70 and 281–336.

23. Neumann offers the following summary:

> The male collective is the source of all the taboos, laws, and institutions that are destined to break the dominance of the . . . Great Mother. Heaven, the father, and the spirit go hand in hand with masculinity and represent the victory of the patriarchate over the matriarchate. This is not to say that the matriarchate knows no law; but the law by which it is informed is the law of instinct, of unconscious, natural functioning, and this law subserves the propagation, preservation, and evolution of the species rather than the development of the single individual. . . . The situation of the males fortifies the ego and consciousness, just as that of the females fortifies the instinct and the group. Hunting and war are conducive to the development of an individual ego capable of acting responsibly in a dangerous situation, and equally conducive to the development of the leader principle.

Neumann, *Origins*, p. 147; see also pp. 104–05, 158–59, 220, 293–94, 310–11.

24. Mead, *Male and Female*, p. 190.

25. Fustel de Coulanges, *The Ancient City*, trans. Willard Small (New York: Doubleday Anchor Books, 1956), p. 36.

26. *Ibid.*, p. 27. To comprehend fully the symbol of the Sacred

Fire and its capacity to bring man into such communion with the animating god who animates it, see Book I, chap. iii.

27. *Ibid.*, pp. 34–39 and 90–93. In exalting the father and elder son, the code of the Sacred Fire insists on a complete denial of feminine rights; the maiden become wife must undergo a prescribed ritual which divorces her from the Sacred Fire and ancestral worship of her father so that she may be properly assimilated into the ancestral family of her husband and his father's gods. This denial of matriarchy even takes a legal form. Agnation is recognized as the only legal form of kinship; all property rights belong eventually to the god of the Sacred Fire, and thus the "alien" woman in early Greece and Rome is completely dispossessed. Even her younger sons have no rights, because as the fruits of natural affection, they are somehow tainted. Thus, primogeniture, a concept entirely foreign to the all-embracing matriarchal Physical Hearth, becomes basic to the hierarchical ordering of the Sacred Fire and the Ancestral House. Once the male attains authority as Father, Elder, and property owner, he becomes not only priest but judge; and as he himself is judged before the tribunal of the city for any crimes committed by his family, so he administers justice to his wife, sons, and daughters in matters of recognizing or rejecting a child at its birth, keeping or repudiating a wife, emancipating or adopting children, appointing guardians, and apportioning property.

28. *Ibid.*, pp. 101 ff. See also pp. 107, 112–15, 128–29 (applied to Athens), and 132.

29. *Ibid.*, p. 185. By contrast, the phenomena of nature which appear to man as the baffling actions of the Dragon of Mystery are correlated with the Physical Hearth and its threat of chaos, or explained by the capricious figures of the Olympians, gods and goddesses of physical nature, venerated for their obvious power, but absorbed into the patriarchal canon by enduing them with a volition similar to one's own. The distinction between the patriarchal worship of the gods of Olympus and that of heroes and *manes* is summarized by De Coulanges (pp. 121–22).

30. *Ibid.*, p. 191. See also pp. 167 and 211–12.

31. C. M. Bowra, *Early Greek Elegists* (Cambridge, Mass., 1938), pp. 59–70.

32. Fragment 9, lines 10–20, 27–32, E. Diehl, ed., *Anthologia Lyrica Graeca* (Greek edition); translated by C. M. Bowra, *Early Greek Elegists*, pp. 63–64 and p. 67.

33. *Early Greek Elegists*, pp. 69–70.

34. See C. G. Jung, *Two Essays On Analytical Psychology*, pp. 186–87 (for the negative aspects of this relationship, see pp. 196–201); and Neumann, *Origins*, pp. 200–13, especially pp. 203–04 where he comments:

> The rite of marriage derives from the part played by the king in the old fertility ritual. The union of the Earth Goddess with the god-king becomes the prototype of marriage, and only with the institution of this symbolic ritual did the act of sexual union, endlessly repeated for millions of years, begin to be understood consciously. It now became evident, as an ideal and in actual fact, that the hitherto unconscious union, previously regulated only by instinct, has a meaning. Its link with the transpersonal invests a mindless natural occurrence with the solemn significance of a ritual act.

35. See Therese Benedek, "The Emotional Structure of the Family," in Anshen, *The Family*, pp. 204, 206–09, 223.

36. Joseph Campbell summarizes:

> . . . When the child outgrows the popular idyl of the mother breast and turns to face the world of specialized adult action, it passes, spiritually, into the sphere of the father—who becomes, for his son, the sign of the future task, and for his daughter, of the future husband. Whether he knows it or not, and no matter what his position in society, the father is the initiating priest through whom the young being passes on into the larger world. And just as, formerly, the mother represented the "good" and "evil," so now does he. . . .
>
> The traditional idea of initiation combines an introduction of the candidate into the techniques, duties, and prerogatives of his vocation with a radical readjustment of his emotional relationship to the parental images [*The Hero with a Thousand Faces*, p. 136].

37. Neumann, *The Great Mother*, p. 16.

Chapter II. *Inceptions in Greek Tragedy I:* Oresteia

1. C. M. Bowra, *The Greek Experience* (London, 1958), p. 28.

2. Neumann, *The Great Mother*, pp. 268–69, 306–07. See also De Coulanges, *The Ancient City*, pp. 132–33.

3. In this chapter, all line references are based upon the standard Oxford Greek texts of the work cited. The translation employed will be cited at first usage as here: E. V. Rieu, *The Odyssey* (Baltimore: Penguin Books, 1946).

4. George Thomson, *Aeschylus and Athens* (London, 1941), p. 245.

5. *Ibid.*, p. 276.

6. M. P. Nilsson in his *Minoan and Mycenaean Religion* (Lund, 1950) has demonstrated that the Mycenaean (Athenian in Athens) Athene, and her divine counterparts in other Mycenaean sites, were patronesses of the local kings. Cf. W. K. C. Guthrie, chap. ii, "The Divine Family," in *The Greeks and Their Gods* (Boston, 1950).

7. Gilbert Murray, *Five Stages of Greek Religion* (London: The Thinker's Library, 1935), p. 58. See also pp. 29–30, 39–78; and Erich Auerbach, *Mimesis*, trans. Willard Trask (New York: Doubleday Anchor Books, 1957), p. 18.

8. See Jane Harrison, *Prolegomena to the Study of Greek Religion* (New York: Meridian Books, 1955), pp. 283–85. See also pp. 279 and 302. Despite new trends in anthropological research, this volume affords many valuable insights to the literary critic studying myth and symbol.

Comparable to the figures cited are the Agave of Euripides' *Bacchae* (a Terrible Mother), and mythic figures from other cultures used to explain the origin of evil—Eve, Lilith, or the fearsome figure of the Indian Kali. In Greece, the Gorgons, the Erinyes, and the very creation of Olympus itself attest to a probable usurpation of actual matriarchal cults by a variety of masculine cultures.

9. As summarized, "The Oedipus Complex and the Oedipus

Myth," in Anshen, *The Family*, pp. 340–41. See also Bachofen, *Das Mutterrecht*, II, 171–263, especially pp. 178–99.

10. Richmond Lattimore, trans., *The Oresteia* (Chicago: University of Chicago Press, 1953, 1956).

11. Thomson, *Aeschylus and Athens*, p. 35; see chap. ii, "Exogamy," pp. 23–36.

12. Ego-narcissism, then, may be considered as leading to the acquisition of status, authority, and wealth; ego-benevolism, to the possibility of realizing the potentialities of the spirit. Ego-narcissism is, symbolically, the unfruitful seed which seeks to absorb all nourishment within its narrow cellular structure and which yet refuses to bloom itself or give birth to any further life; ego-benevolism, the fruitful seed that takes life to give life, growing into maturity, blossoming, and bequeathing new seed. Supposedly, the motivations of higher patriarchy result from ego-benevolism in its urge to sustain and order life for the continued welfare of both individual and society; the motivations of lower patriarchy spring from ego-narcissism in its urge to gratify the personal ego at all costs. The positive Father seeks maturity and power over his ego so that he may give of himself to others; the negative Father seeks power over others so that they will afford him self-gratification. Cf. Patrick Mullahy, *Oedipus: Myth and Complex* (New York, 1948), p. 151.

13. Rex Warner, trans., *Medea* (Chicago: University of Chicago Press, 1955).

14. Richmond Lattimore, trans., *The Trojan Women* (Chicago: University of Chicago Press, 1955).

15. Thomson, *Aeschylus and Athens*, p. 279. See also pp. 35–36, and Harrison, *Prolegomena*, pp. 213–36.

16. *Aeschylus and Athens*, pp. 279–80; see also Neumann, *The Great Mother*, pp. 147–50.

17. *Aeschylus and Athens*, p. 278; see also pp. 282–83.

18. *Ibid.*, p. 284. According to Thomson, citing *law* as a solar ideal,

> The Athenians claimed that their city was the first to establish laws; that of their laws those relating to homicide were the oldest and best; and that of all their legal institutions the Court of the Areopagus was the most venerable, distinctive and august. It was the

"overseer of all things" and "guardian of the laws"; it had in its keeping "the secret depositions wherein lay the salvation of the city"; it was charged to uphold sobriety and good conduct, on the principle that good government depends, not on a multiplicity of legal enactments, but on the maintenance of justice within the hearts of men. . . .

19. *Ibid.*, pp. 43 and 288–89.

20. Dionysos, the god, is mythically considered the son of Semele, a Great Mother figure, from whom he learns the fundamentals of manticism, prophecy, and spiritual communion. Despite the barbarities earlier associated with his worship, the later basis for participation in his mysteries (as seen in his Eleusinian adaptation) involved the eating and drinking of cereal and wine intoxicants, sacred rites originally employed to gain fertility but now used to achieve a heightened state of spiritual perception. Jane Harrison bears witness to these rituals as foreshadowings not only of Christian Mysteries but also as reflections of the emotional communion to be found in a Family Covenant:

> There are some to whom by natural temperament the religion of Bromios [Dionysos], son of Semele, is and must always be a dead letter, if not a stumbling-block. Food is to such a troublesome necessity, wine a danger or a disgust. They dread all stimulus that comes from without, they would fain break the ties that link them with animals and plants. They do not feel in themselves and are at a loss to imagine for others the sacramental mystery of life and nutrition that is accomplished in us day by day, how in the faintness of fasting the whole nature of man, spirit as well as body, dies down, he cannot think, he cannot work, he cannot love; how in the breaking of bread, and still more in the drinking of wine, life spiritual as well as physical is renewed, thought is reborn, his equanimity, his magnanimity are restored, reason and morality rule again. But to this sacramentalism of life most of us bear constant, if partly unconscious, witness. We will not eat with the man we hate, it is felt a sacrilege leaving a sickness in body and soul. The first breaking of bread and drinking of wine together is the seal of a new friendship; the last eaten in silence at parting is more than many words. The sacramental feast of bread and wine is spread for the newly married, for the newly dead.
>
> Those to whom wine brings no inspiration, no moments of

sudden illumination, of wider and deeper insight, of larger human charity and understanding, find it hard to realize what to others of other temperament is so natural, so elemental, so beautiful—the constant shift from physical to spiritual that is of the essence of the religion of Dionysos [*Prolegomena*, pp. 452–53].

On the other hand, the more tenuous topic of Orphism is regarded by Harrison as a form of worship emphasizing those ascetic attributes which divorce the worship of mystery gods from the irrationality of the Feminine (*ibid.*, pp. 454–77; see also pp. 572–623 and 624–58). Orphism reflects that struggle of patriarchy to find communion in areas divorced from the physical intimacy of flesh with flesh and its emotional-spiritual ramifications. Thus all "solar spirituality" manifests a striving for "heaven" in some transcendent or "ideal" form, even under "inspiration." Cassirer summarizes:

> . . . In Orphic theology the ecstasis was no longer understood as mere madness; it became a "hieromania," a sacred madness in which the soul, leaving the body, winged its way to union with the god. The One divine being has been dispersed by the powers of evil, by the rebellion of the Titans against Zeus, into the multiplicity of men. But it is not lost; it may be restored to its original state. This is only possible if man sacrifices his individuality; if he breaks down every barrier that lies between himself and the eternal unity of life [Ernst Cassirer, *The Myth of the State*, trans. Susanne K. Langer (New York: Dover Publications, n.d.), p. 51].

But the "sacrifice of individuality," as we have noted, constitutes one of the chief injunctions of the Tyrtaean mode of patriarchy; and thus we meet in Orphism, as in medieval Christianity, a heightening of hierarchical status and a concomitant demand for conformity from those who are to be subordinates. The logic employed in this behalf becomes illogical; those who preach self-subjection become, perhaps unwittingly, the victims of pride and self-aggrandizement (*Prolegomena*, p. 658).

See also E. R. Dodds, *The Greeks and the Irrational* (Berkeley, 1951); G. R. Levy, *The Gate of Horn* (London, 1948); and Neumann, *The Great Mother*, pp. 234 and 281 ff.

Chapter III.
Inceptions in Greek Tragedy II: Oedipus and Creon

1. Bachofen early recognized a disparity in patriarchal pursuits and distinguished solar masculinity from what he termed "chthonic" (phallic or worldly) masculinity, a distinction amplified by later analytical psychology to separate the symbolism associated with the head and a concern for mankind's higher aspirations from symbols associated with the phallus and man's preoccupation with the physical and the material (cited in Neumann, *Origins*, pp. 158–59). The term *chthonic* embraces both the satisfactions of appetite and that materialism which logically extends to a desire for wealth, status, and secular achievement. See also Neumann, *Origins*, pp. 104–05, 220, 293–94.

Neumann traces ego development from an unconscious stage through a narcissistic stage of self-gratification to a phallic stage of aroused masculinity which finally culminates in a stage of higher "ego consciousness" wherein the head or the rational-spiritual components predominate:

> The development of ego consciousness is paralleled by a tendency to make itself independent of the body. This tendency finds its most obvious expression in masculine asceticism, world negation, mortification of the body, and hatred of women, and is ritually practiced in the initiation ceremonies of adolescents. The point of all such endurance tests is to strengthen the ego's stability, the will, and the higher masculinity, and to establish a conscious sense of superiority over the body. In rising above it and triumphing over its pains, fears, and lusts, the ego gains an elementary experience of its own manly spirituality. To these tribulations is added an illumination by the higher spiritual principle, whether this be vouchsafed by spiritual beings in individual or collective visions, or by the communication of secret doctrines.
>
> The goal of all initiation, however, from the rites of puberty to the religious mysteries, is transformation. In all of them the higher spiritual man is begotten. But this higher man is the man possessed of consciousness or, as liturgical language expresses it, of the higher consciousness. In him, man experiences his fellowship with a

spiritual and heavenly world. Whether this fellowship takes the form of an apotheosis, or the initiate becomes one of God's children, or a *sol invictus*, or the hero becomes a star or an angel among the heavenly host, or whether he identifies himself with the totem ancestors, is all one. Always he enters into an alliance with heaven, with light and wind, cosmic symbols of the spirit that is not of this earth, bodiless and the enemy of the body.

Heaven is the dwelling place of gods and genii, symbolizing the world of light and consciousness as contrasted with the earthy, body-bound world of the unconscious. Seeing and knowing are the distinctive functions of consciousness, light and sun the transpersonal heavenly factors that are its higher condition, and eye and head the physical organs that are correlated with conscious discrimination. Hence in the psychology of symbols the spiritual soul descends from heaven and in the psychic body scheme is apportioned to the head, just as the loss of this soul is mythologically represented as a blinding, as the death of the sun-horse, or as a plunge into the sea—in other words, the overthrow of masculinity always follows the path of regression. It entails dissolution of the higher masculinity in its lower phallic form and therefore loss of consciousness, of the light of knowledge, of the eye, and a relapse into the body-bound chthonic world of animality [*Origins*, pp. 310–11].

Speaking more generally, the Savior-Hero is a man who has overcome both the debilitating containment of his consciousness in the infantile womb of impulse *and* the inhibiting forces of lower patriarchy which would seek to imprison him within his own ego. He is one who has progressed to that higher level of ego-benevolism which synthesizes rational order and the *caritas* of the Physical Hearth. His orientation to life expresses a strong ethical component as differentiated from an obedient conformity to particularized cultural dicta. From the positive Father, he has learned that justice and the other cardinal virtues are to be the true end of his quest; from the Good Mother, he has learned that the quest cannot be accomplished without the demonstration of selfless giving. Such love, though it originates in the love of specific individuals, the Kore or the Hero, or the members of one's family, when properly extended leads to the love of mankind. Participation in emotional intimacy enables a man to utilize his powers productively as a social being for all men are members of his family. This is a productive orientation not readily achieved, but if the Hero in an *Imitatio Christi* labors for beneficences external to himself, if he seeks to grow and assist growth in others, then he may be said to have achieved some semblance of the Jungian "True Self" in the role of Savior-Hero. See Jung, *Psychology of the Unconscious (Collected Works)*, p. xviii; *Two Essays on Analytical Psychology*, pp. 186–209; Neumann, *Origins*, pp. 50 ff., 141–49, 154–55, 158 ff., 174–78, 196, 202–03, 231, 249–50; *The Great Mother*, p. 294; and Patrick Mullahy, *Oedipus: Myth and Complex* (New York, 1948), pp. 25–29, 107, 128, 136–37, 149–53, 168–72, 225–27.

2. Lord Raglan, *The Hero* (New York: Vintage Books, 1956), p. 203; see also pp. 173–217. Cf. Murray, *Five Stages of Greek Religion*, pp. 23–26; Campbell, *The Hero with a Thousand Faces*, p. 174; and Jung, "The Mana-Personality," in *Two Essays on Analytical Psychology*, pp. 231 ff.

However, once the Hero achieves the status of Ruler, his actual authority is limited to the perpetuation of old tribal laws and customs of which he is only the incarnate embodiment. The egocentricity of such a role betrays its spiritual circumscriptions and hints at the roots of the debilitations manifested by the later organized forms and doctrines of an authoritarian lower patriarchy.

3. Pages 245–46; see also pp. 193–243.

4. *The Faerie Queene*, "Cantos of Mutabilitie," VI, 1–6. Spenser's allegorizing of MUTABILITIE echoes the doom of a damning Original Sin which may be looked upon in other terms as man's penchant to commit evil through ego-narcissism, inadequate understanding, or human frailty. Whatever leads to a living death as an unintegrated personality is as much a manifestation of man's subjection to MUTABILITIE as is the tendency of his body to decay.

5. One might cite in witness the all-embracing idealism of the American Constitution or the idealism which conceives of the United Nations as "a family of nations." Thus, to be a truly

productive personality, the Hero must employ his own transfiguration to illuminate the darknesses of lower patriarchy. To
avoid the pitfalls of tyranny, excessive regard for his own status
as Elder, or the illusion that the status quo already embodies
perfection, the Statesman as Savior-Hero must modify his authority with the tenderness of the Physical Hearth to establish the
just society which embraces all and yet maintains the order
necessary for growth. Within the fertile seedbed of such a
properly nurturing State, the new Youthful-Hero may blossom
as a productive, fully integrated personality himself, repeating
the process whereby the Father as Statesman-Hero became capable of ego-benevolism on a social and political level. The State
can function well only when it is constituted of mature individuals, each possessing personal wisdom and integrity. See Neumann, *Origins*, p. 418 and Appendix I, pp. 421–35.

6. H. D. F. Kitto, *Greek Tragedy* (New York: Doubleday
Anchor Books, 1954), p. 148.

7. The Oedipus complex is conceived of by Adler as resulting
from the suffocating possessiveness of the Terrible Mother. Rank
sees it in terms of a mythical situation providing analogies to his
theories of primal anxiety. Karen Horney, in minimizing the
sexual aspects of Freud's classic description, points out that
certain describable conditions in the family relationship provide
the real causes for a favorable or unfavorable development of
personality. The theories of Jung, Neumann, and Fromm are
dealt with in this chapter; for the work of Harry Stack Sullivan
and others, see Mullahy, *Oedipus: Myth and Complex*.

8. The editor (Pearson) of the Oxford text brackets this
passage and notes that there is some ambiguity as to who utters
this speech. *Oedipus the King*, trans. David Grene (Chicago:
University of Chicago Press, 1954, 1957).

9. "The Oedipus Complex and the Oedipus Myth," pp. 334–49.
Because of Oedipus' ignorance of his true parentage, there is
naturally only the briefest mention of matters pertaining to the
code of the Sacred Fire and the Ancestral House.

10. "The Oedipus Complex and the Oedipus Myth," pp. 355–
58.

11. *Ibid.*, pp. 349–53. Translation of *Antigone* by Elizabeth Wyckoff (Chicago: University of Chicago Press, 1954).

12. For an excellent analysis of the authoritarian personality, see Max Horkheimer, "Authoritarianism and the Family Today," in Anshen, *The Family*, pp. 371–72. Horkheimer points out certain dominant characteristics: adherence to conventional values; disregard of personality through categorizing people in terms of obvious hierarchies; the measuring of human values by success, popularity, and similar criteria; the rejection of any form of self-examination or the possible worth of any type of subjectivity; and a continuing concern with the manipulation of others to enhance one's own status.

13. "The Oedipus Complex and the Oedipus Myth," p. 350.

14. See Mead, *Male and Female*, pp. 145–50; and Neumann, *Origins*, pp. 198–99.

15. Harrison, *Prolegomena*, p. 319.

16. Though sharing with other primates many common instincts, we, as humans, possess one significant trait: "The nurturing behavior of the male, who, among human beings everywhere, helps provide food for women and children" (Mead, *Male and Female*, p. 145). A small distinction, perhaps, yet because in every known human society the young male must come to recognize this demand, we have the inception of the human family, the adoption of a lengthy responsibility on the part of one whose fulfillment is often felt to lie elsewhere.

Thus, in the family there seems to be no absolute separation of the symbolic complexes of the Physical Hearth and the Sacred Fire; in reality, there is an unending interaction between these basic modes and the images and symbol groups which represent them. When the patriarch of the Sacred Fire acts as Nurturing Father, he adopts matriarchal emotional responses and attributes; when the woman as maiden or mother becomes completely subordinated to a particular code of the Sacred Fire, as has been the usual case in Western culture, she accepts the social customs of her patriarchal society as her own just as in ancient times she left her father's Sacred Fire for her husband's.

17. See Jung, *Psychology and Religion* (XI) and *Psychology*

and Alchemy (XII) of the *Collected Works*. See also Neumann, *Origins*, pp. 209–11; and in their entirety, Section B, "The Hero Myth," pp. 131–91, and Section C, "The Transformation Myth," pp. 195–256; and *The Great Mother*, pp. 55–63, 221–22, 286, 325–36.

18. *Oedipus at Colonus*, trans. Robert Fitzgerald (Chicago: University of Chicago Press, 1954, 1957).

19. Kitto finds this mentorship exemplified primarily in the Theatre of Dionysus:

> . . . Athens and the Theatre of Dionysus are, in a very real sense, its Unity of Place. Not only were the plays performed in this theatre, not only was nearly every dramatic poet of eminence an Athenian, not only does the art as a whole bear indelibly the mark of Athenian intelligence and plastic imagination; beyond all this Greek Drama is in a special degree the work of the Athenian people. . . . To the dramatist the significance of the Festival was that it gave him as his audience nothing less than the Athenian people. That same people which, in a practical and political mood, met a few hundred yards away to discuss and determine high matters of state, met in the Theatre, in a more exalted mood, to watch plays; and the dramatists themselves appeared almost as their chosen laureates. Thus the dramatist, tragic or comic, was always writing for a big occasion, one which demanded and made natural big ideas and serious utterance, one which made impossible in comedy as in tragedy, private themes and clever coterie-literature. . . . But Attic tragedy was not restricted by creed or convention (the dramatist could take a political and contemporary subject if he chose), nor was it in any way an official art, an adjunct to politics. It was necessarily in close touch with its audience, as any living art must be, and its audience had come not as individuals looking for entertainment but as the City; an audience accustomed to handle the biggest issues in another place, not afraid of them therefore in the theatre [*Greek Tragedy*, pp. 421–22].

See also De Coulanges, *The Ancient City*, p. 149; Cassirer, *The Myth of the State*, p. 66; and Thomson, *Aeschylus and Athens*, p. 283.

20. Fromm, "The Oedipus Complex and the Oedipus Myth," pp. 354–55.

21. *Anatomy of Criticism*, pp. 220–21; see also pp. 111–12, 209, 214, and 218–22.

Although Sophoclean irony indicates that Oedipus' obsessive desire to purify Thebes from the plague leads him relentlessly to his doom, we are still caught in admiration at his display of integrity, his good intentions, and his perseverance. We are convinced that though these very virtues may destroy the hero, still they are of value, and more often constructive than destructive. Because Oedipus plays his human role well, the dignity of mankind is reaffirmed. In possessing the capacity both to think and to feel, and to unify both modes in a greater understanding, Oedipus becomes both matriarchal and patriarchal hero. To Kitto, Oedipus is great because he surmounts his fate and his agonies to impose himself on the gods by his very "stature as a man" (*Greek Tragedy*, p. 420). To Fromm, Oedipus is great because, as the hero of the older matriarchal cults posited by Bachofen, he demonstrates the capacity to love in his concern for his own and the family of mankind ("The Oedipus Complex and the Oedipus Myth," pp. 344–45). Oedipus, then, as a model of mature, integrated personality, represents the most laudable aspects of both the Sacred Fire and the Physical Hearth.

Chapter IV.
A Shakespearean Corroboration I: Hamlet

1. A. C. Bradley, *Shakespearean Tragedy* (London, 1949), pp. 244–47. Citations of Shakespeare are from *The Complete Works*, ed. George Lyman Kittredge (Boston, 1936).

2. *Shakespearean Tragedy*, pp. 261–69.

3. *Ibid.*, p. 326.

4. In addition to Bradley's discussion of the tension-producing imagery based on comparing man to the lower animals (*ibid.*, pp. 266–68), we may also note Caroline Spurgeon's perception of "an atmosphere of buffeting, strain and strife" (*Shakespeare's Imagery* [New York, 1935], pp. 338–43) which heightens the

emotional effects of the play through the use of a "general 'floating image'" of a human body in anguish. Cf. also W. H. Clemen, *The Development of Shakespeare's Imagery* (Cambridge, Mass., 1951), pp. 133–53.

5. See Neumann, *Origins,* pp. 412–15, and Jung, *Psychological Types,* def. 51.

6. The assumption that revenge is justifiable, deriving from Saxo Grammaticus and Renaissance adherence to Old Testament attitudes, would certainly have been accepted by an Elizabethan audience. Ironically, however, it is just before Hamlet's interview with the Ghost in the fifth scene that he speaks at length concerning that "vicious mole of nature," that congenital flaw, unbalanced humor, or socially determined "habit" which makes an otherwise good man fall victim to the "dram of e'il" which destroys his "noble substance . . . to his own scandal" (I. iv, 23–38). May this be interpreted as a prelude to Hamlet's own fall as a result of the "vicious mole of nature" within him? One must ask whether Hamlet's tragic flaw inheres in his indecision and three acts of reluctance, or in his fifth-act renunciation of all Christian precept for the patriarchal purposes of vengeance? Cf. Harry Levin, *The Question of Hamlet* (New York: Oxford University Press, 1959).

7. Bradley, *Shakespearean Tragedy,* pp. 23, 37–39, 110–13.

8. See above (in this text), pp. 32 and 44. See also Jung, *Two Essays on Analytical Psychology,* pp. 186–209; and Neumann, *Origins,* pp. 195–213.

9. See *Hamlet and Oedipus* (New York: Doubleday Anchor Books, 1954), pp. 51–79, wherein Hamlet's incestuous attachment for Gertrude is interpreted as causing an identification in guilt with Claudius which inhibits his murder of the usurping rival.

10. See Jung, "The Psychology of the Unconscious," in *Two Essays on Analytical Psychology,* pp. 24–28, 29–36, 64–65, 94–95.

11. See Jung, "The Relations Between the Ego and the Unconscious," *ibid.,* pp. 155–56.

12. See Bradley, *Shakespearean Tragedy,* pp. 147–48.

13. Cf. Jung, *Two Essays on Analytical Psychology,* pp. 108–

11, 236–38; and Neumann's discussion (amplified from Jung) of the Hero's path of individuation (*Origins*, pp. 412–15), as a basis for viewing Hamlet's failure to accomplish the act of self-generation.

Chapter V.
A Shakespearean Corroboration II: King Lear

1. Cf. II. iv, 56 and the use of the term, *mother*, to indicate chaos of the emotions or hysteria; cf. Kittredge's note on this passage.

2. Bradley, *Shakespearean Tragedy*, p. 301. See also p. 304.

3. *The Great Mother*, p. 78.

4. Cf. Edgar's speech (III. iv, 86–104) as he adopts the disguise of a "serving-man" fallen through lust and treachery to the state of Poor Tom.

5. Maud Bodkin, *Archetypal Patterns in Poetry* (Oxford, 1934), pp. 15–16.

6. Bradley asks, "Should we not be at least as near the truth if we called this poem *The Redemption of King Lear*, and declared that the business of 'the gods' with him was neither to torment him, nor to teach him a 'noble anger,' but to lead him to attain through apparently hopeless failure the very end and aim of life?" (*Shakespearean Tragedy*, p. 285).

7. To assume that mankind is inherently depraved, compelled as a biological organism to inevitable self-seeking, would be to deny the nobility manifested by such figures as Cordelia, Lear, and Oedipus. It would seem that, like these, men may be blind, weak, or unfortunate; even warped, crippled, and crushed by social circumstance and the pressures of their egoism, but they are not thereby doomed to the designation "evil." Even Goneril and Regan, not to mention Edmund, are not fully "motiveless in their malignity;" their ego-narcissism is motivated by a need for recognition.

8. For additional Jungian conceptions which would allow us to portray Cordelia in the symbolic role of a Redeemer, exercising

"the transformative powers of love" and providing the means of a "uniting symbol" for herself and her father, see Jung, *The Development of Personality*, (XVII, *Collected Works*), pp. 180–86; *Psychological Types*, pp. 601–10; Neumann, *Origins*, pp. 413–14; and *The Great Mother*, pp. 325–36.

Through the transformative power of human love, functioning as a dynamic spiritual force, man is rendered capable of realizing his potential and finding the self latent within him. Failure to love separates man from all that is necessary for growth and communion with his God-Source, the anima of his Kore, the Good Mother and Nurturing Father of his Family Covenant, and all those other beings with whom he must communicate for the integration of his personality.

Failure to love, it has been acknowledged, leads man to Blake's "separation," Tillich's "estrangement," and a divorce from all moral contemplation; it tends to destroy man's vitality and to make of him a "thing" instead of an individual, a victim of the "group" rather than a creative personality, a man whose actions no longer share in what the Renaissance would term the angelic or holy.

9. *Shakespearean Tragedy*, p. 291.

Chapter VI. The Subjective Response

1. C. G. Jung, *Contributions to Analytical Psychology*, pp. 225–28. For Jung's definition of feeling, see *Psychological Types*, def. 20.

2. *Contributions to Analytical Psychology*, p. 240. Cf. Wayne Shumaker, *Literature and the Irrational: A Study in Anthropological Backgrounds* (Englewood Cliffs, N.J.: Prentice-Hall, 1960).

3. *Contributions to Analytical Psychology*, pp. 246–47.

4. Trans. Susanne K. Langer, p. 97. Reference should also be made to Cassirer's great work *Die Philosophie der symbolischen Formen* (3 vols.; Berlin, 1923–31).

Such a notion necessarily involves a recognition of the Jungian principle that libidinal energy can be transformed into art (i.e., a productive source for the understanding of experience) rather than remaining a mere instrument of sexual expression or repression. Cf. Jung, "On Psychical Energy," *Contributions to Analytical Psychology*, pp. 45–50, 51–70, and 248; and *Two Essays on Analytical Psychology*, pp. 46–47, 86, 88, 114, 142, 211, and 219 ff.

5. *Language and Myth*, p. 98. Cf. Neumann, *Origins*, pp. 294–95.

6. *Language and Myth*, p. 99.

7. The "tradition of wit" which Cleanth Brooks posits as a means whereby English verse is to be judged by its use of vigorous metaphor, dramatic shifts of tone, and an incorporation of the difficult and unpoetic undoubtedly enhances our awareness of the truly multiple levels of experience, but its language, "the language of paradox," in which the connotations admittedly play as great a part as the denotations, will be but partial unless it be recognized that the modes of expression characteristic of the Hearth and Sacred Fire (intuition and logic) may, in their interpenetration and opposition, provide the very sources of such "wit" and ironic contrast. Cf. Brooks, *Modern Poetry and the Tradition* (Chapel Hill, N.C., 1939), pp. 18–38, and *The Well Wrought Urn*, pp. 3–20, 62–73, 176–96, 197–238.

8. Brooks, *The Well Wrought Urn*, p. 68.

9. It is conceivable that, as we seek meaning in language, we are "victimized" by certain archetypes which reflect emotionally induced associations grounded in our exposure to the family; that, through such contact, we receive awareness of certain parental images and patterns of behavior which, as a gift or curse, we project into the future in the lives of our children.

The literature, then, which depicts the differing roles of the masculine and the feminine functioning within crucial family episodes will rely upon these archetypes, and their symbols, for emotional dynamism. In its representation of these polarities, in its exploration of such universal attitudes as tenderness and authority, such literature not only informs these experiences with a significance beyond that of the exclusively intellectual, but it also contrasts the knowledge gained by insight with that derived from logic in such a way that we may distinguish (and employ critically) matriarchal and patriarchal modes of expression.

10. Bodkin, *Archetypal Patterns in Poetry*, p. 14.

11. Kitto, *Greek Tragedy*, p. 151. Kitto cites Professor Una Ellis-Fermor, *Frontiers of Drama* (London, 1946), p. 133, on the notion of catharsis being inherent in perfection of form. See also Thomson, *Aeschylus and Athens*, pp. 372–84.

12. "Preface to Shakespeare," in Walter Raleigh, ed., *Johnson on Shakespeare* (Oxford, 1940), pp. 11–12.

13. *Ibid.*, pp. 14–16.

14. Page 19. See the entire chapter, "Odysseus' Scar," for Auerbach's qualifications; and chap. xiii, "The Weary Prince."

15. "Shakespeare and the Stoicism of Seneca," in T. S. Eliot, *Selected Essays* (New York, 1950), p. 115.

16. *Ibid.*, pp. 117–18.

17. *Ibid.*, p. 118.

18. Bradley, *Shakespearean Tragedy*, p. 316.

19. *Ibid.*, see Lecture I, "The Substance of Tragedy," pp. 31–39.

20. *Ibid.*, p. 324.

21. The finest literary works are never fully the product of conceptualization, the masculine element of the psyche. Their vitality often depends to a large extent upon their capacity to stimulate the undisciplined emotional responses of the reader, to probe and activate the unconscious, the feminine element:

> . . . the psychological stage ruled by the unconscious is, as we saw, matriarchal, its emblem being the Great Mother who is overcome in the dragon fight. The association of the unconscious with feminine symbolism is archetypal, and the maternal character of the unconscious is further intensified by the anima figure which, in the masculine psyche, stands for the soul. Consequently the heroic-masculine trend of development is apt to confuse "away from the unconscious" with "away from the feminine" altogether. This trend towards patriarchal consciousness is reflected in the supersession of feminine moon myths by masculine sun myths and can be traced far back into primitive psychology. Whereas the moon myths,

even when the moon is masculine, always indicate the dependence of consciousness and light upon the nocturnal side of life, i.e., the unconscious, this is no longer the case with the patriarchal solar mythologies. Here the sun is not the morning sun born of the night, but the sun in his zenith at high noon, symbolizing a masculine consciousness which knows itself to be free and independent even in its relations with the self, i.e., the creative world of heaven and spirit (Neumann, *Origins*, fn. 15, p. 340).

See also pp. 141–49, 196, 202–03; *The Great Mother*, p. 294; and Jung, *Contributions to Analytical Psychology*, pp. 225–28.

22. *Shakespearean Tragedy*, pp. 324–25.

23. C. G. Jung, *Two Essays on Analytical Psychology*, pp. 108, 219–24, 236–38; *The Development of Personality*, pp. 43, 49–58; *Psychology and Alchemy*, pp. 41, 172–74; and in its entirety, *The Integration of Personality*. See also Neumann, *Origins*, Part II, "The Psychological Stages in the Development of Personality," pp. 261–418, especially, pp. 409–18; and Appendix I, "The Group and the Great Individual," pp. 421–35. The term Self has been used here to suggest an equation of "Self" with "Soul," indicating a midpoint of personality between consciousness and unconsciousness around which all other systems gravitate, as around a magnetic nucleus, to lend stability to the total personality and order to the psyche (cf. *Two Essays on Analytical Psychology*, pp. 219–24.)

Selected Bibliography

Aeschylus. *Oresteia*. Trans. Richmond Lattimore, in David Grene and Richmond Lattimore (eds.). *The Complete Greek Tragedies*. Chicago: University of Chicago Press, 1954.

Anshen, Ruth Nanda (ed.). *The Family: Its Function and Destiny*. New York: Harper & Bros., 1949.

Auerbach, Erich. *Mimesis*. Trans. Willard Trask. New York: Doubleday Anchor Books, 1957.

Bachofen, J. J. *Das Mutterrecht*. Vols. II and III of the *Gesammelte Werke*. Basel: B. Schwaben & Co., 1948.

Benedict, Ruth. *Patterns of Culture*. New York: Mentor Books, 1948.

Bodkin, Maud. *Archetypal Patterns in Poetry*. London: Oxford University Press, 1934.

Bowra, C. M. *Early Greek Elegists*. Cambridge, Mass.; Harvard University Press, 1938.

————. *The Greek Experience*. London: Weidenfield & Nicolson, 1958.

Bradley, A. C. *Shakespearean Tragedy*. London: Macmillan Co., 1949.

Briffault, Robert. *The Mothers*. 3 vols. London, New York: Macmillan Co., 1927.

Brooks, Cleanth. *Modern Poetry and the Tradition*. Chapel Hill: University of North Carolina Press, 1939.

————. *The Well Wrought Urn*. New York: Reynal & Hitchcock, 1947.

Brown, Carleton (ed.). *Religious Lyrics of the Fifteenth Century*. Oxford: Clarendon Press, 1939.

Campbell, Joseph. *The Hero with a Thousand Faces*. New York: Meridian Books, 1956.

Cassirer, Ernst. *Language and Myth*. Trans. Susanne K. Langer. New York: Dover Publications [n.d.].

————. *The Myth of the State*. New York: Doubleday Anchor Books, 1955.

Clemen, W. H. *The Development of Shakespeare's Imagery*. Cambridge, Mass.: Harvard University Press, 1951.

De Coulanges, Fustel. *The Ancient City*. Trans. Willard Small. New York: Doubleday Anchor Books, 1956.

Diehl, Ernst (ed.). *Anthologia Lyrica Graeca*. Editio tertia. Lipsia: Trubner, 1949–52.

Eliot, T. S. *Collected Poems, 1909–1935*. New York: Harcourt, Brace & Co., 1936.

————. *Selected Essays*. New York: Harcourt, Brace & Co., 1950.

Euripides. *The Medea*, trans. Rex Warner; and *The Trojan Women*, trans. Richmond Lattimore; in David Grene and Richmond Lattimore (eds.), *The Complete Greek Tragedies*. Chicago: University of Chicago Press, 1955, 1958.

Frazer, J. G. *The Golden Bough*. Abridged edition. New York: Macmillan Co., 1942.

Fromm, Erich. *Escape from Freedom*. New York: Farrar & Rinehart, 1941.

————. *Man for Himself*. New York: Rinehart Co., 1947.

Frye, Northrop. *Anatomy of Criticism: Four Essays*. Princeton: Princeton University Press, 1957.

Gardner, W. H. (ed.). *Poems of Gerard Manley Hopkins.* New York: Oxford University Press, 1948.

————. *Gerard Manley Hopkins: A Study of Poetic Idiosyncrasy in Relation to Poetic Tradition.* New Haven: Yale University Press, 1948.

Hall, Calvin S., and Gardner Lindzey. *Theories of Personality.* New York, London: Wiley, 1957.

Harrison, Jane. *Prolegomena to the Study of Greek Religion.* New York: Meridian Books, 1955.

Heilman, Robert B. *This Great Stage: Image and Structure in "King Lear."* Baton Rouge: Louisiana State University Press, 1948; Seattle: Washington Paperbacks, 1966.

Higham, T. F., and C. M. Bowra (eds.). *The Oxford Book of Greek Verse in Translation.* Oxford: Clarendon Press, 1938.

Hooker, Richard. *Of the Laws of Ecclesiastical Polity.* Books I–V. New York, London: Everyman's Library, 1907.

Huizinga, Johan. *The Waning of the Middle Ages.* Trans. F. Hopman. New York: Doubleday Anchor Books, 1954.

Jones, Ernest. *Hamlet and Oedipus.* New York: Doubleday Anchor Books, 1954.

Jung, C. G. *Collected Works of C. G. Jung.* Trans. R. F. C. Hull. (Bollingen Series XX.) London, New York: Pantheon Books, 1953–. I have used the following volumes: V, *Symbols of Transformation* (1956); VII, *Two Essays on Analytical Psychology* (1953); IX, *Archetypes and the Collective Unconscious* (1959); XII, *Psychology and Alchemy* (1953); and XVII, *The Development of Personality* (1954).

————. *Collected Papers on Analytical Psychology.* New York: Moffat, Yard & Co., 1917.

————. *Contributions to Analytical Psychology.* Trans. H. G. and Cary F. Baynes. New York, London: Harcourt, Brace & Co., 1928.

————. *The Integration of the Personality.* Trans. Stanley M. Dell. New York, Toronto: Farrar & Rinehart, 1939.

————. *Modern Man in Search of a Soul.* Trans. W. S. Dell and Cary F. Baynes. New York, London: K. Paul, Trench, Trubner & Co., 1933.

————. *Psychological Types.* Trans. H. G. Baynes. New York:

Harcourt, Brace; London: K. Paul, Trench, Trubner & Co., 1926.

——, and C. Kerenyi. *Essays on a Science of Mythology.* Trans. R. F. C. Hull. (Bollingen Series XXII.) New York: Pantheon Books, 1949.

Kitto, H. D. F. *Greek Tragedy.* New York: Doubleday Anchor Books, 1954.

Kittredge, G. L. (ed.). *The Complete Works of Shakespeare.* Boston: Ginn & Co., 1936.

Levin, Harry. *The Question of Hamlet.* New York: Oxford University Press, 1959.

Lewis, C. S. *The Allegory of Love.* London: Oxford University Press, 1938.

Lovejoy, Arthur O. *The Great Chain of Being.* Cambridge, Mass.: Harvard University Press, 1936.

Malinowski, Bronislaw. *Magic, Science and Religion.* New York: Doubleday Anchor Books, 1955.

——. *Sex, Culture, and Myth.* New York: Harcourt, Brace & World, 1962.

Matthiessen, F. O. *The Achievement of T. S. Eliot.* New York, London: Oxford University Press, 1947.

Mead, Margaret. *Male and Female.* New York: Mentor Books, 1955.

Mullahy, Patrick. *Oedipus: Myth and Complex.* New York: Hermitage Press, 1948.

Murray, Gilbert. *Five Stages of Greek Religion.* London: The Thinker's Library, No. 52, 1935.

Neumann, Erich. *The Great Mother.* . . . Trans. Ralph Manheim. (Bollingen Series XLVII.) New York: Pantheon Books, [1955].

——. *The Origins and History of Consciousness.* Trans. R. F. C. Hull. (Bollingen Series XLII.) New York: Pantheon Books, 1954.

Pfeiffer, Robert H. *Introduction to the Old Testament.* New York: Harper & Brothers, 1948.

Raglan, Lord. *The Hero.* New York: Vintage Books, 1956.

Raleigh, Walter (ed.). *Johnson on Shakespeare.* London: Humphrey Milford, 1929.

Rank, Otto. *The Trauma of Birth.* New York: Harcourt, Brace & Co., 1929.

Sophocles. *Oedipus the King,* trans. David Grene; *Oedipus at Colonus,* trans. Robert Fitzgerald; *Antigone,* trans. Elizabeth Wyckoff, in David Grene and Richmond Lattimore (eds.), *The Complete Greek Tragedies.* Chicago: University of Chicago Press, 1954.

Spenser, Edmund. *The Poetical Works of Edmund Spenser,* J. C. Smith and E. de Selincourt (eds.). London and New York: Humphrey Milford, Oxford University Press, 1947.

Spurgeon, Caroline. *Shakespeare's Imagery.* New York: Macmillan, 1935.

Thomson, George. *Aeschylus and Athens.* London: Lawrence & Wishart, 1941.